CATARACT

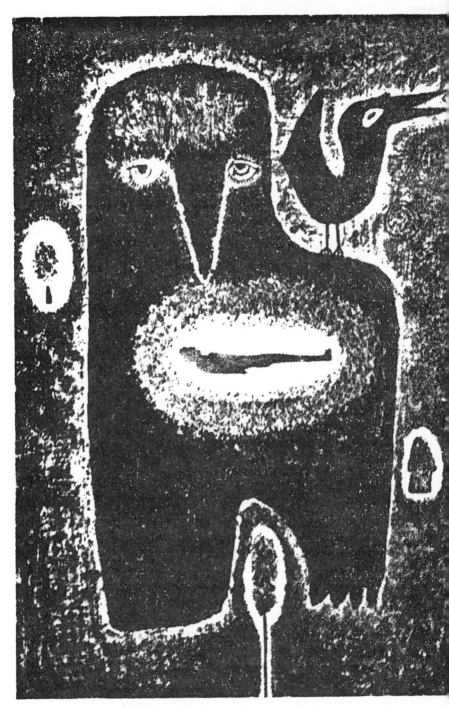

The Sad Raven by Ivan Marchuk

MYKHAYLO OSADCHY

CATARACT

Translated from the Ukrainian,
edited, and annotated by
MARCO CARYNNYK

A Helen and Kurt Wolff Book
Harcourt Brace Jovanovich
New York and London

Printed in the United States

Library of Congress Cataloging in Publication Data

Osadchyĭ, Mykhailo Hryhorovych, 1936–
Cataract.

Translation of Bil'mo.
"A Helen and Kurt Wolff book."
"The aftermath (V. Chornovil's view of the trial, letters from
Yavas, etc.)": p.
Includes bibliographical references and index.
1. Osadchyĭ, Mykhailo Hryhorovych, 1936–   —Biography.
2. Political prisoners—Russia—Personal narratives.
3. Russia—Politics and government—1953–
4. Ukraine—Politics and government—1917–   I. Title.
PG3949.25.S3Z513   070.4′092′4   [B]   75–34371
ISBN 0–15–116115–1
ISBN 0–15–615550–8 (pbk.)

Distributed in Canada exclusively by Cataract Press

A B C D E F G H I J

Contents

Translator's Note

Mykhaylo Osadchy's memoir reached the West by indirect routes, and the four Ukrainian editions differ significantly. Some of the variants may represent Osadchy's revisions. Others —particularly in punctuation and spelling—seem to be corruptions introduced during the neo-scribal process of distributing "bootleg literature," as *samvydav* or uncensored writing is called in Ukraine. Dialogue, for example, is often run together, and punctuation is sprinkled so erratically that it is sometimes difficult to tell where one speech or train of thought ends and another begins.

The only textual divisions that can be definitely attributed to Osadchy are "Part One: The Comedians" and "Part Two: The City of the Sun." As editor, I have divided the text into paragraphs and sections, compiled the documents by and about Osadchy in "The Aftermath," incorporated material from all four editions, supplied all the notes except note 63 on page 229, which appears to be the author's, and corrected some garbled names.

Osadchy's scriveners and publishers like to trot out a Victorian dot-dot-dot whenever an obscenity occurs, forgetting (or not understanding) that his four-letter words are *political:* the zeks—prison-camp inmates—hear them first from their KGB educators and ply them as one of the few weapons of self-defense at their disposal. Verbal jujitsu, if you like. So as translator, I have restored the "mother words," rendering them into colloquial American.

For transliterating Slavic names I have used the system of the United States Board on Geographic Names but omit the "soft sign" (indicated by an apostrophe) from all but the titles of books and periodicals. Ukrainian names are transcribed directly from the original and not, as the decreasingly common custom has it, via Russian. Thus I spell Osadchy's first name as "Mykhaylo," although the old guard might prefer "Mikhail," and write "Lviv," "Kharkiv," and "Ivano-Frankivsk," when gazetteers show "Lvov," "Kharkov," and "Ivano-Frankovsk."

Yuriy Darewych, John Mežaks, and Andriy Semotiuk supplied me with information on obscure points. John Kolasky and George and Moira Luckyj commented on the translation and editorial material. Wolfram Burghardt called on his six-language lexicon and devoted a week of all-nighters to a *very* close reading which radically rectified every page of the translation. The remaining flops and bungles, naturally, are not theirs.

The frontispiece is Ivan Marchuk's *The Sad Raven* and is reproduced by courtesy of *Suchasnist'*. The Committee for the Defense of Valentyn Moroz in Toronto and the Ukrainian Studies Fund at Harvard University generously supported my work. To all of them—my appreciation. My greatest gratitude, however, is to Marta Horban, who put up with the exigencies of intimate collaboration, and to the memory of my father, who taught me what I know.

M. C.

Caliban's Education

1.   *. . . I am subject to a tyrant, a sorcerer,*
      that by his cunning hath cheated me of the island.

In late August 1965, several weeks before the arrest of Andrey Sinyavsky and Yuliy Daniel, which led to the greatest *cause célèbre* of recent times, a swift tightening of controls and a wave of arrests swept unnoticed over Ukraine, the second most populous Soviet republic, putting an emphatic end to the tortuous twists of Nikita Khrushchev's celebrated liberalization campaign. In a synchronized swoop on major cities, the KGB—the Soviet security service—caught up for questioning hundreds of people from almost every section of Ukrainian society. Scores of them were subjected to searches and confiscations of written material, and at least twenty-five were remanded for further investigation. Early in 1966 eighteen of these people—among them Mykhaylo Osadchy—were tried behind closed doors for subversion, "anti-Soviet agitation and propaganda," and "bourgeois nationalism," convicted almost without exception, and shipped off to labor camps in the Soviet hinterland.

The arrests of 1965 were not the first in the country. With a population now of some fifty million, a territory slightly larger than that of France, an independent history and culture going back to the early Middle Ages, a Westward orientation, and the economic potential to go its own way, Ukraine has long resisted Moscow's intention to turn it into another Russian province. The country became a dependency of the tsars only in 1654, and vestiges of autonomy survived until the late eighteenth century. The nineteenth century, as elsewhere in Europe, was marked by the rise of a modern national consciousness, and the growing *indépendiste* tendencies culminated in the establishment of a Ukrainian People's Republic during the revolution of 1917. The communists tactically acknowledged Ukrainian national demands by proclaiming a separate Ukrainian Soviet Republic. After crushing the People's Republic with armed force and incorporating the Soviet Republic into the USSR in 1922 the Bolsheviks continued their policy of recognizing non-Russian national demands by initiating an "indigenization" of the cultural life and the Party and government apparatus. In Ukraine, the native language was on the ascendant after centuries of tsarist restrictions; publishing, education, and scholarship flourished, and a remarkable literary revival began to take place.

This brief but intense period of cultural reconstruction was cut off by Stalin's rise to power, and it can in fact be said that nowhere else did the evils associated with his name wreak as much havoc as in Ukraine. Compulsory collectivization of agriculture in 1932 and 1933 killed some three to six million peasants, and the "Great Terror" of the next few years—mass arrests, secret trials, and execution or long terms in concentration camps—claimed another two million victims, chiefly among intellectuals and in the Party. The policy of encouraging the native language and culture was replaced by one of Russification, and literary activity was brutally trimmed down to meet rigid standards. Of 259 writers who were published in 1930, for example, only 36 were still being published eight years later. World War II claimed a further four million victims in Ukraine, but the postwar period brought no relaxation. Famine occurred again, and in the recently annexed Western provinces there were mass reprisals against entire villages accused of aiding anti-Soviet guerrillas. Justifying his Ukrainophobia with the claim that he was eradicating "bourgeois nationalism," Stalin struck at the very heart of Ukrainian national existence, making it that much easier for his heirs to enunciate their policy of bringing the Soviet nations nearer

and nearer together until their "complete unity" with a common culture and language (Russian, of course) could be
achieved. "From past and recent history," wrote a critic of the
regime's nationalities policy, "it may be seen that in the
Ukraine it was permissible to label as 'nationalist' anyone possessing an elementary sense of national dignity, or anyone
concerned with the fate of Ukrainian culture and language,
and often simply anyone who in some way failed to please
some Russian chauvinist, some 'Great Russian bully.'"[1]

Hopes for a more tolerable way of life were raised throughout the Soviet Union when Stalin died in 1953 and even more
when Khrushchev, in his "secret speech" to the Twentieth
Party Congress in 1956, denounced the Father of Nations as a
mass murderer whose ideology was riddled with lies. By the
end of the 1950's the Russian intelligentsia was emerging, if
not quite intact, then at least viable enough to express meas-
ured indignation at the brutalities of Stalin's era. In Ukraine,
however, the bogey of bourgeois nationalism continued to be
used to quash all independent thought. Aware that his data
may well be incomplete, one writer has estimated that "at
least five or ten persons have stood political trial every year
since 1956, some seventy in 1961–2, and twenty in 1966."[2] But
the repressions of 1965–1966 were different in one unforeseen
respect. "People are as ever thrown behind bars and as ever
transported to the East," wrote Valentyn Moroz, a young intellectual arrested in 1965. "But this time they have not sunk
into the unknown. To the great surprise of the KGB men, *public opinion* has risen up for the first time in recent decades."[3]

This rise of public opinion was instigated in great measure
by the generation that emerged in the early 1960's. Inevitably
dubbed the "Sixtiers," these young intellectuals brought about
a dramatic renaissance of national identity and self-respect.
Challenging the philistine banalities of official culture, they
revitalized the language and rediscovered their roots in the
proscribed past (rehabilitation of Stalin's victims was proceeding much more slowly in Ukraine than in Russia). Born under
the Soviet regime, educated in Soviet schools, members in

many cases of the Communist Party, they believed that their proudest aim was to be citizens—that is, to express their views calmly and with dignity.

This kind of civic courage was notably displayed by Vyacheslav Chornovil, a twenty-eight-year-old television reporter whose efforts in revealing the true extent of the 1965 arrests made him a central figure in the Ukrainian resistance. He first became involved in protest over the repressions when he was sent to Lviv to cover several trials, including the one of Osadchy. Chornovil, who seems to have sincerely believed what he had been taught about the inviolability and fairness of Soviet law, was outraged by the blatant violations that he witnessed: arbitrary arrest, harassment, censorship, provocation, and cruel interrogation. When he saw, too, that the standard charge of "anti-Soviet propaganda" amounted to reading and passing around books which had been published abroad and articles which, from a Marxist viewpoint, deplored Ukraine's colonial status and the consequent stunting of its culture, Chornovil could restrain himself no longer.

Marshaling all the evidence he could get his hands on, Chornovil sent to the top authorities a dossier in which he indicted the KGB and the courts for serious infractions of justice. He noted that the regime was persecuting intellectuals for their beliefs, and he argued that according to Marxism hostile ideas could not take root in a soil that was not socially, economically, and politically ripe for them. Finally, he appealed to Soviet law and "Leninist norms," to the guarantees of the Constitution, and to the United Nations' Universal Declaration of Human Rights. In subsequent months Chornovil put together a second collection of materials, written by twenty of those who had been arrested in 1965 and composed in many cases in the prison camps. Borrowing the title of a nineteenth-century Russian satire, he called his collection *The Misfortune of Intellect* (or *Woe from Wit,* as the phrase is also rendered), adding another dose of irony in the subtitle: *Portraits of Twenty "Criminals."*[4] For his efforts Chornovil was sentenced on 15 November 1967 to three years in a labor camp. A general amnesty reduced his sentence to eighteen months, but in 1972 Chornovil was arrested and brought to trial again. He is now serving a sentence of seven years' labor camp and five years' exile.

Chornovil's insistence that Soviet laws be observed testifies to the intellectual affinity between the Russian dissident movement and the national movements in the non-Russian republics. Like their Russian colleagues, the Ukrainians are anxious to win basic democratic freedoms. But as an oppressed national group they have, in addition, their own goals. They object both to the over-all lawlessness and lack of freedom and to the drastic violations of national rights: the systematic reduction of Ukrainian courses in schools, the dearth of Ukrainian publications, the conduct of almost all official business in Russian, the deliberate neglect or distortion of Ukrainian history, the emasculation of the Ukrainian Party and government, and the de-Ukrainianization of the population through the steady infusion of Russians. This concern for both individual and national rights, which are ultimately inseparable, is particularly marked in the writings of Ivan Dzyuba.

A scholar and critic of literature by training, Dzyuba won attention with his defenses of the experiments of young poets and his articles on major writers of the past. But his outspoken, forward-looking ideas made him an enemy of the conservative mediocrities in the literary establishment. As early as 1962 he was accused of distorting Ukrainian literature and uttering "politically erroneous statements" and threatened with expulsion from the Writers' Union. On 4 September 1965, only a few days after the KGB had made its arrests, Dzyuba strode to the stage of a Kiev motion-picture theater and made a trenchant appeal to the Party leaders and the people of Kiev —the first in Soviet times—to stop the purge and support its victims. Officialdom made no response to the plea. Nor were there answers to the inquiries addressed to the Party's Central Committee by prominent people. Instead of clear official statements, rumors about the arrests of "nationalists" gained ground, and yet another campaign of intimidation against the independent intelligentsia was launched. By the end of the year Dzyuba had submitted a memorandum to the Party authorities.[5]

Convinced that those arrested in August were not "bourgeois nationalists" but people genuinely concerned for their country and himself witnessing "an indefatigable, pitiless, and absurd persecution of the national cultural life," Dzyuba analyzed in his memorandum the social and political situation in the USSR and documented the oppression of non-Russian nationalities. The Ukrainian unrest, he asserted, is much more widespread than appearances indicate. This is a direct result of Moscow's policy of encouraging "Russian great-power chauvinism" and at the same time suppressing any expressions of local national feelings, no matter how innocent. With thorough scholarship and a bold style Dzyuba exposed the Soviet leadership's nationalities policy as being un-Leninist, contrary to the present historical trend of national emancipation, and liable to lead to disaster. Mere declarations about "proletarian internationalism" will not do. Leninist principles must be reestablished, and an open and honest discussion of all unsolved problems is essential.

No open discussion took place, of course. When Dzyuba's memorandum was published in the West, the authorities waited over a year to admit its existence. They did this, typically enough, in the form of a refutation which was made available to Western readers only.[6] Laced with abusive language and based on falsified evidence, the refutation ignored the substance of Dzyuba's analysis and established his guilt by the principle of association: if the enemy praises you, you must be doing something wrong. In August 1969 the press and the Writers' Union mounted a fierce campaign against Dzyuba. Articles appeared belittling his talent, casting aspersions on his character, and ominously accusing him of providing "imperialist circles" and especially "bourgeois nationalists" with a weapon in their anti-Soviet warfare. In 1972 Dzyuba was arrested and held for interrogation for almost a year despite poor health because of tuberculosis. In March 1973 he was tried by the Kiev Provincial Court and sentenced to five years' imprisonment and five years' exile.[7]

Another major figure to emerge in the 1960's was Valentyn Moroz. Son of peasants, he was born in the Volyn Province in 1936, studied history at Lviv University until 1958, and later taught history at teachers' colleges. Arrested in August 1965, Moroz was tried the following January for "propaganda directed toward the separation of Ukraine from the USSR" (he had argued that Ukraine should have the same rights as other socialist countries) and sentenced to four years in a labor camp. There in the camp prison he managed to complete his devastating essay, "Report from the Beria Reserve," in which the frame of reference effortlessly encompasses Borneo tribesmen, Plato, Slavic myth, Stalin, and international law.[8] In the nine months between his release in 1969 and his rearrest in June 1970, during which he underwent nearly continuous police harassment, Moroz wrote three more essays and several sketches of his prison experiences. At his trial in November 1970 (he had been charged with writing and disseminating his essays) Moroz received a sentence whose severity revealed the authorities' concern for the ideas he was expressing: six years in prison in strict isolation, three years in a labor camp, and five years in exile.

Moroz's chief crime, like that of his colleagues, is that he opposed Stalinistic abuses of power in general and the regime's nationalities policy in particular, exposing the latter as lightly veiled Russification and cultural genocide. In "Report from the Beria Reserve" he espouses a "socialism with a human face" and describes his fellow prisoners as "people who think differently or who simply think and whose intellectual world could not be forced into the Stalinist molds which are so assiduously defended by the KGB." He scathingly denounces the lawless brutality in the KGB's vast complex of camps in Mordovia, and he speculates on the struggle between despotism and individualism. Soviet society, he says, is an "empire of cogs" in which fanatic Stalinists produce programmed men on a totalitarian conveyor belt:

The cog is the cherished ideal of any "totalizator." An obedient herd of cogs can be called a parliament or an academic council, and you will have no trouble or surprises from it. A cog called a professor or an academician will never say anything new, and if it does produce a surprise, it will do so not by new words, but by the lightning-swift change of its conceptions. A herd of cogs can be termed the Red Cross, and it will count calories in Africa but not say a single word about famine at home. A cog will emerge from prison and immediately write that it was never there, and what is more, it will call the person who demanded its release a liar (as Ostap Vyshnya did). A cog will shoot at whomever it is told to and then, on command, campaign for peace. The final and most important advantage is that once people have been turned into cogs, you can blithely introduce any constitution you want to, give them the right to anything. The exquisite point is that it will never enter a cog's head to wield this right.[9]

But Moroz believes that the new generation will refuse to be intimidated and turned into cogs. At his trial in 1970 he firmly told his jailers that they are powerless:

Nothing has contributed so much to the quickening of public life in Ukraine as your repressions. Nothing has attracted attention to the Ukrainian renaissance as much as your trials. . . . The national renaissance is the most profound of all spiritual processes. . . . Your dams are strong and reliable, but they stand on dry ground, by-passed by the spring floods. . . . Your drawgates are closed, but they stop no one. . . . You stubbornly insist that all those you place behind bars are dangerous criminals. . . . You can pursue this absurd policy for, let us say, ten more years. But then what? These movements in Ukraine (and in the entire USSR) *are only beginning.*[10]

2.   *You taught me language; and my profit on't*
       Is, I know how to curse. The red plague rid you
       For learning me your language. . . .

Like most of the Sixtiers, Mykhaylo Osadchy appeared to be
a model child of the Revolution. Born on 22 March 1936 in
the Sumy Province of northeastern Ukraine, his parents collective farmers, Osadchy went to Lviv University to study journalism. Graduating in 1958, he embarked upon what promised to
be a long and rewarding career. He was conferred a job as
editor, later senior editor, at the Lviv television studio. Two
years later he was appointed a lecturer in the Journalism
Department of the university, then promoted to senior lecturer.
By 1963 he had been admitted to the Party and the Union of
Journalists, and he was recruited by the local Party Committee
to lecture to the public on the duties of the Soviet press. He
was entrusted with editing the university newspaper, and as a
deputy secretary in his department's Party organization he was
responsible for "ideological education."

Osadchy was also beginning to realize his scholarly and
literary ambitions. In the four years before his arrest he published some forty items—papers at university conferences,
articles on newspaper and television reporting, scripts, book
reviews, and literary criticism—and he was writing a handbook on television production for his students. He was also
regularly placing his verse and poetic prose in the local press,
and a Lviv publishing house undertook to put out a typically
slim first volume of his poems, *A Moonlit Field*. Most im-
pressively, without enrolling in a graduate program and without a faculty supervisor, Osadchy wrote and successfully defended a candidate's thesis (the degree is approximately
equivalent to a Western Ph.D.) on the journalism of Ostap
Vyshnya, a Ukrainian satirist who had been extremely popular
in the 1920's but then fell into Stalinist disfavor. So in the
summer of 1965 things looked quite good for Osadchy: his
degree would be confirmed in a few months; his first book of

poems would be published in a few weeks, and he would soon be married.

But on 28 August came a KGB knock on the door. Within an hour Osadchy had been hustled off to prison, where he stayed, under "preliminary investigation," for almost eight months. His arrest prevented the publication of two papers he had read at university conferences, and the entire print run of his book was either pulped or stored in a warehouse. There was no question, of course, of receiving his candidate's degree: the Supreme Attestation Commission in Moscow, the official body responsible for confirming higher degrees, promptly refused to grant it. The two KGB officers who conducted the investigation, Captain Klymenko and Major Halski, were seasoned police officials who expertly applied to Osadchy the classical Pavlovian approach of alternating humiliation and decency. Promises of leniency in exchange for repentance and cooperation were followed by physical and verbal abuse. Long before the trial Osadchy knew that he would be convicted and dispatched to the political prisoners' camps in Mordovia.

One reason for this severity with the Ukrainian dissenters was that they read material which presents Ukrainian history in other than the official light (all the books confiscated from Osadchy fall into this category) and collected evidence of what they called "distortions of the Leninist nationalities policy: anti-Semitism, Ukrainophobia, [and] national discrimination." A case in point are the two articles that Osadchy was charged with possessing (but not actually reading or passing on): Dwight D. Eisenhower's speech at the unveiling of a monument to Taras Shevchenko in Washington in June 1964 and the anonymous pamphlet, "The Trial of Pogruzhalsky." Both texts circulated widely in Ukrainian circles and frequently figured in the charges against dissenters.

The second of these texts dealt with the trial in August 1964 of a senior librarian who three months earlier had set fire to the largest library in Ukraine, the State Public Library of the Academy of Sciences in Kiev. The official explanation of the arson was that it had been an act of private revenge against the library administration. The pamphlet maintained that the crime, which led to the destruction of some 600,000 books and archives relating to Ukrainian history and culture, was in fact a deliberate act of Russian chauvinism aimed at the spirit of Ukraine. It cited facts suggesting that Pogruzhalsky had not operated alone and that the court had hushed this up. The pamphlet also pointed to similar fires in two national libraries in Central Asia.[11]

When his trial opened, at the Lviv Provincial Court, on 16 April 1966, Osadchy was joined in the prisoners' dock by Myroslava Zvarychevska, a proofreader and editor, Mykhaylo Horyn, an industrial psychologist, and Horyn's younger brother Bohdan, a literary and art critic. Like Osadchy, they had been charged under Article 62—a catch-all provision of the Ukrainian Criminal Code—with conducting "anti-Soviet agitation and propaganda" by circulating manuscript articles and Ukrainian books published abroad. Clearly, though, their real crime—for which they were never tried—was to have expressed the view that the regime's policies in economics and national relations contradicted the tenets of Marxism-Leninism that they had absorbed in school. When Chornovil asked Osadchy's interrogator why Osadchy had been sentenced to two years in a labor camp, the KGB captain replied: "Well, if only you knew what he wrote in his diary!" Yet no diary, as Chornovil points out, was mentioned in Osadchy's verdict, only the two "seditious" articles.[12]

The trial of Sinyavsky and Daniel in Moscow was at least theoretically open to the public (although in practice the courtroom was packed), and there was publicity in the press (although all the reports condemned the defendants in advance as traitors). Osadchy's trial, however, took place as if in an occupied country. There was no audience at all, and the press never mentioned the case. Extraordinary security measures in various cities prevented friends from gathering outside the cordoned-off courthouse, and those who broke through the obstacles were closely watched by a full complement of army troops, police, KGB agents, Komsomol trouble-makers, and plainclothesmen who photographed everybody for the security files.

Many of the dissidents' trials in Russia have been reported to us by members of the audience who surreptiously took shorthand notes. In Lviv this was impossible, and we know nothing about Osadchy's trial beyond what he and Chornovil (who was called as a witness) tell us. The pattern, however, was apparently the same. The trial was held behind closed doors in clear violation of a law which requires open trials except in certain limited cases. Witnesses were browbeaten, the judges were sleepily indifferent, and the defense attorneys were impotent. The State prosecutor, Borys Antonenko, Legal Councilor of the Third Rank and author of a book about the "supreme justice" of Soviet courts and the "valiant Chekists" (KGB agents like to stress their descent from the Cheka, the secret police of Lenin's day, by calling themselves Chekists), displayed his insulting ignorance of Ukrainian affairs by grossly misquoting writers who had written on patriotic themes.

Things were no better outside the courtroom. KGB men hectored the people who had managed to gather in the street, and when Mykhaylo Horyn's wife tried to point him out to their two-year-old daughter as he was being led to a police van, a KGB major covered her mouth with his hand. Some people did succeed in getting up to the floor where the trial was proceeding, but a colonel of the militia tricked them into leaving by ordering them to go downstairs and promising that he would notify the relatives when the verdicts would be read. (Soviet law stipulates that even at a closed trial the verdict itself must be read in public.) When the people descended to the ground floor, however, they found themselves boxed in. Policemen kept them from returning upstairs while armed soldiers blocked their way to the street. The people were held there until the verdicts had been read and the defendants had been led out a back door to the waiting vans. Then trucks and water hoses were used to disperse the crowd.

All four defendants had in the meantime been found guilty.

Mykhaylo Horyn was sentenced to six years, his brother Bohdan to three, Myroslava Zvarychevska to eight months, and Osadchy to two years. In the Soviet Union sentences of deprivation of liberty are normally served in "corrective labor colonies." There are four types of these camps with increasingly harsh regimes: general, hard, strict, and special. Most offenders are sent to camps of the first two categories, but some habitual criminals and all political prisoners are sent to strict- or special-regime camps. Osadchy and the Horyn brothers were to serve their sentences in strict-regime camps.

Early in June 1966 Osadchy was dispatched to such a camp in Dubrovlag, the largest labor-camp complex in the Soviet Union. With stopovers at transit prisons in Kharkiv and Voronezh, he traveled in the infamous Stolypin railroad cars, which have been used to transport convicts since tsarist times, to the village of Yavas in Mordovia, an autonomous republic in the Russian heartland, some 350 miles southeast of Moscow. Mordovia's entire southwest corner is crisscrossed with the barbed wire, fences, watchtowers, and searchlights of Dubrovlag. In the 1960's it was known to hold some 30,000 prisoners, including criminals. Camp No. 11, to which Osadchy was assigned, contained in 1966 about 4,000 prisoners, almost all of them "politicals." (It has since been dissolved and the inmates distributed among other camps.)

The criminal codes of the various republics state flatly the following basic principle of penal policy: "Punishment does not have as one of its aims the incurring of physical suffering or the lowering of human dignity." But this principle is so much bluff, and the regulations in effect are clearly designed to inflict pain and degradation. Although Osadchy paid for his food and clothing by working as a joiner—the camp manufactured furniture—he was kept on a meager diet of bread and rotten cabbage soup and soon contracted a stomach disease. Even in these conditions he remained the bookman that he had been before his arrest, avidly devouring Goethe, Apollinaire, nuclear physics, existentialism, and Central Asian writers. He was, in his own phrase, stuffing his battered head and dreaming of doing independent work as a poet, translator, or critic. And when he adds that his wings have been clipped, the phrase is not simply a metaphor for imprisonment: during a search at the camp in December 1966 he had confiscated from him a notebook. It contained translations and free renditions of Garcia Lorca and of poets from the Baltic republics, as well as original poems.

Shortly before his release Osadchy was brought back to Ukraine and made to testify at the trial of Vyacheslav Chornovil, who had earlier so enraged the authorities by refusing to testify at Osadchy's illegally closed trial. Despite the heavy pressure—he must have been aware that a new charge could always be brought against him—Osadchy retracted whatever earlier testimony he may have given and spoke out in Chornovil's favor. Osadchy was released from confinement in March 1968. The difficulties that he then faced are described in "The Aftermath."

Cataract, the memoir of his arrest, trial, and imprisonment that Osadchy wrote after his release, is more than a factual account of repression and injustice, important though that aspect is. It is also the work of a skilled literary artist who brings a new vision to what has become a depressingly familiar theme of East European writing. This is not the place to discuss Osadchy's sophisticated narrative technique, his precise and evocative language, his charging of the smallest details with emotional significance, or his *arrière-plan* of meanings. But some mention should be made of several pivotal passages in the book—the section about Scythian rock paintings, the "cubist" portrait of Chornovil, and the scene in the crypt—if only because they have been understood until now as sloppy writing at worst or hallucinations at best.[13] In fact, the passage on Scythian art and the frighteningly fractured sketch of Chornovil attempt to reproduce in literature the experiments of young painters in Kiev and Lviv in the early 1960's. Ivan Marchuk's painting, *The Sad Raven*, reproduced as the frontispiece of this book, is an excellent example of this kind of "surrealistic" art with a social message.

The scene in the crypt is a political allegory, a fierce parable about a revolution gone astray and an aborted de-Stalinization. Drawing on such symbolism as Christ's wounds, St. George the Conqueror, patron saint of Imperial Russia, and the KGB's official color of sky blue, Osadchy depicts the USSR as a coffin for the Ukrainian people. The early Ukrainian communists' dream of a "transmontane commune," a brave new world free of national and social inequality, has been perversely realized in the *univers concentrationnaire.* The portent is for increasing doubt that this system can be regenerated from within. The gray-suited, fedora-hatted revolutionaries in the Kremlin are frightened of change, especially within their own borders. But by throwing all the best people into camps and prisons they may be making radical political change inevitable—not now, not perhaps for many years, but some time.

Ultimately, however, the theme of *Cataract* is that explored by every chronicler of imprisonment and suffering: resistance and the survival of human values. When Osadchy describes a dissident who throws his "No!" at a kangaroo court, or when a zek refuses to acknowledge guilt despite the threats and blandishments of the KGB and Osadchy comments with grim understatement that "even [prison] gruel can be savored if it is eaten by choice," he has reached an impressive level of moral utterance. Osadchy is not bitter about his imprisonment: there is perhaps even some ultimate satisfaction in having shared agony with others. His tenderness, his touches of irony and humor, and his level indignation impregnate *Cataract* with a force that flares up in the final lines. Still aware that he is a "savage and deformed slave," "a thing most brutish," he also achieves Prospero's perspective on the tempest he has survived. He sees in the "cloud-capped towers, the gorgeous palaces, the solemn temples" of the world around him only an "insubstantial pageant faded." He finds fresh meaning in Prospero's final affirmation that man is, indeed, "such stuff as dreams are made on."

M. C.

CATARACT

W E are surrounded by streetlights. Only streetlights. They are cleverly distributed along the road we have been bidden to follow. The road is artfully paved with luminous cobblestones that charm our eyes like lodestars. The streetlights and the cobbles are of the same blinding color. Somehow it gets inside us and takes us into captivity. We are made to feel exceedingly important, but empty, too—like clay jars. We can pace this luminous path in our lighthearted, unseeing existence for a year, two, ten, or a whole lifetime, and nothing can halt our steady, confident tread.

On top of these clay jars sit tight-fitting lids—our hats. But one day I jumped for joy, dislodging my lid, and into my being, my empty clay jar, slipped reckless thoughts. They roused my submissive spirit, and suddenly I was seized by an impulse to see what was happening beyond the streetlights.

Shielding my eyes against the dazzle, I glanced behind the scenes. Only for a second and with just the corner of my eye, but this act cost me dearly. Little people scurried around me and in their fright trained all the lights on me. The glare blinded me, and I began to fling myself about in that phantasmagoria until I collapsed exhausted on the paving.

Only then did I realize that there were no cobblestones, merely ordinary sand which adroitly reflected the lamplight. To distract myself I began to write all sorts of words in the sand. No, only one word—man. At first I wrote it in lower-case letters. Then in capitals: MAN. Suddenly I burst out laughing so hard that tears rolled down my face. But my laughter only brought shame on me. It was worse than theft, treason, or murder. I began to stamp on the sand like a madman, trying to crush it into still smaller grains. I did not leave a single grain untouched, but that did not make me feel any better.

That nightmarish frenzy, that evil apparition which caused me so much grief, is still haunting me. I almost went mad and had to save myself. In my despair I grasped at a straw— a scrap of paper. I gave it my sleepless nights, my dignity, and the injustice that was done to me. I told it the truth. That hellish, desperate truth must not leave you unconcerned.

Part One

THE COMEDIANS

THE doorbell buzzes insistently. Then once more. Someone is trying to get in, impatiently shifting from one foot to the other. Who could it be at this ungodly hour? A sense of foreboding grows in me: something must have happened to someone.

I open the door, and a tall fellow with a pampered face enters the room, pushing me gently aside. He smiles enigmatically as he studies me, and I am struck by his strange glance, which seems to drill through me with a smooth assurance. Two other men walk in before I can shut the door. They cross the room in a few quick bounds and close the windows.

"Sit down," orders the tall man. "Right here, beside your wife, and don't move!"

"What . . . " I try to speak, but he cuts me off brusquely and shoves a document under my nose. "The bearer of this permit has the right to carry arms," I manage to read. They must be armed bandits, I suddenly think with horror, robbing me in broad daylight. Robbing me, a proletarian! I begin to laugh hysterically.

His eyes still warily on me, the tall man nervously extends another document. A search warrant. I feel relieved, although I still fail to understand what is going on. Surely there must be some mistake, I think. Perhaps they got the apartment numbers wrong. Yes, that's entirely possible.

But my visitors are no longer paying any attention to me. They are scrutinizing my books, moving them in a disorderly manner from pile to pile. Then they begin to hurry, and I see their dissatisfaction grow with each passing moment. What could they be looking for so persistently?

The telephone rings, but they do not let me answer it. It rings and rings while they keep going through my books and papers. Now I feel like a small hunted animal, paralyzed with fear. My wife sits beside me, equally small and frightened. From time to time the searchers cast venomous glances at me. Then I feel my feet shaking uncontrollably with cold. Reality is dawning on me.

Suddenly one of my visitors lets out a cry of joy. Hardly bothering to conceal his excitement, the youngest of them holds up "The Trial of Pogruzhalsky." The men are jubilant. It seems they will break into dance and drag me, with my glass legs, into their circle.

One of the strangers sits down to write out a search record. The others throw some of my books into a valise: Kulish's *The Black Council*,[1] Hrushevsky's *History of Ukrainian Literature*,[2] several collections by Lepky,[3] and other old imprints. On top of the pile they place the article about Pogruzhalsky with a great deal of ceremony. Minutes later I am being sped into the yonder in a sky-blue Volga sedan.

My visitors sit beside me, corpulent and haughty, now and again exchanging meaningful glances with each other. Sometimes their looks rest on me and their bodies press mine painfully and revoltingly, as if it were held in a vise. I cannot stand it and close my eyes. Later someone shakes my shoulder, and when I open my eyes I see that we have driven up to the gray, three-story corner building at One Peace Street, formerly Stalin Street.[4]

I am a table now, a small, awkward table that does not fit anywhere. People grab me with their hands and hurriedly push me somewhere, then abruptly take me back and move me to a different place. Corridors, offices, corridors, staircases, doors, corridors, officers coming and going, corridors: my eyes glaze over and the floor and ceiling flow together. People change, their faces become different. I feel as if I have been wrapped in a bolt of cloth and rolled across the floor. Some-one pushes me with his feet, and from above I hear an angry voice reproach me: "What more did you want? You're young, you have a degree, your whole life was ahead of you. . . ."

"When the cat's away, the mice will play. You sonofabitch!"

"What did I do?" I try to grasp at something, but every-thing rolls away from me. I try to stop myself from rolling. I want to be stubborn and mulish, but instead become com-pletely helpless and can only whisper feebly, "What did I do? What . . .?"

At last all grows quiet. Hands hastily shove me somewhere and unroll me from my bolt. I see a bare room and a young, tired-looking man whose bored eyes blink at me lifelessly.

"Young and bald, bald and young," I say to myself and cringe at the waggish twitching of his lower lip.

"Sit down!" he orders, stalking away from me toward his desk.

My God! I wonder as I slowly move toward him, have I in fact unwittingly committed a crime? Am I another Heros-tratos?

He swivels about unexpectedly and bores into me with half-crazed eyes.

"Do you know, my precious little scholar," he ejaculates, "that your typewriter was used to type thousands of leaflets? You go about pretending to be honest . . . sneaky devil, you! But we've known all about you for a long time. You won't tell? We'll get it out of you! Will we ever! We've had some real highfliers in our day, and they ended up on their knees, tear-fully begging forgiveness. Not like you, you lousy craphead!"

I still don't understand anything. I try to remember at least a few words of this tirade, but the words pelt me like hail-stones, and I listen only to those painful passages that refer directly to me. Then with the hopeless, stupid look of a drown-ing man, I gaze at the people who dash in and out of the room, shrilling like a covey of rapacious cormorants.

The ordinary rectangular tabletop floats before my eyes. It is the only calm and silent thing in the room, reminding me by its very stability of reality as it surfaces from the Kafkaesque whirlpool. I try to distinguish between the faces and voices that stubbornly keep demanding something from me, but they are all as alike as peas in a pod. Five, three, two, one—it seems the tabletop is a stage, and sets for a lavish production are being thrown up, but instead of powerful basses and tenors and womanish trebles I hear from the prompter's box in the wings the gabble of a damaged tape recorder in which the tape breaks from time to time.

I try to answer these people. Perhaps I do say something and object, because they grasp at my words. Afterward I seem to be sliding down from the chair, which is bolted down against the backdrop of a blank, insurmountable wall.

"What, Malanchuk?[5] We'll bring the Provincial Party Secretary here, and you, his shitty underling, will tell us everything you did! You'll confess all your vile deeds!"

"What, think you're a genius? Lectured at the university, a Candidate of Sciences? Ha! We know all about you scholars. We had more important candidates than you in the thirties, and we wrung their necks like chickens'!"

"Why should we be telling him this? He knows it himself. He even wrote his thesis about one of them—that shitty humorist Vyshnya.[6] Ha-ha, you want to make nationalists famous?"

I object, I really object to this senseless tirade of sneers and taunts. "But how dare you . . . a prominent Ukrainian . . . seven volumes of his work about to be published . . . nominated for the Lenin Prize . . . long since rehabilitated . . ."

"Rehabilitated?" They gape at me as if I have told them of a new Pompeii. They refuse to grant credence to my words and burst into laughter. They actually double up with laughter and point their fingers at me as if I were some sort of freak. Oh, how they laugh!

I look in consternation at these petty, carefree creatures who have descended upon me like a colonizing expedition from another planet, flaunting their youth, cruelty, and insolence. They know their worth, these supreme and exalted protectors. They are not in the least embarrassed by this. On the contrary. Now a thought dawns on me: My God! they're unspeakable jokers, laughing at me simply because they decided to have some fun. And I'm carrying on like a prim girl who longs to push these ruffians away. I am so overcome by this feeling that before I know it I am laughing with them. I must certainly look like good old Vyshnya, who could not get used to the deadly serious interrogation and tried to laugh it all off: "But sirs, why do you consider me a terrorist? If you're so anxious to convict me, why don't you try me for the rape of Clara Zetkin?"

The rectangular tabletop, symbol of permanence in the commotion that has whirled around me, continues to float before my eyes. The table is the only thing that connects me with reality and prevents me from falling into the deep pit that I clearly feel beneath my feet. I am afraid to move a muscle lest I slip and plunge below. Well-fed men, whose fine physiques no doubt stir the imagination of many a lady, circle in confusion around me. I listen to their importunate giggling, catch their enigmatic glances, and overhear fragments of their sentences. At times these surge forward insistently to overwhelm me, then recede into oblivion. I am a simple-minded spectator to all this, unable to grasp or understand anything. At this very moment I am far from this building, standing in a public square, my arms and legs shackled, patiently waiting for the executioner to come and hack my head off. People are chattering, spitting, and crying. Everything blurs over as I stand naked on the scaffolding, my shoulders hunched to ward off the cold.

The executioner arrives and calls to the crowd, "Who wants to save the life of this thief by marrying him?"

A murmur passes through the assembled people. Someone shouts, "I do!" But then the crowd becomes deadly quiet.

"Why?" I puzzle. "Why didn't she come forward? Why has her voice died away?"

"Who wants to marry him?"

I see the executioner, the platform, and a few wasted old people who hasten to lower their eyes.

I am surprised at the silence that unexpectedly fills the room. No one is left around me, but I did not even notice when everyone went out. I am alone. My head feels painfully flattened. You have left and taken me with you, I think.

I realize that darkness has fallen. The noise in the street is slowly subsiding, and I haven't had a bite to eat all day. I have a little change in my pocket, enough to get a light snack on the way home. The thought appeals to me so much that I even get up from the chair and take a step or two. But the barred windows appear before me, and someone asks with a sneer, "Where to, my good man?"

Really, where to? I think and lean on the table. If I don't spend my money on a snack, I can take a taxi home, where my wife is anxiously waiting for me. But if I buy a snack, I won't have enough even for the streetcar. I look at the windows, then at the door. I am a naïve hermit who amuses himself with empty prattle like a gossipy old woman.

Someone comes in. Yes. I don't even turn my head. "Come with me." I hear the authoritative voice and obediently get up to follow.

The clamor keeps up around me until I finally find myself in a large room. I am politely greeted by an ostensibly calm man who introduces himself as my interrogator. I immediately feel well disposed toward him. He is the slim straw that I must clutch at like a drowning man. Now, after all these hours of abuse, I'll finally find out what's happening to me. What can all this mean? Is it a mistake? Am I the victim of some bungling clown?

"You, Mykhaylo Osadchy," says the interrogator after graciously offering me a seat beside him, "are suspected of disseminating anti-Soviet nationalist literature in Lviv. We are presently looking into this, and you have nothing to worry about. A little more patience and you'll soon be able to go home. But it all depends on how honest you are in making a clean breast of everything."

I have nothing to make a clean breast of—that's what I tell him. He looks at me reproachfully as he jots something down. At times he gets up from behind the table and stares out the barred window while toying with his fountain pen. Then he turns toward me slowly—very slowly—and peers intently into my eyes. I sense in this look a kind of carefree skepticism and even unabashed cynicism. The realization is particularly keen when he casts a tired glance at the bars, bluntly reminding me that I'll have a chance to develop a closer acquaintance with them.

As time passes our conversation progresses so far that I no longer see the purpose of it. We are like old friends who meet after a long separation and in a brief encounter blurt everything out, only to worry afterward about what they have actually said. And yet nothing definite has really been said. We touch on various topics in literature and art, but the conversation breaks off abruptly because he is interested in something else, something that neither he nor I have a clear notion of. It seems to me that having begun this conversation he feels obliged by politeness to continue it.

I talk to him about freedom of speech, about the new concept of the dictatorship of the proletariat which, according to the Party Program, "has accomplished its historical mission and from the viewpoint of internal developments ceased to be indispensable in the USSR." I remind him that "the State in the present era has been transformed into a State of all the people, an instrument for expressing the interests and the will of all citizens."

He cuts me off in mid-sentence although I could recite almost the entire Program from memory. He is nervously biting his lips, and his voice is high-pitched, but I am so indifferent to everything that I hardly notice.

"There always was and always will be a dictatorship," he remarks with a sly squint.

"Excuse me," I attempt to contradict him, "but I am a young communist, and surely I ought to take the Party's word sooner than yours."

"Communists, even young ones, don't wind up in here," he replies, a smile quivering at the corners of his thin lips. "And as for what you said, I'm not certain whether it was stated by the Party or by Khrushchev."

To tell the truth, such a distinction staggers me. It is so insolent that for a moment I can't even object. Having been employed by the Lviv Provincial Party Committee, I knew that Khrushchev had resigned because of ill health, and I had even heard from reliable sources that he had committed errors in domestic and foreign affairs. But to say that Khrushchev and the Party were at opposite poles—that seems paradoxical to me!

"How can you indulge in such distinctions?" I ask my interrogator in astonishment. "For ten years Khrushchev headed the Soviet State and Party. For ten years he was a faithful Leninist, the leading authority in the world communist movement, an active . . ."

"Stop, stop!" the interrogator grimaces. "There's no use pretending you're a flounder leaping out of the frying pan! Do you know where such leaders belong?"

He is toying with his fountain pen again and swaying lightly on his feet. I wait for him to continue his train of thought, but he says nothing more. At the end he is once again looking with his characteristic bluntness at the window whose bars are outlined against the twilight. Bars—the only work of art that has undergone no change in thousands of years.

At about nine o'clock I am led into the adjoining room, ordered to undress, and thoroughly searched, even in places I'd be embarrassed to mention. In the guards' faces I see again the disappointment of people who stubbornly search for something but cannot find it. I feel washed out and sleepy. Occasionally I am roused from my stupor by clammy fingers that crawl over my body like restless leeches. I can't keep anything in focus, and only one thought keeps appearing and receding: if they're searching me, then they're going to let me go to sleep. Sleep! Sle-ee-ep!

Barely able to stand on my feet, I am led to Cell No. 64,

tiny, uncomfortable, and stifling. I collapse without undressing on the dirty, sheetless mattress, which seems so inviting at this moment, cover myself with an old blanket, tattered by time and the fates of many others, and fall into a frightening, fitful sleep. I dream about horses. They are thin and sickly, standing in deep snow and breathing halos of vapor to keep me warm. Perhaps they feel better now, I think. The earth is the best blanket of all.

A pounding on the door and a strange voice roaring in Russian wake me in the morning. "Reveille! Reveille!" the voice calls, at first down the corridor and then at my cell.

I lie in bed not understanding anything. The tone reminds me of another voice, one that I used to hear long ago in my village when the ragman rode along the street in his wagon, bellowing at the top of his lungs, "Anything to go? Anything to go?"

I jump up and gasp with pain: my entire body is covered with red splotches that burn and itch unbearably. What could have caused them? But before I can examine them my attention is caught again by the unfamiliar shouts resounding in the corridor.

"Fall out for toilet call! Out for toilet call!"

These words have a strange music to them, and they finally bring me back to reality. Now I remember yesterday and recognize the cell. It is filled with the hurried sounds of shuffling and hissing which seep in from all sides. People seem to be rushing somewhere, as if they were working on a top-secret project, and I hear insistent whispers: "Sh-sh-sh! Quiet, I tell you, quiet! No talking!"

The bolts at the top and bottom of the door rattle, and the huge lock screeches like an asthmatic old man coughing on the hearth. I am being guarded like a mummified pharaoh in a pyramid, weighed down with a heavy slab of stone. The idea makes me laugh, and I feel myself puffing my cheeks out with pride, thrusting my chest forward, and flexing my legs. The ancient tyrants were nothing by comparison. The stones piled on top of their treasures can hardly compare with the countless massive locks and bolts that secure the steel door to my cell.

"Toilet call!" a toy soldier with red-striped shoulder boards calls out sternly from the door. "Move along! Shake yourself!"

Tom Thumb hands me two scraps of paper and politely says, "Please," then patiently stumbles after me. A pharaoh really is nothing by comparison with me. Did anyone ever say "Please" to him in Russian or guard his trip to the toilet so assiduously?

Prison gruel! I stare at my food in bewitchment. It seems to have glued itself to the black, smutty, and misshapen metal dish. You can find one like it on any city dump. I dip my wooden spoon into the greenish-yellow liquid and bring it toward my mouth. But halfway up I stop and carefully examine this eternal companion of prison life. This specialty of the house must have been invented by a master chef who spent many a night poring over the Old Russian counterpart of *Larousse Gastronomique.* His invention has survived all wars and revolutions and still remains the same. Leonardo da Vinci invented the sewing machine, but his model was so crude that it can't even be compared to today's machines, which perform innumerable operations—stitching, buttonholing, sewing on buttons, darning, and embroidering. Yet the inventor's name has not been forgotten, and we still pay him homage. But what an injustice to the inventor of prison gruel! He has been ungratefully consigned to oblivion, even though his invention may have been the greatest of all—it has survived the centuries without any need for refinement.

I bring the spoon closer to my mouth, but then lower it in sudden surprise. My nose is being assailed by such a bouquet of fragrances that I grimace involuntarily. I turn away from the food and think once more with gratitude about the superb chef who invented it. If I could have presided over an ancient culinary art contest, I should have certainly awarded him the title of *Chef extraordinaire.*

I decide that the subject of my next thesis will be prison gruel, a dish that can be savored in any country regardless of its social system. The inventor's name must be discovered. I am very pleased with myself for having decided to make the anonymous chef famous and to link my humble name with his.

My scholarly reflections are interrupted quite inopportunely by a guard at the barred Judas hole. Rounding his *o*'s in the central Russian manner and using mimic gestures to draw me toward him, he calls in a goodnatured way: "Name with *O!* Name with *O!*" I realize now that to prevent inmates from learning each other's identities, they are not called up for interrogation by their surnames—only the first letter is used. In such cases the prisoner must run to his cell door and whisper his name. I obediently rush to the door and identify myself, even though I feel rather funny because I am all alone in the cell.

"Let's go! Hands behind your back, I tell you!"

My escort clomps behind me, stopping me at corners to look down the corridor and make sure no one is coming, then taking up his position behind me again. All the while he is snapping the fingers of both hands with a skill that makes me envy him, just as I would be envied at this moment by a pharaoh whose only accompaniment on his walks was the rataplan of drums and the tantara of trumpets.

Yesterday's acquaintance, with whom I conversed so politely last evening and who opened my eyes to the realities of our political life, is seated behind a massive desk supported by two pedestals and covered with a blue blotter. I have always been fond of this color: it reminds me of skies and open spaces and puts me in a calm and cheerful frame of mind. The interrogator smiles at me, and I immediately perk up. No doubt everything has been looked into just as he promised, and now they'll release me since there's no point in keeping me here any longer. I sit down across from him, look him trustingly in the face, and return his smile. I really do like this man. I can hardly restrain myself from telling him how I'm less gloomy when I'm with him. He's sure to be pleased.

"One moment, just one moment," the interrogator drawls as he bends over his blotter and begins to fill out an interrogation report. "Everything appears to be clearing up, only a few more questions, then we'll send you home with a few good whacks on your bare behind. But don't let us catch you again! I know you haven't been up to anything, but others certainly have."

I don't know what others have been up to. I'm simply pleased that things are being cleared up so quickly and that I'm being proven innocent and will soon go home. Home, away from the dismal, stale-aired cell, away from this gloomy building, away from reveille and toilet calls. Soon I'll be out on the street breathing fresh air again. I probably won't take a streetcar or taxi but will walk down Suvorov, Dzerzhinsky, and Lenin Streets, turn right along Mechnikov, and thus reach my own long-awaited Nekrasov Street.

"Yes," says the interrogator, raising his gray eyes to me. Suddenly I glimpse a shadow of ill-concealed hostility in them. "What anti-Soviet literature did you receive from Ivan Svitlychny in Kiev and from Bohdan Horyn in Lviv?"[7] (He is using the polite form of address, as he does when he is taking testimony. Otherwise, he uses the familiar form.)

I know both of them well. Svitlychny appeals to me as an intelligent, sober man and a talented critic who inspires others by never compromising his principles. I know he is a man of learning; I envy his knowledge of Ukrainian cultural history, and I am captivated by his literary tastes, his aesthetic inclinations, and his wit. And his warm personality has always appealed to me.

"I didn't receive anything from them," I reply calmly but immediately regret my words. Tall, corpulent, and menacing (he reminds me at this moment of Peter the Great), the interrogator jumps from his seat (what has happened to his calm smile and gently playful voice?) and fills the room almost completely with his bulk. His eyes bore down into me, and his breath is on my face. He can barely control himself. (But he does. He has trained himself to do so.)

"Careful now, careful! Your life depends on what you say. Everything depends on you. You'd better remember that!" He paces the length of the room in silence, sits down behind his desk, and picks up his fountain pen.

"I wanted to release you today," he says with emphasis, "and what do you do? Here I'm doing my best to wrap this case up, but you refuse to say anything and insist on playing the fool. You think you can pull the wool over my eyes? What did you receive from Bohdan Horyn?"

"If you're so interested in these things and if my life depends on them, then I can say—"

"That's a smart fellow! Tell me all about it!"

"—that I remember borrowing a book about the painter Novakivsky,[8] a study titled *Napoleon and Ukraine*,[9] and also *The Treaty Between Bohdan Khmelnytsky and Tsar Alexis in 1654*."[10]

"Hold it, hold it!" The interrogator dashes behind his desk. "You're in such a hurry you'll trip over your cock. I believe we shall write it down thus: 'Received from Bohdan Horyn anti-Soviet literature—*The Treaty Between Bohdan Khmelnytsky and Tsar Alexis in 1654*.' "

I am reminded of a pathologically jealous man who drove his chaste and honest wife to the brink of insanity. He imagined her surrounded by lovers who seduced her but wouldn't even pay a few miserable coins for her favors. He called her a tramp, although adultery never entered her mind. He beat her, and she remained meek and silent, not daring to contradict him in anything, since he refused to listen to explanations, arguments, or proof. He was like an artist or a poet who in a burst of creative energy is transported out of the real world by his vision. In this case it was a vision of jealousy and infidelity. These complexes of persecution, jealousy, and death are common ones. Finally the woman went off on a spree. She acquired numerous lovers and took great delight in their good looks and virility. From a persecuted, cowed, insignificant little thing she turned into a person again.

I envy that woman. I envy her fanatically, senselessly. I detect a mania of envy growing in me. I begin to loathe that woman because she succeeded so easily in slipping away from home for an hour or two to be with her lovers. But I cannot escape these walls, cannot use languid eyes and bared knees to rouse desire in someone. But then that's not what I need.

They are trying to turn an honest man into a criminal. Stubbornly and systematically they act out a charade in which the spectators and the players have exchanged places. The spectators perform without the slightest talent, although they refuse to admit this. They continue to act while the real actor closes his eyes in the empty theater and pulls his hair out in helpless dismay.

I never committed any crimes. I did not even know how to treat people basely, and now they are trying to convince me of the opposite. They are proving to me that I am a criminal and merely conceal my guilt like a child who has broken a glass but insists to everyone that it broke by accident. Stubbornly and tediously Major Halski tries to convince me of my guilt. He is doing this with such conviction and with such a strong desire for some unexpected discovery which keeps escaping him, but in which he continues to believe, that at times I feel sorry for him.

I sincerely want to help him, want to make myself a criminal just to humor this drug-crazed maniac who imagines every telephone pole is a felon. He carves his Galatea like a sculptor who rages because she is so beautiful and has no criminal traits, whereas he wants to create only the image of a criminal. He is ready to chop his hands off because they are creating beauty against his will. Oh, how I envy that woman who went wrong and at last became what her husband had imagined her to be!

I am filled with such an uncontrollable desire to help Major Halski in even some small way that I can hardly restrain myself from rushing to the window, wrenching out the iron bars, dashing to the Lviv stadium, where the intellects of our society—the soccer fans—are always gathered, breaking up by force their manic congregations, climbing on the stands, and shouting:

"People, I am your enemy! I am a lackey of West German imperialists! I am a spy! Perhaps you didn't know it, but I was carrying out the heinous assignments of the *Obersturmbannführer* long before I was born. Major Halski, tell them his name! And tell them how I participated in the 'small circle' that prepared the illegal meeting in Yevpatoria.[11] Major Halski, please! Stand beside me and tell them what you know. You have to tell them, because no one, not even the participants, knows anything about this meeting except you!"

Oh, how I envy that woman!

I am standing on the platform again. Beside me the executioner raises high his bloodied ax. It flashes before my eyes, and I close them.

"Who wants to take this thief for a husband?" I hear a voice ask, but it dies away almost immediately, and all becomes still.

But no. From somewhere on the side comes secretive, malicious giggling, and whenever it pauses I clearly hear someone reciting. Familiar and beloved verses creep into my consciousness. Assuming a Pushkin-like stance, Major Halski is reciting from memory my poem, "I Stood in the Carpathians," which was published in the Lviv newspaper *Vil'na Ukrayina* [Free Ukraine]. He pauses for a moment to catch his breath from laughter and then continues to recite. Nearby evil, unpleasant-looking faces are also gloating, and I want to hurl something insulting at them.

I wasn't thinking about poetic quality when I wrote that poem. But even if it turned out as a crude verse, I did express in it my love for Ukraine, my native land. Now, when Major

Halski is ridiculing my poem, I realize that he and the others are not laughing at it. Oh no, they are laughing at my love for Ukraine.

"He, the universe, and Ukraine! Ha-ha-ha! You know what you can do with that, you miserable, motherfucking moron!"

Major Halski did not study at the Gorky Literary Institute where he would have learned to dissemble his literary opinions. He is as blunt and searing as a pint of Russian rotgut. Leaning against the table, he continues to recite my poetry, pausing only to give everyone a chance to laugh. He even knows poems that I have completely forgotten about. I am astonished by Major Halski's total recall, his literary erudition, and his sincere enthusiasm for my poetry. This is the first time I've been face-to-face with a fan of mine.

"You goddamn motherfucker, you double-dealing scoundrel, you political prostitute! You stooge of West German imperialists! Who carried out the assignments of the *Obersturmbannführer*? Who took part in the 'small circle' that set up the illegal meeting in Yevpatoria? You'll tell us everything! We know everything! How? We had your ass bugged, you scurvy little scholar!"

I feel like a small, shy boy who sees a wooden hogshead and cannot resist getting into it. Quickly climbing a nearby tree, he closes his eyes and jumps into the barrel. Suddenly the unexpected occurs: the barrel shudders like a horse that has been dozing, shakes itself, and gallops off. It plunges madly down the hill, careening off rocks and tree stumps. Sometimes it is on its side, then it straightens up. It falls down, then seems to be flying through the air. The boy is numb with fear, unable to shout or cry out. He can only stare wide-eyed as the barrel, like a yearling biting down hard on its bit, plunges headlong to the land of no return.

What kind of horse is this? And why this silence? I diligently examine the walls of the barrel, which do not move but remain steady before my eyes. I notice also that the staves are covered with soot, rather gray, and too commonplace for a barrel. Close to the rim I see a shaft of light dissected by bars. Why should there be bars in a barrel? Then I see before me a short, broad-shouldered man enveloped in a cloud of smoke.

"I sold the raven horse, you know," he is telling me heatedly. "It had white dapples, a very fine animal indeed. There I was walking down the road and I saw a cart horse stop dead in its tracks. No matter how the driver urged it on, that horse wouldn't budge. I turned around, and the horse was staring at me and grinning just like a person. They're supposed to be dumb animals, and here it recognized me five years later. What a splendid little horse that was!"

I must be regaining consciousness. A weight seems to lift from me, and I sigh with relief. The interrogation apparently is over, and I am back in the cell. But I am not alone: the broad-shouldered fellow is furiously chain-smoking and incessantly chattering about horses.

"And what are you in for?" He peers at me intently as he purses his lips. "Where did you work until now?"

"Me? I was a lecturer at the university, in the journalism department. Have you ever read anything by Vyshnya, have you heard about this amusing writer? He was the author of . . . " I have unexpectedly become carefree and cheerful, and my tongue is loosened. Then I forget about Vyshnya and talk about something else, and the more I talk the more quickly I return to reality. I feel pleased as I sense that the viscous mass that has filled my head is slowly receding and in its place consciousness is seeping in.

"What were you thrown in for? Did you take a bribe? Did you try to get somebody admitted to the university?"

"What are you talking about? Mine is an Article 62 case."[12]

"You had a printing press? Put out pamphlets?"

"Come now, what printing press, what pamphlets? They came, took a few books about history and art, an article . . ."

"They used Article 62 for owning books? You must be kidding! It's for people who belong to illegal organizations or try to overthrow the government or spread illegal literature. Something's very fishy here! Maybe you stuffed your students' heads with the wrong kind of ideas?"

"How can you say that? I only taught them what was in the syllabus!"

My cellmate throws his head back and roars with laughter. "If you're not lying, old man, you'll go home tomorrow." He narrows his eyes and falls silent for a moment. "But these days they don't pick you up just like that. Something seems to be wrong here, eh? I understand, something's not quite right, so they go out and bring in a few people. And you scuttle to your burrow and lie low. That's how I got caught. For three whole months I tried to cover up my tracks, led the prosecutor by the nose, confused the investigators, and would you believe it? They had known all about me from the very beginning!"

He puffs on his cigarette bitterly, then adds angrily, with a belated repentance, "So I really messed it up for myself. What an idiot I was! Now I'd gladly kick myself to kingdom come if I could."

I feel a rush of inexpressible sympathy for my cellmate. The man's obviously in trouble, and I, like any oppressed person, feel sorry for him and want to help him in some way. He's been sentenced to twelve years. A wife and two children are waiting at home for him, a wife without a husband, children without a father—separation is particularly keen in the prison cell, when you are cut off from the entire world, driven among four mute, cold walls.

"I had another dream about a clock last night," he says. "It was standing on a table and not ticking. My wife must have betrayed me again last night. It's always like that. Every time you dream about a clock, your wife is being unfaithful. But I don't blame her. What can you do? It's nature. You can't change nature. Michurin managed to, that's true, but he wasn't dealing with a woman.[13] Are you married?"

"Almost," I reply, "almost."

"But those horses are just like people. For five years I didn't see it. I stop, the old man is whipping it, and it stands there smiling at me. Those animals are so funny with their affection and fidelity for people."

"Won't you offer me a cigarette? Permit me to light mine from yours."

"Here are the matches, please."

"No, I'd like, if you don't mind, that is—"

". . . You're young and pretty, with a university education, you're a mathematician. Who are you holding on to? He'll rot in prison, and you—how will you survive without a man? Do you know what lonely nights do to a woman? You can't imagine the suffering they bring! God, you're so young—born in 1943! And you want to throw your life away? Why don't you just let him go to hell? Find yourself another man, one who's big and strong. Do you know what a real man means to a woman? 'Love lives in cottages as well as in courts,' they say. But that's only with a real man. What good will Osadchy be to you even if he does get out of prison someday? An invalid with dystrophy and stomach ulcers?"

"But he'll soon be a father!"

"Oh, that's nothing! Why worry your pretty little head about these things? It's so cheap these days to . . . "

"—May I offer you a light?"

I look at his broad back as he stands by the window, his short legs straddled far apart, and continues to talk about horses. I decide that I must write a poem about his horses and give it to him.

"My name is Palyha, Volodymyr Petrovych Palyha. I'm from Velyki Chuchmany, that's near Buzk [in the Lviv Province]."

"I'll write a poem about your horses."

"Listen, when they clap horse thieves into jail, every idiot knows what they're in for. But what are you poet boys doing here? Is it really for those harmless little books you mentioned? If that's the case, those guys are insulting the good name of prison."

I doubt whether Campanella would have written *The City of the Sun,* that extraordinary book about the society of the future, if he had not spent twenty-seven years in prison. Oppressed by authority's walls in some wretched hole, he let his restless spirit range over sunlit expanses to the glowing horizons of his imaginary city.

My own thoughts are managing to evade me. Perhaps I never had any, or they were inadvertently picked up during the search and locked away in a safe. So many talents are lost to this world simply because people have no time to write and waste their minds. During the day they are occupied by their jobs; in the evenings they go out or spend time with their families. People barely have time to walk around and think. Themes crowd in, but disappear quickly if not fixed. Probably they go looking for their real master.

Here in the prison cell your restlessness is always with you, especially when weeks pass by without interrogation and you feel forgotten by the whole world. You can invent a new mathematics or a second multiplication table and write innumerable *Cities of the Sun.* If we want to have a great many writers, mathematicians, physicists, and scholars, we ought to imprison people for five, ten, or twenty-five years and forget all about them. Let them create freely in their cells. They might starve, but in the end that is not really important. The important thing is that their names and their work be preserved, because they are so vitally necessary for the prestige of our country.

I ask for paper and a pencil, carefully arrange them on the small table, and become lost in thought. Volodya sits by the window reading. If he sat somewhere else, I think, I might get some ideas. But there he sits, blocking the light out. Perhaps my mind is afraid of his broad shoulders and is wandering around outside. . . .

It's no good at all! I am not Campanella. But then his window was not covered by frosted glass—it probably hadn't been invented yet—and if he couldn't find delight in *The City of the Sun,* then he could at least enjoy a ray of real sunlight. But now they think of everything. My grandchildren will probably not get to read a new *City of the Sun.*

But my attempts to distract myself are futile. I am neither Campanella nor even a proper suspect. As I play with my paper illusions, I sense a mounting trepidation in my breast. My heart treacherously skips a beat, and my eyes will not leave the table. "Young and bald, bald and young," I say to myself. "What's happening in that place of his which should be covered by hair?"

He raises his narrowed, prickly eyes to me, then lowers them at once. Now they scurry across the pages of the strange book lying on his blue blotter. The pages are closely covered with elegant handwriting in green ink. But the color does not soothe me at all. On the contrary, it troubles and disturbs me: they've cooked up something against me again!

"Well, well! Little Mykhaylo is very quiet, very modest. Who'd believe that . . ." He mouths the words as his fingers follow the writing, his eyebrows lifting occasionally in surprise. He grows happy, then frowns. Sometimes he folds his hands and slowly lifts his heavy eyelids.

"To tell you the truth, it isn't so important any more to have you talk. That's not really necessary now. You've already told us everything you know. Even if you wanted to repeat the conversations you had with your acquaintances, you couldn't do it any better than what we've got . . ." leaning with both arms on the heavy book, which resembles an ancient Bible, he sighs with satisfaction, ". . . written down here."

"What do you think 'UHVR' might mean?"[14] asks my interrogator as he opens the door a crack. Apparently he has been listening closely to our conversation from the hallway and now, seeing an opportune moment, is trying to throw me off balance.

"Uwerherr?" I repeat. "Is that a surname?"

"We're hiding, my boy, we're shamming," the interrogator shakes his head reproachfully. "We're not coming through nicely at all. We pretend to be honest, but we forget about decency."

He nods to the "young and bald one," who reads from the "Bible" in a dignified tone: "6 May 1965. All talented artists and poets are now resorting only to national forms."

My mouth drops with amazement. How do they know these exact words? I said them once in my own home to the young artist Ivan Ostafiychuk.[15] Perhaps they had questioned him, and he had told them. But surely not word for word? A sudden realization makes me turn cold with loathing: they had me bugged! Yes, they had me bugged. But how? My apartment is on the fifth floor. Maybe the telephone, the tape recorder, a microphone in the attic or near an open window? Anything was possible.

I feel my entire body revolting at the thought: they had *bugged* me, a staff member of the Provincial Party organization, a lecturer at the university! What could they have wanted to know? I never harbored any secret ideas that might have a seditious potential. I always came out with whatever was on my mind. I spoke openly with friends, colleagues at the university, and fellow Party members. I have been maintaining this throughout the interrogation, but they refuse to believe me. In any case, there was never any sedition. Why can't they trust people? Why do they have to spy on them and make them into criminals? Other people speak out much more vehemently than I about the shortcomings of our society. They're all decent and honest people with respectable jobs as scientists and artists. Are they also here? Here, in adjoining cells? Are the guards spying on them and even writing down how long they sit on the toilet? Are their asses bugged too, as Major Halski put it?

I stare at the glowing, triumphant faces of the interrogators and feel that I'm inside the barrel again, plunging headlong from the hilltop. I am small and helpless, and I decide that they have singled me out just because I'm like that. Apparently there are stronger characters than myself, but these are not touched. To frighten them, to cow them into submission and make them lose their civic dignity, the authorities pick out the weak ones and make them into examples of what will happen if people don't stop pointing their fingers at the wolves among us.

"What do you want from me? What do you need?" I shout at my interrogators. I cannot control myself any longer. I am boiling with rage. "You give the impression that God Himself is nothing in comparison with you!"

I feel utterly drained and fall silent. I have no words left. I am nothing to these self-assured interrogators; I am shit. They tell me this to my face again and again. But is it only I? They speak no better of Malanchuk, the Secretary of the Lviv Provincial Party Committee, considered to be the greatest promoter of Russification and "internationalism" in Western Ukraine, and a Doctor of Sciences to boot. Well, all right, I may have said on a number of occasions that here in Ukraine the Ukrainian language receives little encouragement. I may have made myself enemies not only in the interrogators, but in Malanchuk as well. But then how do you explain their contemptuous attitude toward Malanchuk himself? Oh no, I can't understand a thing!

"When horse thieves are clapped in jail, I know what they're in for. But when they imprison these poet boys, they insult the good name of prison."

The cell is always a little easier to endure in the morning, when fresh air wafts in from outside. Perhaps I only imagine the current, but the feeling of lightness stays with me until ten o'clock. "Reveille! Toilet call! Gruel!"—these pleasant-sounding words flow together for me like a concert of Grieg's unfathomable music. I manage to forget about everything, and only occasionally do I think: Something is bound to happen. I can easily guess what it will be, but still it worries and depresses me. Something is bound to happen.

Then I begin to hum half-forgotten melodies which now seem to me as entertaining and enchanting as a pretty girl. Or I close my eyes, lean against the wall, and paraphrase poems. I paraphrase them instead of reciting them because sometimes I cannot even remember their themes or their au-

Cataract

thors. Everything mingles, changes, flows into one. Joy alternating with an unusual sadness fills me to overflowing, and I burst out laughing.

Volodya gazes at me attentively at such moments, and his right eye twitches in surprise. We sit down then on one of the bunks or at the table and play jackstraws. The gambling spirit takes such firm hold of us that it makes us oblivious of everything: the cell, which reminds us of a kennel kept by a bad master; the idiotic questions of the interrogators ("Why did you drink tea? Why did you ride the streetcar? Why did you change twenty kopecks instead of ten?"), and the voice that whispers, "Something is bound to happen."

The game of jackstraws could have been invented only in prison. To a free man it must seem as gray and boring as the world to a color-blind man. Yet here, within these four walls, we get more excited over a round of jackstraws than the most ardent soccer fans do over a world-cup match.

Of the twenty-five matches that we use, four have from one to four notches. Each notch counts for five points. The matches are placed in a box whose bottom has been removed. When the box is raised, the matches are left in a heap on the table. We take turns removing one match at a time from the pile, trying not to touch any of the other matches. Whoever gets the most notches wins the game.

After a while the game begins to pall on us. Volodya and I quarrel over trifles. We turn away from each other and refuse to speak, both harboring insults. But before long an octopus-like apparition begins to swim before my eyes, then creeps over my shoulders and presses me down to the mattress. Its disgusting tentacles slither over my body and worm their way under my skin. I lie face up on the upper bunk and shut my eyes. I feel even more frightened when the walls begin to move together and slide down. The ceiling collapses on my chest, suffocating me, and I jump down gasping for air. Volodya blinks at me again with his blind eye.

"So, you're afraid the nice wall will crush you? You'd better realize, my friend, that this is no kindergarten with fat-assed teachers. This is paradise, but it's full of tailless demons—the KGB men."

Finally, on 28 September, I receive a food parcel from home. I have forgotten much, but this day I shall remember for a long time. Perhaps because the parcel both touches and angers me: it reminds me of something that bothered me even when I was a free man. Not many people know that I was once dishonest with myself and with others. This incident is not for my interrogators; such dishonesty does not interest them in the least. But here in the cell I am particularly sorry when I am reminded of it.

I remember the time when butter and even ordinary cooking oil could not be bought in Lviv. I was working in the Party's Provincial Committee at the time, and like all the other staff members I could easily buy butter and oil in the Committee garage at 59 Zelena Street. At holiday season we would always leave the garage with parcels full of these scarce items. In order not to rouse suspicion in passers-by, we would be driven home in cars, usually in the regular Party car, registration LVB 10–45. Who would have thought that the parcel from home would remind me so unpleasantly of the Party packages? The comparison surfaces quite unexpectedly. Or has Major Halski hammered it into my head?

"You fucking communist! You went around babbling Party secrets! No wonder they ran you out of there!"

I never divulged or sold Party secrets to anyone. I was a loyal member of the Party and observed its statutes strictly. I was only angered by those packages we occasionally got. Sometimes, when I was with close friends, I couldn't refrain from asking why we communists advocate Lenin's frugality but don't practice that virtue in daily life. In times of great hardship Lenin refused all gifts and asked that the sugar and clothing he was sent be donated for the upkeep of kindergartens. But we were driven home with our packages in the regular Party car.

Rummaging about in the parcel, Volodya finds several on-ions. "Now we're going to live it up," he says with a sly wink at me.

I do not quite understand what he means but am immedi-ately caught up by his mood. We decide to become gardeners. Neither of us has the necessary background, but we do have an overwhelming desire to discover a new species of onion. We place the onions in paper boats and float them in a dish of water. This is quite some diversion for us. Every few min-utes we go up to the window to water our garden and to watch the onions send out pale green shoots. Now there is another prisoner in the cell, young and inexperienced like me, but who is not called out for interrogations or accused of counterrevolution, and yet can expect to die like all us sin-ners. Still the onions have a much easier time of it than I, for they are oblivious of all this and continue doggedly to stretch upward.

Our diet of greenish-yellow gruel now becomes more palata-ble. By slicing onion shoots into the thin broth we improve both the color and the taste. We don't even dare to call such splendid fare gruel. This is a nourishing meal, full of calories and vitality. In the free world the onion is a remedy for seven diseases. Here in prison it will surely cure all the maladies that mankind is prone to.

Yet our onions cannot cure one sickness—suspicion. The warden almost has an epileptic fit when he sees the young and sprightly plants on the windowsill. Each shoot reminds him of a cold, sharp weapon. As he gingerly touches the plants and tests their strength, I watch him with bated breath and wonder if he will take them away so that Volodya and I will be left alone again, forced to pass the time playing jackstraws.

"All right," he concludes, having satisfied himself that we are growing only ordinary onions and not steel knives. "Our prison regulations do not cover the growing of onions in the cell . . ."

I am happy—we are allowed to keep our onions prisoner. They continue to grow on the windowsill, dispelling our boredom and bringing in from outside the insolence of life, which can be ended only when the plants are pulled up by the roots.

Volodya resumes telling stories about horses. I lie motionless and stare at the ceiling. Sometimes I screw up my eyes, and then the light that glows almost by my nose sinks lower and burns me. I turn over and feverishly rub my eyes, but my delirium will not go away. It has taken a firm grip on me. I see a sunny field, or perhaps a meadow, not far from the Sula River in my native Sumy Province, with horses grazing on the banks.

"There were twenty-five," announces Volodya.

"Were they your horses?" I ask from the bunk with curiosity.

"Yes, I grazed them on the river bank, and they drank river water."

"They couldn't have been your horses," I contradict Volodya cautiously. "You couldn't have had twenty-five of them."

Kalnyshevsky had twenty-five horses.[16] He grazed them in his deep hole, where the sun never penetrated. His cell had no bars, no frosted glass, no sunlight. It must have been designed by an engineer with all sorts of advanced degrees. For twenty-five years the prisoner sat on a bare rock, begging for water from above to keep his horses from dying of thirst. They grazed beside him, on the bank of a river where no water ever flowed. It could not have been easy for him to graze horses at the age of eighty-four, especially when dense fog descended and the horses could run off. Oh, how difficult it was for him!

At the age of a hundred and nine, Kalnyshevsky saw the light of day for the first time after twenty-five years in an Arctic hole. But he never saw his horses again. They had stampeded, and he was blinded by the light he had dreamt about for a quarter of a century. Catherine II knew how to love men, but she also knew how to hate them. How terrible is the hatred of innocent women! How did you endure twenty-five years in your stone cell, my old hunchback? How did you survive with your thirsty horses? Did you have anything but gruel to feed your sick and wretched body? Anything to give strength to your feeble legs and sagging jaw? Tell me, what was Christ's suffering compared to yours? He was crucified and died peacefully on a hilltop. He saw great distances before him. The sun shone on him, and he breathed fresh air. He died easily in his suffering. You also suffered, but you did not die immediately, and so your suffering was greater than Christ's. Yet Christ became God. His agony was graced by a faith that has inspired believers for almost two thousand years. Christ perhaps did not exist; he may have been invented by those who fanatically needed a Christ. His sufferings may have been invented as well. But you—you were real, and so was your suffering.

You loved men and the earth they live on, but both your name and your purpose in life have been ungratefully forgotten. People pray to icons at bedtime, and it does not even occur to them that instead of supplicating a crucified prophet, they might direct their prayers to you, the last leader of the Zaporozhian Host. Faith in you would be much more justified than faith in an afterlife, a paradise so hard to win and so unreal. You believed in reality, but people fear it and have long since stopped praying to it. Kalnyshevsky in his warped hole, buried alive! That's more horrible than crucifixion.

I cannot fall asleep. It is long past midnight; and the city sleeps, the prison sleeps, Volodya and his horses sleep. He was lying when he said he had twenty-five of them and grazed them on the banks of my river. I don't think he is a very nice cellmate. The wall is pushing me down to the floor, and I feverishly hold on to the bunk to keep from falling. But if I have to fall, I think, better I fall on my hands than on my back. I turn over and grow cold: the opposite wall is right against my face. I grasp at the mattress and the bedboards in frenzy, not knowing what to do to keep the ceiling from coming down on my chest and suffocating me.

"Hey you, go to sleep!" the guard hisses at the door. "You've been mumbling half the night, and you're bound to wake everybody up!"

"Listen, buddy, I'll give you everything I've got." I scramble from the bunk to the door, but something is blocking my path. "I'll give you everything I've got, just let me out into the corridor for a minute," I mumble almost in delirium. "The walls are squashing me! You don't have to do it for free, I'll pay you! Please let me out, buddy!"

The corridor seems huge and spacious to me, and I frantically beg to be let out. "Everyone's asleep now. They won't see me, honest!" I whisper madly. I continue to beg long after the guard has disappeared.

"You piece of shit!" Major Halski roars in a frenzied voice. "Shitty, motherfucking sonofabitch!"

His fist whistles past my face. I barely jump back in time. He swings again, and again I see, or rather feel, the fist hurtle past my head. Major Halski swings time and again, raging because he cannot hit me where it will hurt the most. Each time I manage miraculously to turn my face away at the very last moment.

"Don't be afraid, damn it!" he snorts somewhere beside me or already in back. "I won't hit you, whore!"

Again his fist whizzes past my ear, and again I dodge, running from corner to corner without finding refuge. Flushed with fury, Major Halski leaps and turns around me like a huge, acrobatic spider. At times it seems to me that he is above me, at other times below me, thrusting his fist in my face from all directions.

"Don't be afraid, damn it! Don't be afraid, you idiot!" he keeps on shrieking, and I cannot understand whether he really cannot hit me or is simply not trying to, but merely intimidating me, giving me a psychological working-over. But it is enough for me to glance at his rage-contorted face for his words, "Don't be afraid, damn it, I won't hit you," to sound less than reassuring. He seems to be very anxious not to fail in this interrogation. He reminds me at this moment of a drunken youth who tears off a girl's clothes as he promises in a gasping voice not to hurt her. It would . . . only . . . simply . . . be better . . . if she were . . . naked.

The interrogator tries to restrain Major Halski. He grasps the major's hand halfway to my head and soothingly reproaches him, but the major always gets away, and everything begins all over again.

"What, Drach?"[17] Major Halski screams. "You put this guy on a pedestal, blow him up, and what does he do? Scribbles gibberish. Drach . . . he's shit just like you and all your Svitlychnys and Dzyubas.[18] What, some Kholodny has appeared on the horizon too?[19] We'll make it hot for him here! Repent, you scum, you'll kiss my feet yet, but it will be too late! Pour all the rot out while you still can!"

Major Halski runs from the interrogation room as abruptly as he ran in, and I drop into a chair. Everything begins to swim before my eyes: the interrogator, the rectangular table-top, and the walls. Suddenly it all freezes in a strange pattern and then begins to move backward.

"How dare he?" I whisper. "How can he get away with such behavior?"

"Don't be angry with him. Major Halski is a fine man," the interrogator explains calmly. "But we've been getting a lot of anti-Soviets lately, and some of our people's nerves are on edge."

"If somebody's got problems with his nerves, he ought to go chop wood for some poor widow or take swineherds under his patronage. But to put people through this . . ."

"In your diary you write that you visited Ivan Svitlychny and talked about various things. It's true it says here that your conversation dealt only with literature and painting, but a person as inquisitive as you would hardly limit himself to just these subjects. You surely must have politicked a bit. Svitlychny tried to prove something, you contradicted . . . We understand that you didn't exactly say anything, but even so, he . . . Now you as a decent and law-abiding citizen will tell us all about it.

"You've studied the literary trends of the twenties, for example. I'm sure you were interested in other writers besides Ostap Vyshnya. Here in your diary you mention Mykola Khvylovy[20] and his part in the literary process and make note of his attitude toward Vyshnya. You probably shared these thoughts with Svitlychny. Tell us, what comments did he make?

"He has a large library. What books did you borrow to read, what books did he give you? Did he ask you to pass any on to other people? While browsing through his library you surely must have noticed—as any well-educated person would—the many rare books that it wouldn't hurt to donate to a public library. Why does he hold on to them? Maybe he wants to circulate them himself? Yes, that must be it. There's nothing bad in confirming this for us. And here's another thing: all of you—and you were one of those from whom we confiscated 'The Trial of Pogruzhalsky'—are up in arms about the burning of the library and the destruction of many priceless old Ukrainian imprints, books that are absolutely essential to the nation. Then why doesn't Svitlychny, if he's so concerned about the enlightenment of his people, offer his own books in place of the ones that were burned? He'd be much more useful to society if he did that rather than lend them to one person who then passes them on to another. Surely that's not a serious method of . . ."

The interrogator has a tone of voice as gentle and apologetic as Bulgakov's Azazello.[21] After the stormy "experimentation" by the explosive Major Halski, his tone has the effect of calculated torture on me, as if he took me out of boiling water and threw me naked into bitter cold, so that I lose consciousness without having really regained it. I am falling into a bottomless pit, and as I hurtle down I see phantoms that smile sweetly and lure me into sin with seductive whispers. I seem to be Adam, and an alluring Eve entices me with forbidden fruit. I do not have the strength to refuse it.

"Go ahead and write whatever your interrogator's mind can think up. Write that I'm a follower of Petlyura, or Bandera, or Makhno,[22] or even something much worse than any of those.

Put down that I'm Genghis Khan. Just leave my friends alone. They haven't done anything. They didn't give me any anti-Soviet literature, didn't found any secret organizations or set up any meetings."

The interrogator writes in his report with a bold hand, flipping page after page, then leans back in his chair and reads aloud: "While at the flat of Ivan Svitlychny I could not help seeing his extensive library, could not help realizing that he gives these books to others to read."

My interrogator's style would make him the envy of Faulkner, and the convolutions of his plot are hardly matched by Agatha Christie's. Proceeding entirely by intuitive guesses, he makes the most commonplace things appear in a new light. According to his report, I have, while taking a dozen steps around the room, staged a *coup d'état*. I have not executed it yet, but in that short distance I could inadvertently have thought of doing so. I have not conceived the idea yet, but it certainly could have occurred to me because no one, not even the State, is immune to such thoughts. The interrogator is very pleased with his report and only hesitates about the punctuation and so repeatedly asks me where commas and periods go.

Then, to dispel any doubt I may have about his good intentions toward me, the interrogator beckons me to come closer and with a glance at the door whispers surreptitiously, "Are we so different after all? I'm really just like you. The only difference between us is that you sleep here and I go home. If you like, I won't call the escort guard but will take you to your cell myself."

For the first and only time in my imprisonment no one shouts "Stop!" at me, and no one cracks his knuckles as I walk to my cell. Beside me strolls a friendly, smiling man who is telling me something about the outside world. But I can hardly pay attention. My ears are still ringing with Major Halski's wild screams: "What, you say you're honest? If such men do get here, they're never the same when they leave!"

Sometimes a bird gets so accustomed to its cage that eventually it cannot live outside it. Set it free and it will die. Man is a creature of a higher order, but he has a great deal in common with caged birds: he cannot survive without a cage, whether it be home, job, food, or prison. All these oppress to some degree, but the prison cell is the most onerous of all. The feeling is almost physical: you are shut in by prison walls which are constantly threatening to fall on your shoulders. Four huge walls unexpectedly press down on you, and although there is no real weight, you can hardly keep from screaming.

"Listen," says Volodya to me one day, "wouldn't you like to correspond with one of your accomplices?"

"Is that possible?"

"Sure, it's very simple. I'm a jailbird from way back, and I'll arrange everything for you."

"No, I don't know anyone here. Besides, what would I write about?"

"You don't know anything about the toilet, do you? They always check after us to make sure we haven't left any crap behind or scribbled some shit on the wall. But I know places no guard would ever sniff out."

Volodya goes to such great lengths to persuade me that I soon become suspicious. First his imaginary horses, and now such a very real undertaking.

"No, I really don't want to, if you don't mind."

Offended, Volodya retreats to his bunk and for a time remains silent.

"You're a weird bird," he says finally. "But if you're so scared of this method, there's another one, and it's just as good. Go to the library and get a book and place dots under various letters on the last page to compose any message you like."

Volodya's ingenuousness makes me laugh. "But how do you pass it on?"

"That's easier than spitting on the ground. We'll pass a message through somebody so that your friend borrows the

book next. Say the book has a call number ending in nine—
no sweat."

I walk up to the window and look at the growing onions,
then pick up the cup to water them.

"Give me the cup," says Volodya, "and go stand by the
Judas hole."

"What for?"

But Volodya motions me toward the door and lies down on
his back as if to read a book. Then he places the tin mug
against the wall between us and Cell No. 66 and taps twice
on the wall with his finger.

When his taps are returned, Volodya grasps the mug in the
palm of his hand and yells into it: "Who? For how long?
Where from? Who with? What for? Over."

He hastily inverts the mug and places his ear to the bottom.
I follow his conversation nervously. Suddenly the cover on
the Judas hole squeaks, and Volodya, having pushed the mug
under his pillow, begins to read his book. I start to pace the
cell, casting impatient glances at Volodya or the Judas hole
and wondering whether the guards heard anything. But
Volodya reads on calmly as if nothing has happened, and I
soon settle down a bit. But in a moment this quiet begins to
annoy me.

"Do you know anybody who works in some kind of a
museum?" Volodya peers from behind his book.

"In a museum? But why? What's . . ."

"Well, he turned stoolie, squealed everything. A cellmate
of his passed it on."

Turned stoolie? How, when, what? I am struck by Volodya's
use of such words. Now, after all the interrogations and horrible misunderstandings, when I am always on guard and
expecting something to happen at any minute, every little
thing assumes insane proportions and sometimes simply stuns
me. Coming from a skeptic, even a cynic, Volodya's words
baffle and worry me. A fanwheel begins to whirl somewhere
very close, as if Major Halski's clenched fist were whistling
around my head.

I begin to pay as much attention to minute details and concealed meanings as my interrogator, and now everything that Volodya says to me takes on a great significance. I sense in his last remark an implied question, and perhaps even more. Then I begin to suspect that Volodya has been planted in the cell with me. He is an ordinary stool pigeon, too lazy to rephrase the questions pounded into his head by the interrogator. Two cars are careening along a twisting road, and I am being heaved back and forth between them.

Unexpectedly, out of nowhere, Volodya begins to yell at me the day after the conversation through the cup.

"You motherfucking idiot! I'd take communists like you and hang them all from a withered tree. You told people lies while all along you were hatching fiendish plots in your mind!"

I have heard almost the same words from Major Halski. What is this, I wonder, a telepathic transmission from one mind to another?

Volodya bustles by the door, swinging his powerful, gawky arms about, barely able to restrain himself, then gnashes his teeth and shakes me by the shoulders. I shut my eyes and all at once reach a simple conclusion: I am being worked over not by Volodya, but by Major Halski!

"What's the matter with you, Volodya?" I whisper, pressing my back to the wall. "How dare you speak to me like this? Those fiendish plots are all a lie."

Volodya comes to his senses, gets a hangdog look on his face, and shrugs his shoulders.

"You were scared," he says quickly. "Scared, weren't you? I was just kidding around. And you're such a hero. What are you going to do at the interrogation when they give you the one-two and you find yourself right up against the wall?"

He cannot pull it off. His gestures and his lack of conviction betray him. To cover over his blunder as best he can, Volodya moves away from me and starts to sing. Soon I realize that he has ulterior motives even now as he picks out songs with certain themes. It is sufficient for him to pause meaningfully as he eyes me carefully and hums, "Hey, far away in Volyn, the UPA army arose . . ."[23] for me to understand his implication.

In one of my diary entries I mentioned the translator Yuliy Daniel.[24] I met him quite by chance in Moscow, and we spoke for no more than five minutes. I remember telling him (I wrote down this conversation in my diary, which was confiscated during the search) an anecdote that was making the rounds in Kiev then. The story was about the astrological significance of the number twelve. In 1905 there was a revolution. Twelve years later, in 1917, there was a second revolution. Twelve years after that Stalin established his cult. Twelve more brought the tragic year of 1941. Twelve years later Stalin died and the great cult ended. Twelve more came to this year, 1965, and it would seem that something should happen.

"What more can we have in this country?" Daniel replied when he had heard the story. "We had the Revolution, we had the Cult."

The interrogator relentlessly ascribes great importance to my diary. He is looking for "sedition," but most of the entries are not terribly significant. Yet this incident is never brought up. This puts me on my guard: if the interrogator is looking for sedition, wouldn't he do best to single out this particular anecdote?

One day Volodya and I go on our "excursion" to the toilet. (One of our small diversions is trying to stay as long as possible in the spacious toilet, just to escape for a while from the cramped, suffocating cell.) Until now we have been given, for "official use," scraps of blank paper. This time, to my surprise, we are handed strips of newspaper.

"Listen," Volodya calls out with excitement, "my piece of paper mentions some trial regarding the article you're accused under."

The first thing I see is the name of Yuliy Daniel. He has been brought to trial. Which Daniel? The one from Moscow? The same one I mention in my diary? The item from Baku does not say where the trial was held, but merely quotes some pensioner's fierce condemnation of Daniel's "irreverent" behavior. If this is really the same Daniel, why hasn't the interrogator attempted to clarify my relations with him? Why has he kept silent?

I look up into Volodya's inquiring eyes. He immediately looks away and rushes off to wash his hands under the faucet. I am beginning to understand a few things. . . .

The supply officer always brings a breath of fresh air into our cell with his army jokes and his razor, sharp as a knife made at Dulledge. Only a reckless fool would shave with such a blade, and that only after placing a sizable wager. Today the supply officer smiles enigmatically as he strides in, tall and at ease.

"Which one of you guys is thinking of getting married?" he asks with a slap on my back. "Come on now, man, shave your Robinson Crusoe or your fiancée will have a heart attack when she sees you."

A fine kettle of fish they're cooking up for me. The razor the supply officer brings today is brand-new, and for the first time he does not stand watch over me when I shave. He has no qualms about my veins today, realizing that you'd have to be an idiot to take your life when your fiancée is waiting for you downstairs and may even prove to be Lady Luck, in whom I have not stopped believing. When I am finished shaving the supply officer says that all I need now is a dash of "Red Moscow" cologne, but this is "against regulations" for politicals.

I walk the length of the corridor and arrive at a large, brightly lit room as wide as a street. (Such comparisons come easily to mind when you've been sitting in a stifling cell.) A T-shaped table spread with a blue baize stands in the middle of the room. Behind it are arrayed several strangers, all of them so elegantly dressed and serious of demeanor that I feel like an ambassador presenting his credentials to a head of state.

"This is the Chairman of the Committee of State Security of the Ukrainian SSR," says someone on my left, and I see behind the table a cheerful, elderly man who is directing an affable smile at me.[25]

"Please sit down," he says briskly in excellent Ukrainian with an Eastern accent. "What did you do? Why are you here?"

I am dreadfully disconcerted, and everything I try to say comes out wrong.

"In May of 1965," I begin quietly, "a friend of mine left me an article titled 'The Trial of Pogruzhalsky.' I did not have time to read it before I was arrested. I was swamped with work because I would soon be defending my dissertation." I want to say more, but the strangers rush to interrupt me.

"He was working for the Provincial Party Committee but failed to inform us! He hid it! He had personal friends among our staff members, but he didn't tell them about it!"

The voices all flow together, and a hubbub fills the room as if someone were beating a barrel with an iron bar. Abruptly everyone falls silent as if on command, and the chairman asks in his pleasant, controlled tone, "Do you have any complaints about your interrogator?"

I cannot get hold of myself, and everything I try to do turns against me. Just as I start to mumble a reply, someone grasps me by the elbow and hustles me out of the room to my cell.

Oh, what an idiot I was! I whisper as I huddle on my bunk. How I hate myself right now! Here was such a splendid opportunity to explain everything, to establish my innocence, to prove that the whole affair had started spinning at the wave of a vindictive magic wand. He would have understood me, he would have ordered them to . . . Everything is mixed up in my mind, and I feel as helpless as a child who is given a piece of candy but immediately has it taken away and is told that he stole it.

And then unexpectedly I hear protracted, piercing wailing. A woman weeps and keens the way peasant women do when they lament for a dead man, making your hackles rise as you listen at the other end of the village.

"Do you hear that, Volodya?" I ask, frightened at the thought that I might be losing my mind. "Such weeping and wailing . . ."

"Yes," Volodya drawls, "she was howling all day yesterday as if she were being butchered."[26]

After my interview with the chairman, everyone begins to speak Ukrainian with me, and the interrogator sweats profusely as he tries to write his report in his native language.

"Did I place the commas correctly?" he asks me. "If you see anything that looks Russian, throw it out to the devil!"

I throw things out, I insert commas. I am both a copy editor and a defendant.

In a moment he adds, "I believe we shall exclude *The Treaty Between Bohdan Khmelnytsky and Tsar Alexis in 1654* from your bill of particulars. I've consulted with my colleagues, and we have decided that it is not an anti-Soviet work. Nor will we mention Ivan Drach any more. He's an honest man and was never involved with you."

Later I read in *Literaturna Ukrayina* [Literary Ukraine] Drach's article, "May You Be Cursed Again and Again," in which he debunks Ukrainian bourgeois nationalism.[27] The authorities obviously lost interest in him after this. His case demonstrates the "schism" in the young generation in Ukraine. His confession is always rubbed into our eyes. "Look," they say, "here's a man who made mistakes exactly as you did, but he caught himself just in time. You see, he even condemned his own foolish views. Now he can really become a great poet. . . ."

It's a strange world we live in. No one can fathom it. Not the artist, not even God. No one can say: Here stood the small child, and here it sacrificed itself, its head thrown back proudly. Only a shortsighted man could venture to do that. Only he could fail to notice how a person does not fit in with his surroundings, how he shines forth like a beacon on a rocky point.

Good old Svitlychny. For some reason everyone is in the habit of referring to him in just this way, as though he were a near and dear friend. The "comfort" of his tiny flat: a table, two chairs, and the four walls of his world lined with bookshelves. This is all his wealth, the wealth of a man who knows its true worth. Here in these books the wisdom of the ages has been laid down by men of great learning. Here is our present and future life. Here you can find out anything at all; it's like reading the stars. You can even learn the future. Weary days, armies of time-servers—objects and nothing more. Hollow bricks drowning themselves in drink. No one can expose the genuine human being or his self-sacrifice. Not the artist, not even God.

Quiet Svitlychny, completely engrossed in his books. If only he realized how he doesn't fit in with them, how comical he looks with his daily problems and scholarly concerns! Something drives him from this world into the countryside, to trees, fields of flowering buckwheat, and busy beehives. One just can't imagine bees not liking this man. No doubt they sleep quietly on his hands and face. He is of average height, lean, and quiet. A feeling of sincere good will radiates from him. He is never possessed by demons. On the contrary, he is by nature calm and concentrated, ready to meet the challenge of being a citizen.

Hemmed in by a squad of strangers who guard him like the Queen of England, he enters the interrogation room and sits down on a chair. Easy and serene in his bearing, he seems out of place here as well. His shining face stands out among the gray, malevolent miens of the KGB men and the grim iron bars on the windows, and again I am reminded of villages and beehives.

We are asked in turn when we met and what we said to each other. The questions are remarkably petty and insignificant. The interrogators are sounding us out, hoping to stumble onto something bigger but not quite sure what it might be. They cast scornful, caustic looks at Svitlychny without making the slightest attempt to conceal their cynicism, occasionally spinning out multi-layered conceits that only the obscene mind of a third-rate lawyer could conceive.

I am asked whether Svitlychny had an influence on me and if so, exactly how and for what purpose.

"The time we met," I remark, "we had a glass of wine together."

"It was on 23 August 1963. The wine was a Cabernet. . . ."

But Svitlychny is rudely interrupted. "Speak only when you're spoken to!"

"Svitlychny sent a young boy from Kiev to you with a note. In the note he said you could discuss everything with the boy. What did you take this note to mean, and how did you interpret 'everything'?"

"Yes," I reply, "I did receive such a note from Svitlychny. But to tell you what I think he meant by those words, I can't. In any case, Svitlychny is here, so why don't you ask him yourself?"

"We're quite capable of asking him without your prompting. The question now concerns only you. Please answer: what did you think he meant in the note?"

They interrogate me about the meaning of the note for an hour. I explain everything that there is to be explained and finally fall silent. What can I say about the things they are demanding from me?

"I gave him my poems," I say. "Some of them were later published."

"What was your motive in giving him your poems to read?"

"He is a literary critic, and I wanted his opinion."

"You could have given them to someone else. Why did you give them to Svitlychny?"

"I had read many of his articles. I liked their objectivity; I was impressed by the uncompromising quality of his criticism."

I am reminded of Shevchenko's trial in Tsarist Russia.[28] His interrogators asked him the very same sort of questions: "What was your motive in writing poetry? Why did you incite Kostomarov in Kiev? Who are . . . and why in their letters did they call you . . .?" Shevchenko was interrogated 118 years ago, but I realize that criminal investigations have not changed in the least during all this time, nor have the nature of the questions, their phrasing, or the people who ask them.

The interrogators have exhausted their stock of loaded questions and now find themselves at a dead end. For a moment there is silence. I see that the interrogators are not in the least interested in knowing where Svitlychny and I met or what we discussed. They only want to know whether Svitlychny influenced me and whether he deliberately planted seeds of sedition in my mind.

Svitlychny is sitting across from me, and I notice his new white woolen socks. He seems to guess the question in my glance and says unexpectedly, "My wife sent these over. I think I'm warmer than you."

"Silence!" the Lviv prosecutor thunders. "Do you want us to cut this confrontation short and take you out of here?"

Now they leave me alone and start to question Svitlychny.

"Would you believe I don't remember anything about this," he says. "I've been having terrible attacks of amnesia lately. I can't even remember my last few jobs and have had to jot them down on index cards."

Sometimes the nonsense seems to be annoying Svitlychny, and then he helps the interrogators to compile their report.

"Write whatever fits the Criminal Code best," he says. "It's all the same to me. But leave other people out of it. I don't want anyone else held responsible for my 'actions.'"

At the end we are allowed to talk freely for a minute.

"Your cheeks are glowing as if you'd just come in from the outside," I remark.

Svitlychny smiles.

"Our 'seniority' here is almost the same."

He departs, leaving me with a kind of quiet joy and with faith in myself and in elementary justice. His smiling face, the only human and natural face I have seen in several months of imprisonment, stays with me for a long time. Svitlychny has been ground through the interrogation mill, but he has managed to stay cheerful. He must have realized much earlier than I the medieval absurdity of the "case" that the plain-clothes comedians have cooked up against us. He understands that everything can be falsified, that we can be convicted on the silliest imaginable charges, even of crossing the street at a legal crosswalk. Everything depends on a magic wand that someone holds ready. The wand was instrumental in the black deeds of the thirties and is still in the hands of the same people. Nothing has changed except the date. Another wave of the wand, and again trainloads of Kalnyshevskys, Khvylovys, Kurbases, and Dray-Khmaras will set off.[29] Later . . . later, the dead can be rehabilitated, labeled "Victim of So-and-so," and recognized to have been important men. These are strange times we live in. Children are playing at politics—proud, pompous, cruel, and vindictive children.

"How do you like Svitlychny?" I ask the interrogator when I am alone with him again. "This was the first time you met him, wasn't it?"

"Oh, he still needs a lot of work before we get him into shape," the interrogator retorts. "He may yet become a real literary critic."

One day when I am feeling particularly wretched, Volodya gets up the nerve, over a game of jackstraws, to tell me about his adventures. His horses can hardly rival the story of his life. I gasp when I hear that he is a "criminal of two republics."

In the early fifties, Volodya was suspected of a connection with the Banderites and was sentenced to life exile in Central Asia. (In those days they could rivet twenty-five years or life exile on you regardless of your "contacts.")[30] He served his time until the Twentieth Party Congress and after that great upheaval got his case reviewed and was allowed to return home to Lviv Province. Later he and his friends organized a group that began clandestinely to print anti-Soviet leaflets and pamphlets.

He was on his way to Transcarpathia when the KGB caught

him with a gun in his pocket and a suitcase full of these pamphlets. Volodya tried to deny everything. He claimed that the pamphlets in the suitcase were not his and that the revolver had been planted on him by the KGB. But the authorities had the pocket cut out, and a panel of forensic experts established that a gun had indeed been carried in it for a long time. During the investigation it was also discovered that Volodya had committed a whole chain of crimes while living in Central Asia. He was guilty in particular of disseminating Ukrainian nationalist songs and ideas. For all this he was branded a "criminal of two republics" and sentenced to twelve years' "deprivation of liberty." He served time at Dushanbe, the capital of the Tadzhik Republic. Now he has been called up as the chief witness in the case of Dmytro Kupyak, a former chief of the Banderite Security Service, who settled after the war in Canada. The Soviet government has repeatedly sent notes to the Canadian authorities demanding that Kupyak be extradited to stand trial as a war criminal.

I look at Volodya in wonder. Until now his conduct has led me to believe that he is a common criminal accused of stealing or speculating. As if sensing his superiority over me, Volodya sprawls on the bunk, one leg thrown over the other, breaking wind in a manner hardly befitting an intellectual.

"Would you like me to tell you how many years they'll stick you with for your little escapades?" he asks me.

Without waiting for an answer, he draws one circle, then a larger one around it, and divides them into seven parts (for the seven years sanctioned by the article I am charged under). He places a cup of water in the center, stirs it, and drops in a match. As the water grows still, the match floats to the surface, its head striking the side of the cup and pointing to one of the numbered partitions. The augury is for three years.

"I swear by my own and my grandfather's horses that you won't get any more than this."

On 11 February 1966 we are transferred to Cell No. 70. I measure it carefully and find that it is eight meters long.

"We're in paradise," Volodya laughs. "All we need now is some broads. . . ."

Another prisoner is put in with us, a small, portly Jew, placid and not very talkative. A few days earlier Volodya told me that he would leave my company for good in a day or two, because his case had been "cleared up." But no sooner does the new man arrive than Volodya, after his regular visit to the interrogator, announces that he will have to stay at least another month because new and very unfavorable evidence has been unearthed. He says this with emphasis, but I do not find him to be upset in any way.

Our paradise seems like the Hermitage Museum to me, although it doesn't have any paintings on the walls, of course. By pacing the cell and counting my steps carefully as I go, I can walk six kilometers a day—the distance from my home to the main department store and back. I entertain myself by walking up and down the cell and even rejoice like a child over my discovery. I actually feel a bit livelier. Sometimes my steps vary in length, and then I count two steps as one.

But even this little game cannot distract me from the weeping that has been tormenting my ears for almost a week now. My gut roils with nausea at the sound of the woman's cries, and a frightful worry gnaws at my heart. I pace from door to window, counting my steps over and over again, but the crying never stops.

"We seem to be in a jungle and not a prison. We've been isolated from the whole world, dumb Tarzans whom the apes have decided to drive out from the underbrush with mad wailing."

Volodya continues to read silently. His lower lip twitches oddly, and he casts stealthy glances at our new cellmate from time to time.

"Excuse me," he says finally, unable to restrain his curiosity any longer. "Under what article are you here, if it's not a secret?"

"There are no secrets here," replies Naum quickly but doesn't offer anything more.

Volodya is frustrated. He lies on his bunk, swallowing his saliva and wheezing, then tries to start up the conversation once again, but still doesn't get anywhere. The next day Volodya announces that everything is "clear" now, coolly bids me good-by, nods to Naum, and walks to the door to await his summons. He stands there for quite a while with his bundle, then seems to remember something and tells me off-handedly, after asking me not to repeat it:

"You'll have a kind thought for me when you get your two years. Do you know the writer Dzyuba? He spoke in your defense at the Writers' Union not long ago. He was roundly booed. Then Ko—Ko—Koza—Kozachenko[31] told him: 'It's not our Writers' Union that's malodorous, Dzyuba, it's yours!' Everyone jeered and whistled. Oh yes, there's another thing I heard. They put people like you on trial not long ago in Lutsk.[32] The public was outraged and raised a hue and cry in the courtroom. 'Send them to prison! Send them to prison!' The accused hung their heads in dejection and said they were already serving time. Penitents!"

"That man is dishonest," declares Naum as soon as Volodya has been led away from our cell. "I knew he was no good the very first time I looked at him. Besides, is that how you say good-by to someone you've just spent six months in jail with?"

Naum is a changed man. He becomes so talkative that I can hardly get a word in edgewise. He repeatedly tells me how to conduct myself at the trial and how to answer the questions. I stare at him with astonishment. We talk in whispers long past lights out. As I go to sleep I decide that I just don't know how to tell good people from bad, that I know nothing about human psychology, and that I don't know how to recognize a true friend.

The loathsome weeping that has racked me for so many days, haunting my dreams with its monstrous self-evidence, that I have so stubbornly tried to silence by counting steps single-mindedly, reciting poetry, or humming tunelessly—this weeping suddenly breaks off during my talk with Naum like a tape that snaps or like a phonograph needle that finally lifts itself out of a twisted groove.

Man was created to be written about. He walks, works, loves, sleeps a blessed sleep, and sometimes even dreams. In order to become cultured and educated he must read a lot, widely and deeply. When he reads something that praises only morning and forgets about midday and night, man becomes one-sided and starts to squint, like Faulkner's Negro when the Indians led him to bury the chieftain's body.

Such a man can be described: he is interesting and knowledgeable; and yet this same person gets portrayed in all sorts of ways. The socialist realists do it their way; the surrealists do it another way; the imagists have their own way, and the impressionists do it differently again. But no matter how they describe a person, that person must be either a negative type, for instance a thief, a drug addict, or a rapist, or a positive one, like the collective farm milkmaid and her cow Daisy, who have both taken the socialist pledge—the milkmaid to produce a certain quantity of milk and Daisy to be milked; like the schoolteacher who has pledged himself to make A-grade pupils out of D-grade ones and, sure enough, gives them A's every time; or like the savant who is so fond of children that he stops them in the street to give them candy and then asks them what their names are. And when instead of saying their first names they tell him their surnames, he flees in a panic, forgetting to give the children their candy, because he has just heard from the children's lips the surnames of people whom he condemned, "some time ago," in secret denunciations written in his own hand, to life imprisonment or "simply" death. Now he fears human justice and smooths his gray hair down and screws up his intelligent eyes.

Man will always be beautiful to such writers and will sit somewhere in the clouds, gazing sadly at the wide world, just as the hero of Joyce's *Ulysses* did when with his stream of consciousness and subconsciousness he filled a novel of several hundred pages in less than twenty-four hours. This happens when real writers get to work. Life would be very sad and uninteresting without them, and the world would lose its color and its *raison d'être*. If it weren't for writers, we would undoubtedly not even know how to love.

There are, however, writers of a different sort, who are no less prolific than real writers. But these do not publish and would not ever want to become recognized. Their writings are kept behind huge, secret locks and are guarded not by a terrible Cyclops, but by humble mortals armed with weapons. If these writings were ever published, they would dismay realists and modernists alike. Even the great Hoffmann, who so loved giving free rein to his imagination, would be humbled and forced to cast down his eyes if he read a few of these pages.

And if the first sort of writers raise their heroes and villains up into the clouds, the latter (and herein lies their greatest artistic value) drive them underground, pushing them along narrow, impenetrable labyrinths, to leave them there at the mercy of fate. One can just imagine how appalling these novels are! They have very modest titles, true enough, but are titles really important to a beautiful work of art? The novel that my interrogator has written about me in six months is titled *Case No. 107* and is the seventh book of an epic comprising nineteen volumes. It is clear from the novel's very first page who is the hero and who the villain. (I might note that this type of classification is obligatory not only for the literature of socialist realism, but also for fiction such as this.) And the role assigned to me is not even that of a minor scoundrel: I have committed every vile deed that a man is capable of. I never had the slightest suspicion of what a hostile element I am, or how hostile my thoughts have been! Even my thoughts about an ordinary needle, if you'll forgive me for saying so, are not what they should be.

My interrogator's *magnum opus*, almost four hundred pages long, mentions every crime that I could conceivably have committed. It turns out that any acquaintanceship or meeting, any greeting made on May Day can be classified as criminal. And if, in the course of an introduction, my back was turned to a building or my hands were in my pockets, then these, believe it or not, are deemed to be criminal acts. If, in addition, I happened to shake my head (epilepsy is not taken into account), then that is outright sedition.

I had an opportunity once to attend the writers' workshop at the Lutsk Teachers' College, where I took a liking to the poems of Anatolia P[anas]. I was unable then to make her acquaintance and requested her, through my friends, to send me her poems. Several of them, accompanied by my short introduction, were published in the Lviv paper *Lenins'ka molod'* [Leninist Youth]. When Anatolia happened to be passing through Lviv, she stopped by to visit me with a mutual friend. I was very busy at that time, so we just introduced ourselves and I gave her my address. All this was painstakingly noted in my dossier. When they asked Anatolia, "What were you doing in his flat in the spring of 1965 and what was the purpose of your visiting him?" she answered, "I read my poems to him." "And what about him—did he say anything?" "No, he only nodded his head." I suppose that if I hadn't nodded then this trivial incident would perhaps have not been recorded for posterity in my dossier.

You can, if you like, imagine life as a mechanism, bristling with all sorts of levers and cogwheels. These wheels are friends, and if you replace one cogwheel by another identical one, the mechanism will continue working. These are twin wheels, twin friends which, you come to realize, are easily interchangeable, and the mechanism will not stop functioning because of the change. A true friend is a true wheel. Take him away, and the entire mechanism will break down.

Ihor Sandursky was a wheel in my mechanism (I hope he will forgive me the comparison),[33] and when this cogwheel was replaced it did not stop the mechanism, but rather caused it to run more smoothly. In short, it was improved. My friendship with Sandursky was of long standing, maybe even of ten years or so. He was a graduate student in the Department of Philosophy at Lviv University. He was well read and erudite and knew a great deal about aesthetics and literature. I gave him quite a lot of help in life and am not ashamed to say so. I even trusted him and regarded him as a very close friend who would help me in trouble. But as soon as I find myself behind these absurd bars, the cogwheel not only falls out of my mechanism, but also breaks, at the same time destroying the mechanism itself. Sandursky turns out to be a coward who lies about people for gain. He used to bunk at my bachelor quarters (he had nowhere else to go), yet he tells the interrogator that I invited him around and gave him anti-Soviet literature to read. He talks about books that I can't for the life of me identify, and he besmirches me from head to foot, in this way assisting the Security people. Having buried me alive, he helps them to drive me into dark and treacherous underground labyrinths. And he does all this with such ardor that the interrogators themselves might envy him. In fact, they can't praise him enough. "Now there's an intelligent man, a true Soviet man." If the Security forces conceive a Soviet man as being capable of both friendship and treachery like Sandursky, then theirs is a very primitive way of thinking.

Such thoughts occur to me as I read *Case No. 107*. There in the record of 5 October 1965 is Sandursky's deposition, with all his philosophical generalizations about the danger I pose to society. When I am free again one day and run into him, as I am bound to, how will he dare to look me in the eye?

At last they let me read the bill of indictment against me: "An ideological saboteur . . . from isolated acts of an anti-Soviet nature progressed to agitating for the secession of the Ukrainian SSR from the USSR. . . . Received anti-Soviet literature from Ivan Svitlychny in Kiev. . . . Had criminal contacts with Bohdan and Mykhaylo Horyn. . . .[34] Distributed anti-Soviet nationalist literature in Lviv. . . ."

"But how dare you write such things?" I ask the interrogator incredulously. "There isn't a bit of truth in any of this."

"Yes, I know," replies the interrogator calmly. "Most of it

has little truth in it, but the trial is still to come, and then all the facts will be sorted out."

"But if what you say is true, then what grounds are there to put me on trial?"

The interrogator does not know what reply to make, but he is spared an answer by the chief of the interrogation department, who walks into the office at just this moment. The chief scrutinizes me and maliciously tosses off:

"Do you really think we've been feeding you government rations for eight months to no purpose? *He* is innocent! Release him, and he'll pretend to the whole world that he's a victim of injustice. But if you get a couple of years, then God Himself won't believe that you're not a camel!"

Rounding the bend of the Middle Ages, the current of history cast the Holy Inquisition onto a high, impregnable bank together with all its accoutrements: imposing carved benches, massive chairs, and black robes. Bulk instilled fear and humility into people when they faced the great; black represented the inquisitors' enlightened aspirations. The world has changed, and there is little left now to remind us of the days of chivalry. Everything has changed beyond recognition. Only courts have not changed. The bulky courtroom furnishings, immutable attributes of drowsy, blindfold Themis, remain the same, and the black robes have not completely disappeared. Elegant suits, bespoken at the finest tailors', do not endow the judges with the necessary severity, and so their faces must always be sullen and disdainful. And should indifference suit any of them—that, too, may be donned.

The judges judge; the judges doze. Today they judge the opponents of the king, tomorrow the king himself; they always judge someone's opponents. The judges judge; the judges are tired of judging, but they must—society demands it. The judges are above this world. They are the ultimate puppet, a tiny state, a toy in someone's bag. No matter whom they try and how they do it, they always adhere to the principles of justice. It is another matter that this justice may not be what one might imagine it. But this, too, does not concern the judges, since they are so much above the very concept of justice.

The judges themselves are never judged, only the period and the environment that harbors them. This period and environment may even be condemned by the same judges after they have entered a different dimension of time and a different environment. And they condemn their environment according to the same principles of justice that existed in the Middle Ages.

The judges judge; the judges doze, holding their trials behind closed doors to keep spectators from devouring them with their eyes and disturbing their dozing. On they doze—and are extremely upset when the accused or the witnesses rouse them from their lethargy.

"I protest against the holding of this court session *in camera.* The Constitution of the USSR and Article 20 of the Code of Criminal Procedure guarantee that trials of this kind must always be held in public. This court is infringing the Constitution and the Code. Therefore, I consider the trial null and void, refuse to give evidence, and am handing you this brief to that effect."

This is a bolt from the blue, shattering the somnolent judges and enraging the corpulent prosecutor. He leaps up from his seat and hurls the brief in Vyacheslav Chornovil's face.[35]

"You are an enemy!" he screams, snorting with indignation.

The presiding judge does not know what to do with his hands in their white cuffs, which have eaten up many a pound of starch. "Out with him!" he shouts from the bench. "Take him out at once!"

Vyacheslav is calm and even somehow handsome in his calmness, exuding intelligence and reasonableness. He has been brought to these proceedings from a great distance, and he acts as if he's just dropped by for a minute to see what is going on. He doesn't bother to look too closely at anything. He hasn't the least desire to scratch at the pebble in order to extract the grain of gold in it. He knows the pebble is a dud, a loser, as empty as that nineteen-volume epic so carefully penned by the interrogator. Now the volumes are piled high on the tables, and the judges can doze undisturbed behind them. Vyacheslav does not take offense at anybody: how can one be offended by those who have been slighted by their Creator? His lively gray eyes glint with cunning; his forehead is smooth and unfurrowed, like the calm before the storm.

Vyacheslav goes up to the dock and places a small bunch of red tulips on the railing.

"This is for you from your friends and acquaintances."

"Take those flowers away at once!" someone shrieks. The perplexed guardians of order rush over to the dock, but they snatch the flowers so clumsily that they scatter on the floor. Vyacheslav is expelled, but the spirit, the mood that he leaves behind, cannot be exorcized. It permeates the empty courtroom, vexing the judges and the prosecutor and lighting up our faces.

"I also protest against this trial being held behind closed doors," Mykhaylo Horyn declares, "and I demand that it be opened to the public, as required by Article 20 of the Code of Criminal Procedure on the holding of judicial inquiries in public."

The judges judge. They have been roused from their slumber, and now they just cannot go back to sleep. They forgot their sleeping pills at home.

Anatolia P[anas] has entered the courtroom. She is testifying in the case of Mykhaylo Horyn. She is calm and self-possessed, as if she has arrived for a rendezvous and has plenty of time in hand.

"Did you take anti-Soviet writings from Mykhaylo Horyn?"

"No, I did not."

"But didn't you take from him an article about the Russification of Ukrainian schools?"

"Yes, I did, but surely that's not anti-Soviet?"

"What do you mean, not anti-Soviet? Haven't you read it?"

"Yes, I read it. But everything it says is true."

"True?"

"Yes, indeed. When I was doing my practice teaching in the Crimean Province, our principal ordered us to teach the Ukrainian language in Russian."

"What do you think you're doing? Making fun of us?"

"Look at that! They don't even believe me. Well, ask the principal himself about it. He'll tell you."

Everyone bursts out laughing. Even the judges crack a smile for a second, but, frightened, immediately suppress it. The prosecutor gazes around the room in confusion, wiping his bald patch and coughing irritably. It's been a long time since he has felt so confused and cheated. A bomb is just about to go off but never does.

"Get on back to Lutsk, my girl," suggests the judge, who feels no less cheated than the prosecutor, "and take my advice: don't get into any more mischief."[36]

The trial reminds me of a squirrel endlessly turning around in its cage. More and more quickly it whirls, until squirrel and wheel blur together in a single image. Faces flicker before my eyes. Witnesses enter, say things, and go out. Then everything starts all over again. I lapse into lethargy, and the proceedings flow past me like a swift stream—the trial has been going on for four days now. Sometimes the squirrel pauses briefly, and I have a glimpse of the judges, the witnesses, and the empty rows of seats.

Yaroslav K[endzyor] is being questioned.[37] He is tall and elegant, with a natural bearing and the build of an athlete. At times he shows surprise at the trivial questions being put to him.

"Do you know that you ought to be put on trial for the photocopy you made of that book?"

"Try me if you think it necessary," Yaroslav replies indifferently, as though purchasing a streetcar ticket.

The prosecutor has got everything muddled. He obviously

hasn't studied his dossiers sufficiently, and for the fourth time I am getting questions that should be directed to someone else.

"What was your purpose in instructing Yaroslav K[endzyor] to make a photocopy of that book?"

"What photocopy?" I ask.

"I beg your pardon," the embarrassed judge interrupts the prosecutor. "You are asking the wrong person!"

The prosecutor groans as if he has been cheated again. He keeps on wiping his bald patch and shrugging his shoulders in discomfiture. Carried away by his questions, he forgot to look where he was going and stepped into something unpleasant, and now he wheezes with annoyance.

The squirrel winks at the prosecutor, he looks daggers back at it, the squirrel winks again—and the wheel starts turning once more.

In the morning we are hustled into Black Marias and driven to the provincial courthouse on Pekarska Street. Myroslava Zvarychevska[38] is in a good mood and recites some lines from a poem that Shevchenko wrote in prison 120 years ago:

> Remember, brothers (how I yearn
> That this dark fate may ne'er return!),
> How you and I, in humble doubt,
> Between a window's bars peered out. . . .[39]

"Quiet, you there!" barks a guard, but his shout is drowned in the uproar that unexpectedly envelops our van.

"Hurrah! Hurrah! Hurrah!" shouts the crowd which fills the whole of Pekarska Street (and it is like that on all five days). People throw flowers to us through the police cordons. They fall onto the metal roof of the van and penetrate to us through the cracks in the doors. As we approach the courthouse, we walk on a carpet of fresh spring flowers. We are sorry to crush them, but we cannot sidestep them, because the guards inexorably lead us on, gripping our arms so hard that it hurts. A flower falls on one of the men's peak caps. He is a paunchy soldier who keeps looking around him like a hare brought to bay. Someone points out the flower to him, and he shakes it off his cap with such hatred and fear as if it were a small bomb to him.

"Bear up, Mykhaylo!" shouts Ivan Dzyuba to Horyn from the crowd. "Bear up!" he shouts.

I only manage to catch a glimpse of his face. For a second I see how Lina Kostenko[40] breaks through the cordon of guards and neatly slips a chocolate bar into Myroslava Zvarychevska's hand. The warden rushes to Myroslava like a madman and snatches the chocolate away.

"You never can tell, maybe it's poisoned."

The squirrel stops scrambling and looks at the prosecutor in amazement. Perfumed and solemn (only that damn sweat is spoiling it all!), he is reading from a sheaf of papers:

"Comrade judges! The statistics of our ever-growing industrial achievements ring out ever more resonantly like a swelling hymn of joy. Hundreds of tons of coal over and above the plan . . . cast iron and steel . . . wool and fibers . . . milk and eggs! . . ."

The squirrel blinks in astonishment; the prosecutor darts angry glances back at it, furiously puffing out his cheeks and panting. The squirrel winks at him; his eyebrow twitches, and again dense beads of sweat break out on his bald pate. He clutches at his saving handkerchief, loses the line he is about to read; the squirrel jumps—and once more the wheel begins to whirl and whirl.

I learn the full story of Lina Kostenko's involvement only after I have left the courtroom. People tell me that she is just as impossible for the authorities to handle as her poetry. Her spirit dominates the entire senseless trial. Lina is indignant as only brave and honest people, true citizens, can be when they realize that they are citizens and must battle those who would deprive all citizens of their rights.

Lina has never been able to make her peace with baseness or hypocrisy, especially when they go hand in hand with sarcasm, wreaking havoc everywhere, but cannot be confronted because they cleverly hide behind someone's authoritative shoulders. She is warned and cajoled, intimidated and persuaded. For the first time in her life strangers and acquaintances discuss her great talent, which needs more time to reach full bloom. They tell her that her place is not here, in the courthouse on Pekarska Street, but at home, in a quiet and comfortable room of her own. She laughs in their faces and she rages. This may be her first face-to-face encounter with injustice, not the injustice of the thirties, which she learned about from books, but real, tangible injustice, which is trying to grind her down in its millstones.

Lina is a poet, a good Ukrainian poet, but she is also a citizen. She has forgotten for now that she is a poet (other poets, verse-mongers major and minor, have timidly retreated into their petty worlds to hack jingles that promise them royalties and fame, cognac and Volgas). Now she writes not with her pen, but with her voice. She looks people right in the eyes, trying to find outrage, and may those who lack it forgive her insolence, for she is a woman and women can be forgiven anything. . . .

Iryna Vilde pushes through the crowd toward Lina with open arms.[41] Lina surges toward her with a wild excitement: this prominent Ukrainian writer, this winner of the Shevchenko Prize (named for our first rebel against injustice), this chairman of the Lviv writers' union, will surely stop the senselessness. She'll realize her civic duty, she'll speak her mind, she can do it.

"Lina!" Iryna Vilde tries to shout over the clamor of the crowd. "Don't expose yourself to danger. Your talent is needed to do something good for those poor people. Get away from here!"

Lina bursts into tears: her feelings have been tricked, her civic innocence has been deflowered.

"What people are you talking about in this time of trouble? Why are you trying to lure me into the bushes? This will never happen! Do you hear? Get out of here, you and all your kind!"

But Lina is not alone, not forsaken at some desolate crossroads. Outside the closed doors of the courtroom stand Ivan

Dzyuba, Ivan Drach, Vyacheslav Chornovil, Mykola Petrenko, Yakiv Stetsyuk, Roman Kudlyk, and Iryna and Ihor Kalynets.[42] They too have come to demand justice. But the judges on the high banks of justice doze on, their backs turned to the whole world in indifference, dreaming of fragrant coffee and cognac and new stripes on their sleeves.

The squirrel wheel stops whirling. The prosecutor is delving into the Dark Ages. No, let us be fair, he is not going back that far, only to the times of the Austro-Hungarian Empire. His Ukrainian thickly larded with Russian, he pontificates:

"Here you have these renegades, comrade judges, who don't appreciate the great and beautiful Russian language. I was at Lviv University recently—I often visit this cathedral of learning, as I like to call it. On one of these occasions, comrades showed me a poem by Markian Shashkevych,[43] whom I had known before, of course. To have such a brilliant man emerge from the darkness of the Austro-Hungarian Empire! He was their countryman—can you imagine?—he was the countryman of these filthy renegades! Markian Shashkevych patterned himself on the magnificent Russian language. Just listen to what he wrote about it:

> 'A Ruthenian mother gave us birth,
> A Ruthenian mother nourished us,
> Why is her tongue not dear to us?' "

The squirrel stares in surprise at prosecutor Borys Antonenko. Everyone bursts out laughing, embarrassing the prosecutor.

"He wasn't writing about the Russian language," remonstrates Myroslava Zvarychevska, "but the Ukrainian. There was a time when Ukrainians were called Ruthenians."

The judges lower their heads and shuffle the papers lying before them. The prosecutor summons his handkerchief again to rescue his bald pate from the thick beads of sweat that are breaking out on it.

"Comrade judges!" he calls out curtly with an arrogant shake of his head. "I cannot continue this way. Please restore order!"

The presiding judge stands up, leans on the massive bench, and gazes with half-closed eyes into the distance. "Please come to order . . ."

The squirrel winks at the prosecutor as he nervously flips through his lengthy speech.

"At one time, during the dark and illiterate ages of the Austro-Hungarian monarchy, such a genius, you understand, the likes of which you seldom met, a man like Ivan Franko, you understand, because he loved and advocated Ruthenian literature, was not permitted by the authorities to teach at the university.[44] And who is teaching there now? Just take a look! There before you is accused Osadchy, a former lecturer of this university. So he goes around wailing that the library burned down, that the national treasure of the Ukrainian people was destroyed."

A spectator in the courtroom giggles unexpectedly; the squirrel gives another wink, and the prosecutor is visibly annoyed again. But with his characteristic stubbornness he quickly regains his composure.

"So what could he teach his students? He spoke a great deal about Ostap Vyshnya here. But who was Ostap Vyshnya? I know the thirties very well, you understand, and it's not for greenhorns like you to poke around in some of the misunderstandings of the thirties. So who was Ostap Vyshnya? That this lecturer, you understand—excuse me, this former lecturer —is fascinated by his writing and is researching something in it. . . . Well, one thing is certain, you understand. Ostap Vyshnya deliberately wrote in a pure, refined Ukrainian—that's what provoked his readers! And Vyshnya's fame, you realize, of course, was artificially blown up, and people got funny ideas reading him. No wonder he got it, but good."

Mykhaylo Kosiv,[45] a witness for the defense, states at the trial: "I did not read 'The Trial of Pogruzhalsky' at Osadchy's, and he did not express any thoughts of an anti-Soviet nationalist nature. Thus he cannot be said to have manifested any dissatisfaction with Soviet reality" (p. 85 of the trial transcript).

But the honorable judges tell Kosiv not to try his luck twice. He has been released (after six months behind bars), but he can be clapped into jail again at any time. And in the face of Kosiv's testimony the verdict reads: "The accused Osadchy gave Kosiv to read 'The Trial of Pogruzhalsky.'"

Another witness for the defense, Ivan Ostafiychuk, said five times during the pre-trial investigation that he never read the Pogruzhalsky article at my flat. He strongly reiterates this point at the trial (p. 91 of the transcript). But from their high bank of justice the judges enter into the verdict: "The accused Osadchy asked Ivan Ostafiychuk to read 'The Trial of Pogruzhalsky.'"

My fair-weather friend Ihor Sandursky said during the investigation that I asked him to read "The Trial of Pogruzhalsky." He makes a similar statement to the court, but when the prosecutor, exasperated by the ever-spinning squirrel cage, asks what the article looks like, Sandursky is thoroughly befuddled and replies that he cannot answer the question because he has not read the article and in fact has not seen it with his own eyes. He also says that Osadchy is a "modest man who is interested in Ukrainian literature" (p. 69 of the transcript).

Nevertheless, the judges write in the verdict: "The accused Osadchy gave citizen Sandursky to read 'The Trial of Pogruzhalsky.'" And one of the judges, who wakes from his doze a bit early, adds to the record: "The accused Osadchy gave Mykhaylo Masyutko the anti-Soviet nationalist 'Eisenhower Address at the Unveiling of the Shevchenko Monument in Washington in 1964.'"[46] I had never met Mykhaylo Masyutko, and his name has not been mentioned either during the interrogation or at the trial.

That funny little squirrel in the cage is not a whimsy of mine. I did not make it up. The squirrel really existed, but it was probably much funnier than I have managed to show it.

The squirrel whirls around and around in the multicolor wheel, demonstrating how in motion all the colors of the spectrum blend together as white. On and on the squirrel spins, moving its little paws up and down and twitching its pointed nose. On and on it gyres, showing us how fast time is passing by, while on a makeshift stage in a crowded marketplace itinerant actors are presenting a farcical court trial.

There's the prosecutor, the bungling erudite with the traditional bald head (a sign of higher intellect) and with the traditional beads of sweat on it. There are the judges, who doze as their custom requires because they have long since grown weary of judging people but must keep up with tradition and continue judging because, by God, they are judges. And there are the defense attorneys, who traditionally do not defend anyone, because they take their instructions from the judges and the prosecutor. Just try to cross your superiors and they will just as traditionally cross you.

And there's the audience, which consists of the accused. They huddle in a group and laugh so hard that tears spring to their eyes. This is traditional laughter for a traditional comedy. The accused are so taken with the performance (the performers are very funny despite their traditional amateurishness) that they forget to watch out for the pickpockets who have been waiting for this decadent laughter so that they can brazenly throw their arms over the spectators' shoulders and pick their pockets clean. My pockets are empty, they cannot steal anything from me, so they con me out of two years of my life. Mykhaylo Horyn is swindled out of six years; Bohdan Horyn— three. And all the while the damn squirrel never stops spinning its multicolor wheel and the colors continue to blend into white. The joker of a prosecutor continues to sweat; the judges continue to doze on their high benches, and the scrawny lawyers continue to hold their hands over their hearts as they mumble a prayer under their noses, "Lord, let this chalice pass. . . ."

I am an easy mark for them, like a hick off on his first jaunt to the big city who stands gaping at the sights as his pockets are picked clean. Later, when he discovers his loss, he is so impressed with the neat job and so embarrassed that he goes home silent, registering no complaints and bearing malice toward none. Yes, I am a country bumpkin amazed by the slick operation. The whole trial, perhaps not so much the trial as the prosecutor and the judges, should be awarded the Nobel Prize. With their eyes shut tight they were able to invent in five days accusations that would have thoroughly put to shame the wretchedly unimaginative judges who nailed Ostap Vyshnya to the wall for terrorist activities (not for the rape of Clara Zetkin, though this would have been a much more serious crime).

In *The Story of My Life* Svirsky relates that he loved to lie as a young boy.[47] He didn't lie just for the sake of lying but because he liked to entertain his elders: "Aunt Dvoyre, a woman just gave birth to a baby in the street! It was such a tiny baby, and how it cried!" Aunt Dvoyre rushed out and returned furious. No woman was having babies in the street. Meanwhile, the little rascal was hiding in the bushes, burning with shame and through bitter tears begging God to help him stop lying. But God did not wish to help the miserable child.

I think of this boy and his agony, and I wonder whether judges and prosecutors ever ask Themis, their goddess of justice, to guide them to the path of righteousness. Or are they so far gone that she turns her back on them in indifference?

I come to the conclusion that anyone can find himself being sentenced to life imprisonment for doing just about anything. If I should sit down and squash a bedbug by accident, for example, Major Halski will be sure to say, "You're a scurvy scumbag and you must be wiped out because you maliciously crushed an honest Soviet bedbug with your bourgeois-nationalist ass!" And that's enough of a case to have me nailed to the wall. You want to submit complaints, file appeals? Go right ahead, please—that's part of the package deal, like the shit you're going to get.

I appeal the unjust verdict of the Lviv Provincial Court to

the Supreme Court of the Ukrainian SSR. And what do I get for my troubles? I am acquitted of "falsely imputed" criminal associations with Mykhaylo and Bohdan Horyn, Mykhaylo Masyutko, and Ivan Svitlychny. But the Supreme Court does not reverse the arbitrary accusations the judges have made against me, though they have been denied by the witnesses. I shall still have to serve my sentence.

"You should be happy you got so little," my interrogator tells me after the trial. "Two years—why that's not even a child's sentence. Thank God they didn't stick you with any more than that. These two years will go by like a flash for you. You'll come back, and we'll go fishing in Lake Svytyaz."

A trial purifies you. It cleanses you of suffering, sleepless nights, and faith in decency and justice. It purges you of every imperfection, of everything that has stirred and troubled you in your former life. Suddenly you feel lighthearted, even happy, and your sentence, whether two years or ten, means nothing. You're entirely carefree—as if you've just left the confessional and haven't a single thought about sinning again. Even the narrow, gloomy cell does not oppress you as it did before, and the familiar words "toilet call," "reveille," and "gruel" no longer concern you. You feel absolutely sure of yourself, and the realization that you've been conned doesn't in the least disturb you. You're just like the country bumpkin who was picked clean. He goes home in dread, but the bright memory of tall buildings keeps him from despairing.

To add to all this, I am honored one morning by a visit from my good interrogator. I look at him gratefully, thinking that he belongs not on this assembly line of justice, rubber-stamping verdicts, but rather on an airliner, serving professional smiles and coffee, or behind a counter, dispensing to tourists information, keys, and kindness.

I have lectured at the university; I have been a journalist; I have written poetry, and always I have believed that I understand people, that I can delve into their minds and comprehend them, distinguishing the good from the bad, the sincere from the insincere. Now I throw up my hands in bewilderment because I simply cannot tell good from evil, kindness from plain cruelty. Everything here reminds me of a gigantic chameleon or a constant kaleidoscopic flux. It all spins around and around, and I can't understand anything or reach any conclusions. "To hell with it!" I say. For the first time in my life I sense a distrust of mankind growing in me. Words, even the most beautiful words, lose all meaning for me.

Who would think that at the precise moment when the interrogator is consoling me with the prospect of seeing my wife again, she is waiting a floor below—she has been there for quite some time—and when she asks permission to see me as soon as possible, the very same interrogator nervously blurts into the telephone receiver, "You'll have to wait! I don't have any time now, I'm very busy!"

I don't know what urgent matters of state he is deliberating —maybe he's having a cup of coffee or peacefully napping on his couch—but my wife is kept waiting from ten o'clock in the morning until half past four in the afternoon. My wife is very young, only twenty years old. She is pregnant and expecting her baby at any time. The interrogator knows this and sometimes even expresses concern about her condition. "You've got a very nice wife, you know," he says.

She stands there pale and weak, and ten minutes after she is finally granted permission to see me, she falls into my arms, softly weeping, and begins to slide down to the floor. I think at first that she has collapsed because she knows that she will not see me again for a long time, but the interrogator is much more discerning than I. He quickly grasps her under the arms and leads her to the door. My wife leaves alone and goes to the medical institute on foot because she doesn't have enough money for the streetcar. An hour after seeing me she gives birth to our child.

Let us assume that in the eyes of the interrogator I am a

convicted felon. Then he is certainly within his rights in treating me as such. But why subject a woman to such fiendish torture? Not only a woman, but a mother! And not merely a mother, but a pregnant woman who is going to give birth—this very same day! We celebrate Woman's Day every March 8, bringing women flowers. The interrogator no doubt gives his wife flowers too. If you were to ask him on that day whether he has anything against establishing another organization to fight for women's rights in society and their "equality" with men, the interrogator would certainly give his wholehearted approval. Do I now have the moral right to believe a man like the interrogator? How can I believe the words he utters from his lofty social position? No, my faith has been shattered by the injustice perpetrated on innocent people in the thirties, people who were later rehabilitated and now honestly labor side by side with those who wrote denunciations against them.

I cannot, for example, believe the writer Oleksiy Poltoratsky, editor of *Vsesvit* [The Universe], either as a private citizen or as a public man who fervently campaigns in the press for honesty and encourages his readers to love humanism.[48] Tell me, how am I to believe a man who in the thirties called Ostap Vyshnya a "class enemy," a "glorifier of the kulak peasantry," a "conservationist of the language," and a "zoological nationalist," and then in the sixties calls this great Ukrainian humorist his "dearest friend"? When was Poltoratsky an upright citizen? When Ostap Vyshnya was in a tight spot and Poltoratsky was slandering him from head to foot? Or now, when Ostap Vyshnya has been rehabilitated, when his honest name has been restored to him, and when he has been proclaimed as an outstanding Ukrainian humorist? Does Poltoratsky, the great "psychoanalyst" of his time, have the right to call Vyshnya his friend? Who gave him that right? His civic conscience? The Soviet regime? No, Poltoratsky shamelessly appropriated Vyshnya, committing an even more heinous crime than the one he was guilty of in the thirties!

Such thoughts give me no peace. They only add to the

troubles of my mind, tearing me apart so violently that at times I walk up to the wall, close my eyes, and hammer my fists against the stone in impotent rage. This happens when I am preparing for my first deportation to a hard-labor camp.

Part Two

THE CITY OF THE SUN

IF you stare intently at the ground beneath your feet, you will notice a hole and a pickax at the bottom. You can dig the earth with the pickax, carry it out of the hole by the armful, and pile it in mounds. If you don't get tired and dig long enough, you will reach water. You can fall face down and drink for an hour or two. You can simply refuse to take your mouth away from the spurting fountain for the duration of your sentence. You can sprout roots and become a tree. Then the chief guard will pound his fist on the tree trunk and say, "So, you've found yourself a comfortable spot, you Ukie sonofabitch!" The guard might say more because he is remarkably talkative, but the prisoners pester him and change the subject.

"This is fascism, chief, feeding us herring for two days and not giving us any water. You ought to be hung by your balls for that, you scum!"

"Maybe he doesn't have any balls. What are you going to hang him by then? Your own?"

"Stop fucking around, you sonofabitch," the guard answers calmly, "or I'll take the bread away and you'll have to feed on herring alone. If you're thirsty, go drink your piss!"

"Chief, let me out to piss, or I'll flood the whole compartment and you won't get your holiday bonus, you bastard!"

"Piss over the wall to him, he's thirsty!"

A woman's insanely shrill voice carries through the railroad car: "Hey chief, you with the limp dong! I've been asking you for three hours now to let me out to the toilet. I can't hold out anymore! I've got female problems!"

"The toilet ain't no gynecologist for you," the guard shakes with laughter as he surveys the prisoners. They blink their eyes apprehensively, but when they see only satisfaction in his face, they begin to titter as well.

Mykhaylo Horyn seems to be swimming in a cloud of smoke and stale air. He walks up to the thick steel grating and looks out into the passageway. The train is rolling past fields, posts, houses, and vegetable patches with people bustling around in them. Further on, in a beet field several kilometers long, a solitary, desolate woman stoops to the ground.

"Women," says Mykhaylo as if to himself. "Anya Sadovska and Yaroslava Menkush. . . .[1] They suffered in prison a hundred times more than we did, but they held up well."

"Get your paws off the grating, counterrevolutionary scum, or I'll poke your eyes out!" an escort guard screams. "You didn't want to be a university rector, so chew on your herring now!"

Mykhaylo slowly withdraws and sits down beside me.

"It just dawned on me why our writers like to write about water so much—streams, rivers flowing by . . . It must be that more than one of them was fed this herring and given no water. After a hundred years of such diet the thirst must have got into our blood."

"You're not a beast, chief, you're a human being. Give me some water, my brains are drying out."

"Tell me when your ass starts to dry out."

"I just can't imagine what Semen Shakhovsky, the 'great literary trailblazer,'[2] would yell if he were thrown into a prison train," continues Horyn. "Particularly if he were locked up with those he denounced and helped to dispatch to the other world in the thirties, nailing the lids on their coffins. He was terribly hurt when I said this to him at Mykhaylo Masyutko's trial: he lowered his head and wouldn't look up for the duration of the trial."

"Let the man go to the john; he's dying! Can't you see he's dripping already?"

"I should shoot the likes of him!"

"I'll shoot you first; I'll poke your eyes out before you get me!"

"Is Professor Volodymyr Zdoroveha one of your people?"

"Yes, he lectured on Party journalism in our department. He was known to his students as a 'liberal democrat.' He even occasionally allowed himself to flirt with the subject of the thirties. An ardent Ukrainophile he was."

"Yes, that was quite evident at the trial. He, Semen Shakhovsky, and two others from your department—Pavlo Yashchuk and Kybalchych—busted their balls trying to prove ideological similarities between Masyutko's views and those expressed in papers ripped out of somebody's hands. There was absolutely no criminal evidence against Masyutko, so they 'scientifically' established that he was author of these papers. For this he was sentenced to six years at hard labor.

"You know, Masyutko's trial was like the spring mating of wood grouse when the cocks fight for the hens. Soloukhin, I think, has a brilliant description of this splendid and tragic scene.[3] The best, most worthy males fight over a beautiful female until they collapse dead or exhausted. Then the worst males, who stayed away from the fight because of their innate worthlessness, take the opportunity to steal the hen away. Masyutko defended his innocence like a desperate male grouse. He didn't win, of course, but neither did his opponents. Their mutual defeat was made use of by a third party—the worthless birds, the rejects. They received a fee that will be collected from Masyutko. That's outright robbery! And then in Kiev, you know, Masyutko was formally cleared of these charges because they hadn't been properly substantiated, but innocent as he is he still has to serve his six years. How can those little pricks now teach students and lecture them about decency?"

"What's the matter with you, Mykhaylo?" I whisper hoarsely because my mouth is terribly parched. "Don't you understand that the fee is a lot of money? Three hundred and twenty rubles! You know what they say about money keeping you warm!"

"What money are you blabbering about?" someone yells from the neighboring compartment. "My ass is warm! It's damn hot in here and it stinks! This whole joint is a nightmare. Chief, get away from the grating and stop smelling everything up!"

"Hey, buddy," a zek drums on our wall. "Pass this note to the broad who has female problems."

The guard walks away, and his footsteps echo at the far end of the passageway. Two fingers slip a scrap of paper through the grating. Now the note is passed through all the compartments to the women's section. A few minutes later a reply comes back: "I want you!"

"What? You want me? Crawl over here, you can pick whoever tickles your fancy just like in Georgia. We can even give you a queer from the Caucasus."

"Save the Caucasian for the chief. He'll fuck him so hard his eyeballs will pop out!"

A new voice cuts through the growing clamor in the boxcar: "Keep it down, Banderite, keep it down or I'll rub you out!"

"What do you mean, keep it down?" an angry voice shoots back. "Go keep it down in Moscow. What the hell are you doing in Ukraine? You've jammed the prisons with our people, letting them rot to death."

"What are you bawling for, buddy? How long?" another prisoner calls out.

"How dare you talk to me in Russian! A guy can't get away from you people even here. You Russian butchers clear the hell out of Ukrainian prisons!"

Mykhaylo, who has been carefully listening to this exchange, bursts out with a laugh. "Listen to him. Straight out of Vynnychenko with his sincerity!"[4]

The rebel is brought into our compartment, disheveled and barechested. Without so much as glancing at us he starts to pound on the grating with his fists.

"Don't put people behind bars, you Russky pig, because

tomorrow you might wind up in here yourself. Do you think you'll rule our country forever?"

"Shut up, you bandit! The government spent millions searching you out. We made one croak, so be grateful you're behind bars and not under six feet of shit!"

I am lying on an upper berth in a cloud of smoke and foul smells. I feel sick, and everything swims before my eyes. My swollen, brittle tongue painfully slides across my dry palate. At this moment I fiercely hate fishermen, fish, and salt. I see a caravan of *chumaks*—Ukrainian oxcart drivers of old—slowly ascending a hill, their carts weighed down with mountains of fish, grain, and glistening sea salt, and I develop a passionate hatred for the *chumaks* and their mottled oxen.

I seem to be running and rasping air into my lungs like Faulkner's Negro. Then I turn back and immediately feel better. I can breathe more freely, and my legs aren't quite so weak. I am finally being led out of the compartment by the escort guards. They order me to run; they shove and push me into another compartment; I see a Judas hole open, and wild eyes stare at me.

It must be evening, I realize, and people are being taken out for toilet call. Then a zek is pushed in with me, the one who wrote the note to the woman, I think.

"Valyusha," he says, after firing off a burst of curses at the guards, who keep pushing him away from the grating, "Valyusha, what are you in for? Her?"

"No, Vanya, everything's okay with her. They got me for pickpocketing."

"Who would you shoot, Valyusha, if the Chinese attacked us: them or the pigs?"

"The pigs, Vanya. What about you?"

"Me too, Valyusha."

"Swell, Vanya, I'll sleep with you the first chance I get. You hear? Just you."

Later our "loudmouth" paces up and down the compartment, his hands folded behind his back. I hear him say his name—Semenyuk, Roman Semenyuk. He says that he has been doing time since the age of eighteen. He says that he was sentenced and served eighteen years even though he didn't do anything. Then he explains that he and another inmate named Oliynyk escaped from a camp not long ago.[5] They were at large for three months before they were caught at the home of Oliynyk's sister, near Rivne in Western Ukraine. The sister got a term for not reporting them. Oliynyk had a new case started against him and has probably been shot by now.

"They wanted to start a new case against me too, but they couldn't find the old one, so now they're shipping me back to Yavas to slap on a new term for escaping."

Semenyuk says that he had nine years left to serve, but now he'll have to serve twelve. He sings prison songs: "Hey, buddy, don't hurry, I'll sing a song with you." He says that he got a taste of freedom and now it will be easier to do time, but he thinks he will never be a free man again. He has never been with a girl and doesn't even know how women kiss. Semenyuk sobs and says that he and Oliynyk were the first to notice some rotten posts along the camp perimeter, in the branch of a river. The men pushed the posts apart and swam more than a kilometer under water. Semenyuk sobs and says that he will never again be able to swim so far underwater.

Then a woman prisoner is led down the passageway to the toilet, and a minute later we hear her scream: "You sonofabitch, why are you watching me piss?"

"I'm not watching," the embarrassed guard snuffles. "I'm only standing here according to regulations."

"Give me your goddamn regulations," the woman shoots back with a shrill laugh. "I'll wipe my ass with them!"

"Faster, faster! Everybody out! Link arms, run, run!" Strong hands push me in the back, and I fall headlong on the tracks. My gear tumbles on top of me. I feverishly pull it out from under somebody's feet—feet fly past my eyes like the wheels of an express train—then step aside and freeze, motionless:

huge police dogs are straining at their leashes and baring their black palates in my face. I crawl backwards involuntarily, still trying to get hold of my gear, which will not yield to my weak hands.

"One step out of line and we open fire without warning!" the guards call out. "Link arms, higher, higher, by the elbows! Run, run!"

We are running, stumbling over railroad ties, hurriedly getting up, and falling down again. The dogs course beside us, pulling their handlers along in their excitement at the fresh human scent. Soldiers with submachine guns trot alongside them. The barrels point directly at our faces, and I close my eyes with a shudder, falling on the tracks again and dragging my gear with me. As I lie on the ground for a second, I notice the Moscow–Sevastopol and Kharkiv–Odessa express trains. Fat, anemic, expressionless faces sleeping on thick red necks can be seen in the windows of the well-appointed carriages.

"Ugh! Ten inches of fat, and they get it all off our sweat. I bet my balls a bullet couldn't pierce that!"

"Run, run, run, no lagging, pull up!"

"The bastard didn't bark at the fascists the way he barks at us, and the sonofabitch is supposed to be a Soviet man."

Over thirty prisoners are shoe-horned into a van made to hold maybe sixteen, twenty men. The doors slam shut, and two bolts click into place. Everything swims before my eyes, and I cannot catch my breath—I underwent a serious throat operation as a child. My legs collapse, and I cannot hold back a scream: "Let's go! How long are you going to stand here?"

"Let's go!" the other prisoners yell at the top of their lungs, but the guards have vanished in the oppressive glimmer of heat and sweat.

Later we hear calm voices: we are to be transferred, but the new escort wants no part of us. A quarrel breaks out, and the police dogs begin to whine.

"What's the matter with you, buddy?" Someone is shaking me violently. I resist and say that I've had enough.

"That's it," I say. "Nobody is going to push me around anymore. Do what you like to me, but I'm not getting up. I wouldn't budge even for Stalin himself."

"Bastards!" says a zek. "That fucking broad Catherine put up all these 'big houses,' and now they're only too glad to cram us into the old pigpens."

"Leave the old girl alone. She was no tight little bitch, she did things in a broad way like a true Russian. She'd take on a horse any day! And the prisons she built will last Mother Russia a thousand years."

The guard stares at a young boy who walks past him defiantly, then turns around and walks back.

"Smartass! Not even sixteen yet, and already he's a know-it-all," the guard snorts. "What idiot got it into his head to think up that goddamn law for juvenile delinquents? They lock up kids for getting into mischief, give them six years, no wonder the prisons are jammed. No bonuses, no fucking holidays, just work your ass off night and day."

A scrawny, redheaded professional thief who has been sentenced for the thirteenth time and has a cumulative term of 108 years, says, "Don't rub it in. We'll reform him before his time is up. Maybe we'll even make a real crook out of him so that he won't have to go around a sucker."

"I'd give you a piece of my mind, you shithead, if you weren't taking off tomorrow. I'd have you on your hands and knees, you cocksucker!"

"Yeah, you guys are fine bastards. I've covered Russia from one end to the other, and I've never seen such crummy transit prisons as here in Kharkiv. You scabs are worse than your dogs. You'd eat a man alive. Here, suck on my throat, you louse!"

Dear God, what have I fallen into? I am nothing here, a tiny insect, an earwig. I'm just a creepy little intellectual to these people. I say I'm vermin, but actually I'm much less than that. I have been obliterated. Maybe I don't even exist. All that's left of me is my big ears, which hear everything no matter how tightly I press my hands over them. My hands are so weak, and I can't press any harder. . . .

"Nothing to read. How can I get through the rest of the day?" I ask Mykhaylo Horyn, who has been walking up and down past the windows.

"Weren't you ever taught to learn things by heart?" Horyn sits down beside me and begins to recite the poems of Samiylenko.[6] I repeat them after him but immediately forget what I have recited.

"What are you shits babbling?" someone yells at us from the other side of the partition.

Damn ears! I think. I wonder whether Ostap Vyshnya found all this funny. Maybe he even sat in this same cell, No. 80. Could he still be amusing in the midst of such chaos and degradation?

"Tell me," I address a guard, trying to avoid his bloodshot eyes, "is this the Cold Mountain Prison where Ostap Vyshnya rotted away?" I try to make my words sound like a joke, but it falls flat.

"Yeah, this is the place. Millions were written off here. How can you remember them all after twenty years of work?"

Ukraine stares at the convict with wide eyes, then hastily turns her eyes away because fear of the escort guard paralyzes her pink cheeks. Ukraine is afraid of the convict; she is wary of the guard. There she is, just around the corner. Now she has passed the corner and is gone. She has shamefully retreated into her humdrum existence. She does not feel safe unless she is immersed in the imperceptible passage of days and nights. Chafers and cherry orchards in bloom are much dearer to her heart. But dress those chafers in striped prison garb, shave their heads, and Ukraine will surely come to hate the orchard and will cut down the cherry trees because they breed striped chafers. She will plant willows instead. They won't bear juicy cherries, of course, and there's no profit to be reaped from them, but they seem safer and less troublesome, and the bitter fragrance of the willow leaves is hardly noticeable. Ukraine can get used to this bitterness more quickly than to the shaved heads of the chafers.

Ukraine can get used to anything. Tell that polite farmer that he is a prisoner, and he won't argue with you. Yes, of course, he's a prisoner, and the only thing that bothers him, gnawing at his heart and leaving a taste of ashes in his mouth, is that he won't be able to spade his vegetable patch, graze his cow, or mend his fences. It makes no difference to him what he is as long as he's allowed to rest in his orchard in the warmth of a June night, oh you know, falling in love with the stars somewhere high up in the heaven and, you know, getting excited when he hears his cow chewing her cud in the stall.

Russia, on the other hand, is no match for Ukraine. She likes prisons and is really quite respectful of prisoners. When she sees them huddled on a train platform, she rushes headlong toward them, calling out encouragements. She throws bread and cigarettes to them, turning out her pockets unhappily and cursing herself when they are empty. Russia spares nothing for prisoners—neither tortures nor bread.

There she stands in a long, dirty gypsy skirt, calling out between sobs: "Take it, dear, take it, have some fresh bread! Here, have a roll, I bought it for the children, but you eat it, you've got to keep your strength up, my son. What a bitter fate you've got, what a sorry lot. . . .

"I'm sorry, brother, I can only give you half a pack. I didn't know I was going to run into you."

Ukraine, the prison guard, as well as Ukraine, the farmer, is always one-sided. If she is told to shout, she shouts and shouts much more than is called for. If she is told to be polite to prisoners, she is so polite that it makes you sick. If she takes you for a walk, she says, "Please." And if she escorts you to the toilet, she's also sure to say, "If you please." Ukraine, the guard, like Ukraine, the farmer, is always conscientious.

Russia, the guard, does not deviate from the letter of the law: she yells, she curses, and she swings her fists, but at the same time she inconspicuously slips cigarettes and a bread roll to the crowd of prisoners, furtively looking around to see if the brass have noticed. Russia, the guard, smiles at you and cheerfully runs to post your letter at the railway station. Russia, the guard, walks up to you and says kindly, "Why should I give you a hard time? You're human just like me. Tomorrow you'll be out of here. I'll run into you on the town, and you can set me up for a round."

Ukraine is in awe of the guard and sees her calling in him. But Russia does not like the guard and views his job skeptically, as merely a way to earn her bread. Such work tires and depresses her, and she scoffs at it, yet she never makes an effort to lose it. Such is the Russia of the guards at the transit prisons in every railway station. She is phlegmatic and loves peace. She is displeased when the peace is disturbed. "Wild" Semenyuk has been handcuffed. He walks among us like a rogue elephant, and we take turns carrying his suitcase and putting strong cigarettes in his mouth.

Some words attract, others repel. The word *chefir* neither attracts nor repels but hangs in midair like a crucified Christ in a painting.[7] You raise your eyes to it in secret supplication and become as excited as when you were in the cradle and saw around you for the first time a strange world of colors, sounds, and peculiar beings called humans. Stoned on *chefir,* a prisoner crawls into a corner ready to spit at the barbed wires and the official warnings against escape. He forgets all the vicissitudes of imprisonment and finds himself rushing into his home, kissing his family, and weeping with joy.

Yes, damn it, he's laughing, for this is quite some occasion. The call for lights out rings in his ears, but he lies there like a stone, speeding through the night. He's high, he's stoned, he's gotta talk, he'd talk all night, he'd talk to anybody. And in the morning his cellmates glance at him and ask, "What were you doing, making flicks?"

Chefir. Say something stupid like "wife," "cognac," or "a

blue night," when the prisoner is relishing it from a blackened tin mug, and he'll stare back at you in amazement and spew forth a string of curses that reaches all the way to Red Square.

Getting high is forbidden by the administration. You can drink black coffee, but for tea they throw you in the cooler—fifteen days of concrete carpets. A packet of tea—Georgian, Indian, or Ceylonese—costs two rubles, and you have to be thoroughly checked out to get it. The best tea comes from Ceylon. The older hands can tell the teas apart as readily as wine tasters distinguish vintages.

A group of prisoners huddles around the owner of the tea, who presides over the ceremony like a sorcerer preparing his potions. A small fire is built in the corner of the cell, and a metal mug is hung over it on a spoon. When the water boils, a matchboxful of tea (the only measure in camp) is poured in. The cup of tea is lovingly wrapped in a quilt jacket—even a mother diapering her baby is not so careful—and permitted to steep for five or ten minutes. (It would be ridiculous to compare our suspense to the countdown for the first manned space flight.) Then the mug is carefully unwrapped and all sorts of solemn toasts are proposed: to the United Nations, to a nag's tail, to the health of the pre-revolutionary prisoner, Father Stalin, and to the health of His Holiness the Pope, whose life on earth is easier: he can always see *his* leader securely nailed to a cross. "May they all drop dead!" The prisoners gingerly pass the *chefir* from hand to hand, taking care not to spill a single drop. Each person is allowed two gulps, three if he has just come out of the cooler, but even the most inveterate *chefirnik* wouldn't risk getting himself thrown in the cooler just for an extra gulp.

Nothing brings prisoners together faster than *chefir*. When the empty mug finally stops in someone's hands, the questions begin to fly: "Why are you here?" "Where are you from?" "How long are you in for?"

"What can I give you as a present?" Neeme, an Estonian, asks me. "I like Ukrainians a lot, they're really great people.

Would you like to have my brief case? Where did you work? At the university? Then for an educated man like you only a brief case will do. I'm sorry that it's a bit worn. We'll bunk together tonight. Oh, by the way, I'm in for two years of solitary at Vladimir.[8] Your camp offers a little more freedom. Enjoy it!

"Do you know how to hide a blade, or money, or a needle? You're lost without them. Do you know how to get the best work assignments? If you wind up in Camp 11, God forbid you should go to the cutting room or the machine shop. One's very drafty, and the din in the other is unbearable. You don't have stomach problems, do you? Don't worry, you'll pull through.

"Did you know that Estonia is a thousand years old? Once there were only sixty Estonians left, but Estonia survived. She'll survive the camps as well.

"Have you heard about Daniel? He's in Camp 11. The way he's working, he'll end up in the cooler."

We take each other by the arms and begin to walk around the cell with the other pairs. I can't for the life of me figure out what we're saying, but we talk like old friends who have met unexpectedly after a long separation. We huddle against the wall laughing and listening to one zek, a heavy but surprisingly agile fellow who never stops moving his toothless mouth.

Choking with laughter, he says: "The shithead calls me in and says, 'You cocksucking zek, you're a good guy. Don't just stand there, don't tremble, you pile of shit, have a seat. There's no bad blood between us, we're all your friends here, from the first country of socialism. Come on, you stuck-up sonofabitch, help us figure out your case. The devil only knows what you're here for. We'll give you anything you ask for. Whaddaya want: your freedom? a woman?'

" 'You're no fucking friends of mine,' I says to him. 'Up the ass with your freedom and your fucking woman. Give me a package of tea, you Soviet shit!' " The fellow throws his head back and bellows with laughter. Wiping the tears from his eyes he adds, "What kind of fucking life is it when there's nobody to live with?"

He throws his head back again and gives another roar. His chest and stomach, scarred by barbed wire, glass, and knives, begin to heave as if they had a life of their own. They rise up to follow the thrown-back head, and the zek keeps on laughing. He is high on *chefir,* and now he points to his mangled forehead.

"I had 'Khrushchev's Slave' tattooed here, but the motherfuckers cut him off my forehead and out of my life. Idiot, I should have known that belly-buster would be booted out and tattooed somebody else's name instead."

"You can afford to wisecrack, you lucky dog, they're shipping you to the loony bin."

"Fuck them, I don't care. I can get by anywhere. I only wish those mothers at the top hadn't picked me. Why me? Am I any better than you guys? I wouldn't want anybody to think I finked out."

The zek leans his head against the wall with a chuckle. He is a confirmed loner and laughs only at his own jokes. The gashes on his neck suggest the graffiti on the walls: "Your rights are protected by the UN"; "Kolya from Kineshma two years"; "Ten years for being a queer"; "Vanya from Moscow. . . ."

The prisoners tell each other stories. Sometimes they forget and tell the same stories twice, and then they're even funnier. The prisoners strut about the cell arm in arm, pawing at the concrete carpet more fiercely than any horse or bull with manure under its hoofs. Their heads waver in the smoke. Very high, higher than our friend in the striped recidivist's uniform can toss his head, they keep churning out an ever denser gloom, in which they are finally immured, while their short, headless bodies shuffle aimlessly around the cell. Stripey throws his head back as far as it will go, and it hits the wall with a dull thud, his toothless mouth a gaping hole on a black ground.

"Bylaws . . . I might be illiterate, you bastards, and goofed off through three grades, but I can still read. B as in *brighten up*, Y as in *you*, L as in *lags!* A as in *amnesty!* W as in *work camps*, S as in *scrapped*: BYLAWS! SWALYB: S as in *stop*, W as in *wishing!* A as in *amnesty* and *a*, L as in *lie*, Y as in *you*, B as in *bastards!*"

The gaping hole is fixed against the wall, a thick blackness churning within, as the zek convulses with soundless laughter. "But still, I had them royally screwed! In the loony bin you can at least beat your meat till it's raw."

Then a luminous green circle comes into focus above the black hole, and I read: "Zeks, do not despair! You will soon be home. Zhora from Mogilev."

There is a paradox of beauty: an exceptionally beautiful woman with an uncommonly vulgar nose. She's wonderful to look at full face, but when you see her in profile you can't help shuddering: some sort of monstrous entity is hitting you in the eye. The hell with it, you think.

There's another paradox of beauty: birch groves where the slender tree trunks captivate you with their warm colors, and you hug the bars like an idiot so that the other zeks won't think you're headed for the nuthouse. You smile and personate the man of prayer. There is a painting of Jesus Christ on Golgotha. He sits grasping his knees, and around him is a dark-blue twilight. In any case, it is night because the moon is peering through the clouds. Below are buildings, many buildings with lights inside. Those lights are a symbol of sorrow. Christ is suffering—or perhaps not suffering, but simply resting after his crucifixion.

Here's another paradox for you: resting after crucifixion. Your face shows annoyance, annoyance at the profile of nature: birch groves and then suddenly enormous wooden fences—the labor camp. Concealed behind the fences are rows of barbed wire. Nineteen rows, nineteen camps. Birch trees and labor camps. More precisely, birch trees and barbed wire.

They say there's still another paradox: the birches are young, but they're rotten inside. Dig into one and you'll find rot. They're like beautiful but barren women. The zeks say these birches cannot be otherwise—the soil isn't right for them. Sink your spade a few feet and you come across human bones. Or a skull. Birch trees from corpses. The trees have been rooted in this soil for ages. Since the times of the Terrible One, some say.

"Well, we're fucking well stuck," says one zek. He often talks about it, this zek. "With a birch tree, first you knock it over and then you drag it off. It's a little different with a girl: first you drag her off and then you knock her up. But these shitty fences screw everything up for us."

"Once the bloody queers get you behind their heavenly gates all you'll be able to do is eyeball our Soviet sky. It's my third time here, damn it, and I still get the same old shitty feeling that I'm a mouse being thrown in with a horny elephant. Sometimes I feel so low, just can't get used to it, what a bunch of bastards, I think. There's one old queer here, tough as nails. Every night for two years that mother of a CO brainwashed me. My luck he'll still be there. Who the fuck knows how I'll take it this time."

"What are you in for, politics? It must have been some mindfuck for you. They gave me ten fucking years for rape— now it's going to be a long dry hump. Listen, buddy, is there any way to smuggle in a piece of ass?"

"Sure, you can swing anything here, but with those fucking queers all over the joint you might have to do it in the cooler. When they throw you in for fifteen days they'll screw the hell out of you just like in a French whorehouse. You'll drag your feet like a cockroach. Turns my stomach to think about it!"

"Listen, sonny, what about an old guy like me? Think I'll last ten years?"[9]

"What are you in for, you old geezer?"

"You know, sonny, the war . . . the kind of time it was . . . the Germans . . . no grub . . . you'd do worse things under fire."

"So you sold yourself, you fucking fascist? For that you'll

have two veteran fags riding your ass. They haven't got any horses, the Party brass ate them all up. Now the camp bosses ride to work on the oldsters."

"So you're saying I won't pull through, sonny?"

"Naw, you'll pull through, gramps; you'll even get to bang your old lady again."

The old man huddles in a corner, his knees shaking, and mumbles something about his granddaughters, his wife is gone, as his frightened little eyes dart over the excited, disheveled zeks: that zek is at home here, everyone is afraid of the zek, and he in turn is afraid of the authorities. That's the kind of place it is—everyone is afraid of someone. The old man is afraid because he's getting on in years and the brass have eaten up all the horses. What is it to the other zeks, no one is going to ride them to work. The old man sobs and rolls up his trousers and tears violently at the hairy scars on his leg. Blood spurts over his leg, and the old man is racked with sobs.

You imagine that in half an hour you'll be sound asleep in the barracks, where it's warm and you have your own corner to crawl into, and you don't have to talk to those guys who might sell you for a packet of tea. But there's another feeling, too—of losing your home and knowing that in half an hour they'll herd you into the barracks and you'll never come out again.

What is camp? A comfortable shelter or the loss of it forever? Your mind is disturbed, you're anxious, your legs are painfully weak, and you sit down on a bench.

"It's my third time here, damn it, and I still get the same old shitty feeling that I'm a mouse being thrown in with a horny elephant."

The old man blinks fearfully. Idiot! He's lived all these years and never seen an elephant. He imagines that an elephant is like a huge house, and he moves his anemic arms about on his chest.

"They say there used to be a wide-gauge track here, but

these fucking fences squeezed it in from both sides, and that's why it's so narrow now."

I can feel the tall gray fences pressing in from both sides and the walls of the train closing in on me. Then everything shrinks even more, and I hear the old man's anemic hands fidgeting on his chest. I see a gate. We fly through it as if shot from a cannon. We sense an openness, a roominess before us. Someone is shoving and pushing us from behind. I turn around and see that the gate has been slammed shut. I see bolts and locks. I see a sign overhead: TO FREEDOM WITH A CLEAR CONSCIENCE. The lettering is red and blue. We are at Yavas.

"You'll sleep here," I am told. "Here's your locker. Your bedding is in the supply room."

"Where are you from, buddy? How long?"

"Two. From Lviv."

The zeks are still within earshot when one of them says, "Two years? He must be putting us on. Since when do politicals get only two?"

"He's a rookie. We know the kind."

We are led on the run to the supply room. Yaroslav Hevrych whispers to me—a guard is standing behind us—"Give me your sweater, your underwear, and your beret. They'll take everything away from you."[10]

I pull out my shabby clothes. Yaroslav slips them under his tunic.

"Shove off, you bastard!" the guard screams. "You'll get the cooler for this!"

"Give me your shoes," Hevrych says.

In the supply room I am issued a visored cap. It comes down over my ears.

"A former Beria man," someone jokes.

The bearded supply clerk self-importantly hands me another cap. He feels at home here, but he has nothing to do at home.

Mykhaylo Soroka, phlegmatic but smiling, shakes my hand.[11] "How is it outside?" he asks. "What's new?"

I have no news, but he is still interested in me. "You're a rookie," he says, "but you'll get used to everything."

I am astonished by the camp atmosphere. Actually, there are several atmospheres here: the atmosphere of philosophical contemplation (it could be portrayed in a painting of wise eyes surmounted by a lofty, thoughtful forehead); the atmosphere of tranquility (even the camp pigeons fly seldom, and when they are in the air they fly slowly, without hurrying anywhere); the atmosphere of refined culture (if anyone uses foul language, it's usually the guards, the stoolies, or the non-politicals); the atmosphere of neatness (there are flowers and trees everywhere, and the wooden sidewalks are immaculate; this cleanliness of the camp grounds suggests an inner purity); and the atmosphere of individuality (everyone lives in his own private world and demands that it be respected as an artistic creation). Then there are other atmospheres: of fear, of abject loyalty (to the powers that be), of baseness (purely human), of self-imposed conformity, of withdrawn reserve, and of lonely pride.

In the closed circle of his daily existence a man always has something to amuse him. It may be the movies or a museum excursion. Then again it may be the theater, his wife and children, his friends, or the corner bar. This closed circle exists in the camp as well, but in an idealized form, transcending ordinary materialism because it is based not on being, but on consciousness. It is a complete realization of one's fantasy, one's personal world view. A man lives above things until, unexpectedly, he discovers himself beneath them. Out of this sudden realization he builds a world in which only one man can live. The intrusion of another person brings about a catastrophe, not quite total destruction, but catastrophe nevertheless. A man who has learned to affirm his world can survive all the adversities of camp imprisonment and preserve his mind and spirit.

For example, I am taking a walk. Some cats are sprawled out beside the sidewalk. Someone is bent over one of them—let's say it's a gray cat—and is tickling it with a blade of grass. He tickles the cat for an hour or two or three. Then it's lights out. He goes to sleep and dreams that he is still tickling the cat with a blade of grass . . . Someone else has grown a full beard, and his eyes shine alertly. Suppose you stop him and ask: What about that beard?

The zeks are gathered in the compound. You run into one whose bootleg is always turned down. From afar he looks comical; closer up you see that he is a dark-skinned man with a pencil-line mustache. He always smiles cunningly as he strokes his mustache. This man knows all of Shakespeare by heart but will not contradict you if you say Shakespeare was nothing. He'll merely flash his cunning smile and walk away. Then you'll realize how comical you look in comparison with his turned-down bootleg.

This man is Ivan Rusyn, an engineer from Kiev.[12] He was sentenced to a year in camp when a search in his room produced "The Trial of Pogruzhalsky." The twenty-fivers make him feel guilty, and he tells everyone that he's serving five.

Rusyn knows that Socrates was extremely disturbed when writing was invented and that he predicted civilization and intellect would perish when ideas began to be placed on paper. Rusyn respects Socrates: if the world had listened to the philosopher, people would not be imprisoned today for articles such as "The Trial of Pogruzhalsky." But Rusyn is above all this. He realizes that if writing and even discourse had not been invented, people would still be put in prison. Rusyn walks away, and you can't help noticing again how comical you look in comparison with his turned-down bootleg.

Before supper Rusyn goes for a stroll and approaches us again. He is holding a book of poems by Ivan Drach. His hand behind his back in a theatrical pose, he reads:

On 22 June 1966 at 5:00 P.M.
We were passing Babyn Yar
The sun congealed in sleepy clouds
Villagers sprawled in the bushes
Sucking succulently on dried herring
And washing it down with beer
Near them a Black lounged in the lap
Of a blond teenage beauty
A gray-haired crone hobbled around
Asking if anyone had crosses for sale
The sickly maples suffocated in the heat
And my son slept in my lap
Dreaming of a wild horse in tall grass
Pile drivers pounded dry earth
Shovelfuls of sky were pitched upon me
Hard, full of cloud roots and sun stones
The steel cobras of lampposts
Hid their long necks in the dense leaves
And I instinctively shielded my son with my hands
On 22 June 1966 at 5:00 P.M.
When we were passing Babyn Yar.[13]

"On 22 June 1941 the Germans attacked. . . . On 22 June 1966 Drach passed by Babyn Yar and wrote his poem. . . . On 22 June 1966 two simple Soviet prisoners, Mykhaylo Horyn and Mykhaylo Osadchy, arrived in camp."

Rusyn walks away, and once more I see how comical I look in comparison with his turned-down bootleg.

Losiv is from Nizhyn. He is a Ukrainian with droopy Cossack mustaches, who feeds the pigeons in his free time. The pigeons perch on the latrine roof, unafraid of the zeks. Cooing and dozing, they patiently wait for Losiv to come feed them the glutinous bread we get in our rations. Losiv from Nizhyn would love to sleep on the latrine roof with the pigeons, but he'd get thrown in the cooler for that, so he spends the night on his hard bunk in the airless barracks, whistling in his sleep to his pigeons and startling the other prisoners. Losiv will be released in a few days after serving twenty-four procrustean years. To celebrate his coming freedom he buys coffee and treats the zeks in the machine shop to it for three days.

Ivan Hereha has lived so long that he knows life as well as any clairvoyant. He cannot precisely foretell the future, true enough, but he stubbornly insists on one thing: no one has yet been imprisoned for growing flowers. Hereha is pleased to see me (he's also from Lviv), and he takes me through his flower patch, naming the various species. Hereha is respected —not in the newspaper way, but in the camp way, even by the authorities. He feels lonely with the other prisoners and the barbed wire, and the flowers bring cheer into his life. He manages to stay out of the cooler, and the cook takes the risk of giving him seconds. With his profusion of flowers Hereha doesn't in the least look like a zek, and you can tell where he is located in space only by the fact that he isn't paid for his work.

Hereha has grown a sunflower—the only vision of Ukraine in the camp—and he takes as much joy in it as if it were his personal invention, but he conceals his pleasure even from himself. Mykhaylo Kotsyubynsky was the first to import carnations from Italy.[14] Ivan Hereha was the first to bring the Ukrainian sunflower into the Mordovian camps. The huge head of the plant (sixty centimeters across) is flung back haughtily, and the thick stalk towers over the barracks and the barbed-wire enclosures. Whenever the Latvian poet Knuts Skujenieks walks by,[15] Hereha can't resist crossing his path and asking, "Well, how do you like my sunflower?"

And every time Knuts surveys it as if he's never seen it before and answers, "Not bad, you know. But your creation is not entirely realistic. Why don't you try growing a rope with a hangman's noose on it?"

I don't remember Mahmed's surname, but I know he is a Kazakh and lectured on dialectical and historical materialism at the university in Alma-Ata.[16] In the fifth year of his teaching career Mahmed decided to leave the university. He wrote a statement to the effect that his views did not correspond with those set forth in the curriculum. Mahmed began to search for truth in materialism. He could not set his mind at rest and turned for advice to various authorities, first in Alma-Ata and later in Moscow. There, after a polite reception, Mahmed was told that he lacked a thorough theoretical training. He was erudite and highly knowledgeable, but he lacked a profound understanding of the essence of materialism. Mahmed went home. A few days later he was "assigned" to study that essence for seven years at the Yavas hard-labor camp.

Quite suddenly and unexpectedly, Mahmed set his mind at rest. He became a phlegmatic zek, losing his intellectual urge and forgetting all about the essence of dialectical and historical materialism, and he came to life only when he screamed and cursed at the cooks for serving rotten cabbage at supper again.

Here is another example of human whimsy. Someone at the camp tells a story about a peasant in the Ivano-Frankivsk Province who concealed an army tank in the space below his stable during the last war. For over twenty years he diligently oiled it and kept it free of rust and dirt. Finally he could no longer resist the urge to see whether the tank would really work. So one night he turned the engine on. It was only for a moment, but that was enough for the authorities to hear him. They took the tank away and locked the farmer up. He'll probably wind up in Yavas, too. Such a strange attachment to things is hard to figure out.

Scythian rock paintings that look like a schoolboy's exercises: horses, warriors, spearheads, and oxen. Also birds in flight, huge birds on a slab of rock. The birds are actually quite small, but they seem incredibly large. Their misleading size is the schoolboy's secret, which the teachers cannot fathom. They take a step back, then another, and stare. Finally they leave the cave with sheepish smiles. Then they toss their teaching manuals in the corner and lie face up on their beds. They lie there for whole days. They no longer want to teach those nasty pupils who can draw huge birds on small rocks. "To hell with those pupils," they say. The teachers grow ill. They lie in bed for days, and perhaps they will die, but they will never fathom the secret of the birds. Huge birds on a small rock. The teachers will run down the hill waving their arms. You'll hear their shouts if you listen. Those are shouts of awe. The sick are shouting. . . .

I always approach Mykhaylo Soroka from behind. I want to say hello first. He likes to play the same trick. He appears suddenly at your side—that's quite some trick. Soroka likes the summerhouse on the slope behind the stadium, where Hereha's flowers and the camp birch trees grow. Sometimes I like to be amusing and am inclined to make analogies. I clearly see the slope and the teachers who still have not figured out the secret of the schoolboys' birds.

Mykhaylo Soroka, I think. Sometimes we are enchanted by something but do not know exactly why. I come up from behind and say hello first. He looks up in surprise and squints slyly.

"How's your router treating you? Have they found a man for Daniel's jointer?"

Mykhaylo Soroka, I think. The first thing you notice about him is his very bright eyes. Then you notice that he never slips when he walks on snow. In twenty-eight years in labor camps he has learned to walk straight and to place his feet precisely. He is a skeptic. Not merely a skeptic, but a yoga-practicing one. He has perfected himself in every respect. Even his mind is still, high above the everyday humdrum. Tell him that at nine o'clock tomorrow morning the gates will be thrown open and everyone will get the hell out of here, and he'll reply with a sly squint, "Yes, yes, of course."

He does not believe in anything, this "atheist" who stands over everything mundane while leaning on the cane of skepticism. When you see him standing like that you run away from him the way the teachers ran down the slope.

Mykhaylo Soroka, I think. He's impossible to understand.

Just fall on your bed, close your eyes, and you will clearly see the huge bird on the small rock. Yogis—their teaching is not camp-begotten, but you couldn't survive the camps without it. Ten years of raja-yoga exercises, ten years of alienation. Flowers live apart; the mind is on other shores, and the body is here. You can let them merge, that's yoga too. Yoga and decades snatched from death's jaws. Steely indifference to his surroundings and willpower. Twenty-eight years of labor camps and prisons! The man has an irrepressible desire to survive and be set free.

Mykhaylo Soroka, I think. Five years in the hands of the political police in pre-war Poland. And then something different, closer to home, unspeakable. Twenty-eight years in all. I am in for two years and still sometimes almost go mad. I was one of the teachers, I ran down the slope: how? How long can one survive on prison gruel? The years terrify me. The huge bird and the small rock are here someplace. I have seen them clearly. I have only to close my eyes in the evening.

And to add to this—fate. His wife, Kateryna Zarytska, has spent nineteen years in imprisonment.[17] She's at the Vladimir Prison now. She, too, has survived. Their son is an artist. He grew up without his parents. He visits them sometimes.

Mykhaylo Soroka, I think. He forgets all about his yoga for a month when he receives word from his son. He forgets to be skeptical and walks around with a smile on his face for everyone. He becomes talkative, almost too much so, and recites the poems of Oles and describes his meetings with the great poet.[18] They met in an old café in Prague and drank pilsner. A commemorative plaque is nailed above the table where Oles once sat.

Sometimes the Security people summon Soroka to Kiev or Lviv. They dress him in black tie and take him to the theater to see Korniychuk's *A Page from a Diary*.[19] At the Cybernetics Institute gray-haired professors shake his hand and explain the latest achievements of science to him.

"They shake my hand," Mykhaylo Soroka says with a laugh,

"but they don't realize it's the hand of a zek. They'd forget all their science if they knew what sort of 'Canadian tourist' I am!"

Elegantly dressed men take him around Lviv. He remembers everything, and it is very painful for him. This is no welcome taste of the good life. It's a mockery: they taunt him with the thought that he may never see any of this again, or maybe . . . The choice is his. That's terrible. Not to stroll on a sidewalk or inhale the fragrances of mankind for twenty years. He has grown old; he is no longer accustomed to life outside, and now it exhausts him. Happiness ages him.

There's no youth in that bright face, I think. And when he has calmed down again and gone back to his rock, you can see him leaning once more on the cane of skepticism. Then he slips up to you from the side again and says hello first, squinting slyly in the old way, and tells you about how he was sentenced to a firing squad once. For several months he waited for the execution, imagining his body and the wall behind it riddled with bullets: soldiers sometimes miss their target.

He often thinks about his son. He was upset when he saw Bohdan wearing a wrinkled tie. He was disturbed when he unexpectedly came across Bohdan's dirty underwear. He spent many nights imagining that he was sewing missing buttons on his son's coat. And then for a moment he wishes that everything would change, that just once the day would begin in the evening and not at dawn. Then he'd be able to foresee his own dying, and knowing beforehand what to expect he would find life easier to bear.

Mykhaylo Soroka, I think. He knows several foreign languages; he has an excellent knowledge of modern literature and has his favorite writers. "They can be counted on the fingers of one hand," he says, raising his arm. "The world is not worthy of this hand." He shows his hand to everyone and says that the eternal spinning of the universe is not worthy of one steady hand grasping a spoonful of gruel. Even the Creator of the world is puzzled by what he created. If you ask

Mykhaylo Soroka about this, he'll shrug his shoulders and give
the same reply as Einstein: "Everything in the world is so
complicated that I discovered the theory of relativity but cannot say what it is."

You have a man standing before you. He says something,
and you agree with him although you can't understand a single word. He stands before you, and when he leaves you say,
"Yes, he's quite right." You turn and see him slowly walk
toward the barracks, erect but with a slight humpback. That
hump is his by fate. A childhood accident with a horse—and
he was left crippled for the rest of his life. Such men have
their own characters and, God forbid, their own ideas. And
they have a total, unrelenting hatred.

In such cases physical deformity is also spiritual. Nothing
matters to these men. Life is a figment that can be easily
dispelled. Life is nothing if the nation is in chains. Such men
hate slavery. They hate slaves and slave traders with equal
passion. Such men deliberately seek out minds that stand for
something. Minds that don't stand for anything concern them
as much as clouds in the sky. The only jokes they know are
the ones death plays. They laugh when rifle muzzles are
trained on them and frown when someone cracks a joke in
passing. The maelstrom of war caught them up in its under-
tow and robbed them of their youth. They shot and were shot
at in turn. A tooth for a tooth. It was a tragedy and yet it
wasn't. And there's no way to decide whose tragedy it was.
They defended their country and cannot imagine themselves
apart from it. Their life is hatred. A concrete, specific hatred.
They have their enemies and make no bones about it. No one
denies his enemies. The enemy is so close you can see the
whites of his eyes.

Vasyl Pidhorodetsky raises his arm and says, "This hand
has seen a few things in its time."[20] He says that he lost. The
opposing force was greater, and it crushed him. He does not
deny this. But he is superior to this force. Just listen to the
way he mocks and scorns it! His gibes express the temporary

defeat of a man, but not of his idea. Nothing transcends the idea, the goal of national independence. Bury a man like that in a hole and he'll survive longer than Kalnyshevsky. He finds no joy in freedom or raja-yoga. He has a loftier substance— faith in his rightness and in the rightness of the cause to which he has dedicated his life. Such men are rarities. They, too, can be counted on the fingers of one hand. You can raise your hand to Pidhorodetsky and say, "Every finger is worth thousands." Who are these thousands of men? Pidhorodetsky will smile in return. He knows who they are: a thousand dedicated men. But they are not equal to one of his fingers. Everyone knows this and respects him. The respect comes not from fear but from inability to comprehend. The incomprehensible essence of divine action. That's exactly what Pidhorodetsky says: "divine action." It is in its own way sur-sublime, surpassing the realistic commonplaces of daily life.

They captured Pidhorodetsky in 1953. He was in the Security Service of the UPA. They tortured him in every imaginable way. Three times they stood him before a firing squad. It was psychological torture: he will always remember the trees in the forest and the rifle muzzles. This accursed psychological execution when they fire at the trees is worse than death itself. But he never betrayed anyone. When they threw facts in his face he told them that he had always acted alone and that he alone would be responsible for his actions. Let others answer for themselves. This, too, was his personal conviction.

Then they stopped torturing Pidhorodetsky. They asked him what Shevchenko had dreamt of all his life. A cottage overlooking the Dnieper, he replied. He'd have a three-room apartment near the river, they told him, and the windows would look out over the water. They respected his faith and his idea, and they promised him his life if only he would change his ideal. They respect idealists. Sometimes they played chess with him. "The fucking Banderite is advancing," they'd say when he put them in check. But he was superior to all this and went into a twenty-five-year exile.

In 1955 Pidhorodetsky mounted a revolt in one of the northern camps. They reviewed his case and slapped on another twenty-five years. They would have shot him if the law had permitted. Now he can't start a revolt or try to escape because capital punishment has been reinstated. Pidhorodetsky is quite calm, although he has long since realized that he will never be a free man again. Only once did he cry. His fellow prisoners say that the only time he shed a tear was when he heard that his mother had died. He said that she had always begged him: "Don't let them take you alive, shoot yourself first." He didn't have a chance to shoot himself when he walked into the room in the Donbas region and a bag fell over his head. He didn't know what it was, but he couldn't even move, and he was very sorry that he wasn't able to carry out his mother's request.

Sometimes, when he regrets that he didn't marry and have a family, Pidhorodetsky becomes almost misty-eyed. "You'll have your little Halyna, your pretty dark-eyed girl," they say to him. "Just write a recantation." His sweetheart will always be an old maid. There are some things greater than the joys of family life.

"We can forgive you everything, even our blood which has made your hands red," a colonel says to Pidhorodetsky when they transport him from time to time for reeducation to Saransk, the capital of the Mordovian Republic. They never give up hope of reeducating a man.

"You can see quite clearly that your ideal isn't worth peanuts. Life has gone forward, and our Ukrainian people have long since forgotten you. They're building a new life, an international one, and they don't have time to think about you. Not a single Ukrainian will ever again raise a hand against his Russian brothers."

"Maybe," Pidhorodetsky replies quietly. "Maybe. Anything is possible. But just look at the hump on my back. I wasn't born with it, but now that I have it I'll never be rid of it."

"Yes, even our Russian proverb says that only the grave can cure a humpback. You know, I don't respect your ideal, I simply detest it, but I can't allow myself not to respect you as a man. I must respect your faith and your stubbornness. If all our communists were as stubborn as you, everything would be so much more interesting."

I am assigned to the carpentry shop to work as a joiner. I was told to steer clear of it, but a zek does not decide his own fate. My job involves standing the whole shift at the router, cutting grooves in chair legs. LET'S GIVE THE COUNTRY MORE HIGH-QUALITY HOLES FOR BACK LEGS! a poster shouts at me. The din is incredible. My ears ring as if I were standing next to a moving train. The quota is three hundred twenty back legs and five hundred sixty front legs. We never reach it.

"Give me those grooves or you'll get the cooler," the foreman shouts.

We aren't thrown in the cooler, either.

"You're lucky," says Daniel, the "great writer with the world-famous name," as the foreman ironically calls him. Daniel stands beside me, trimming rungs on the jointer. "You're always in luck; with you I can risk goofing off."

Daniel and I sneak off to the drying room and climb atop a pile of parts that reaches to the ceiling.

"I really like my jointer," Daniel explains to me. "One stroke this way, one stroke that way, and I've got a rhyme. Ten strokes and I've got ten rhymes, industrial-production rhymes. Just listen. . . ."

I envy Daniel. I just can't come up with any rhymes.

"Chuck your router! You'll get the cooler like me, but when you come out they'll put you on the production-rhyme jointer."

A supervisor appears from behind a cart. "Hey, Daniel, warming your anti-Soviet ass again? Quit screwing around and get down here fast!"

At lunch we go to the mess hall. The chow line is unbelievably long. There's a note on a pillar: IF SOMEBODY FINDS A SPOON PLEASE PASS IT ON TO THE THIRD ASSEMBLY SHOP—SLAVE ZADOROZHNY.

I read a little Drozd while waiting for the cabbage soup.[21]

Skimming over a few paragraphs is enough to whet my appetite.

Knuts walks up to me. "Studying the new mess-hall prose, are you?"

"It's high in calories," I reply.

"Then don't forget to throw those calories in the cabbage soup. Look out, you're falling behind."

Someone curses violently. But it's not about Drozd, it's about the cook. "The fucking sonofabitch has stolen the rotten cabbage out of the soup again!"

"Remember," says the Ingush Ali Khashagulgov, "a zek must never let a single crumb of bread fall to the ground." He is holding his slice of bread over his bowl as if it were a baby.

Some of the zeks are cutting up parsley into their soup. It adds a touch of glamor to the meatless broth. Other zeks add oil or shortening. We are in heaven.

"We're going to Hyde Park," Yuriy Shukhevych announces when chow is over.[22] Shukhevych is tall and round-shouldered and wears glasses. His father was a general of the Ukrainian Insurgent Army. Yuriy has been in the hard-labor camps since the age of fourteen because of his father.

"Our movement lost, but you must go on living," his father told Yuriy. "Who knows what the future will bring."

Hyde Park turns out to be a small meadow between the second and third assembly shops. Poplars, birches, and tall grass grow in the park, and there are plywood platforms where the zeks sunbathe their "disgraceful" bodies. The summer has turned out surprisingly mild, and we bask our stomachs in the sun. The guards spend the lunch break racing around the park and yelling, "Leave your pants on, tan only from the waist up!"

When the whistle blows, the guards shout, "Back to work, you cunt louses! Shukhevych, are you pushing for the cooler? Haven't you had your fill?"

Yuriy carelessly throws his tunic over his shoulder and slowly ambles on. He is in no hurry.

"If you were a decent fellow you could be vacationing in

the Crimea, picking up a suntan and screwing broads. This way you're stuck here, smelling the place up!"

The guards are right. If Yuriy had disowned his father, he would have been in the Crimea long ago.

"Get away from me, you scum!" Yuriy retorts. "Get away or I'll give you a residence permit for the Mausoleum!"

Nine grams—that's Vasyl Yakubyak. Nine grams of lead—that's the bullet he'll get instead of freedom when his twenty-five years are up. Vasyl is exceptionally kind to people. Our Social Security system could envy his generosity. Such people never own anything except their own two hands. They give everything else away. There's Vasyl now, waving at us from across the compound.

"Today is Saint Peter and Paul's," he says when we meet. "Rozhko is our Paul. That monkey-faced zek will do for Peter."

About ten of us gather. Someone opens a can of varnish, the only alcohol we can afford in the camp. We drink to happy days. The varnish is strong stuff. The herring we usually can't stand the sight of would be just the thing to munch on now.

"Mykhaylo Zelenchuk has stronger stuff," someone observes. "It's purer."

It is made like this: you mix half a liter of alcohol varnish with an equal amount of water. Then you put cotton wool in the jar and shake the whole thing repeatedly. The cotton wool purifies the mixture by filtering out the varnish. If you let it age for two weeks and then strain it through cotton wool for a final purification, you've got Zelenchuk's stuff.

The zeks are happy now. They prattle and sing quietly and don't even mind the work. The guards think it's fear of the cooler. The foremen are free laborers—they get some, too. Sometimes the zeks get very drunk and wander around, three sheets to the wind.

"What am I supposed to do, boss? We've finished off the front legs."

"How much longer till the end, three hours? Go squash some bedbugs!"

But then you have to keep an eye peeled for the guards,

or else it's the cooler for you. On the job it's hard for them to tell who's oiled: the machines make everybody shake. The problem is getting past the body search. You have to stand there while they frisk you and try not to breathe on them.

"Aha, sonofabitch! You've been at it again! Step aside, motherfucker, it's the cooler for you!"

Barracks, barbed-wire fences, and watchtowers with sour-faced guards and arrogant submachine guns—it's all enough to make you sick. You want fresh air and space. Near the third assembly shop, right beside the railroad tracks, is a mountain of logs. If you climb that pile you can survey everything that grips you with an iron hand. There's the Yavas River. Young people are splashing about in the water, and women are sunbathing on the grassy banks. When he sees the bodies in bathing suits, the zek forgets to breathe and chokes on his cigarette. He's getting so hot he'd go up in smoke himself it it weren't for the guards.

"Come on, you bastard, stop fucking those free girls with your eyes!"

But the squinting, chain-smoking zek can't hear the guard: he's out on the river. He'd go to the dogs if it weren't for the guard. The latter throws a cudgel at him, and the zek climbs down from the woodpile, cursing copiously.

"Sex fiend! Scoundrel!" the guard calls after him.

"Idiot!" snorts Ivan Stanislav. "I didn't climb up there to look. I just wanted to catch a smoke and get some fresh air."

No two zeks are alike. There he is, a graduate student from the Moscow Institute of Forestry, in his fourth year at the camp, pushing a wheelbarrow filled with spare parts. The other zeks blink their eyes and laugh at him. He thinks about Einstein's theory of relativity as he trundles his wheelbarrow. He doesn't know whether Einstein ever read the Bible. The Good Book proves that the theory of relativity was known many thousands of years ago: "And the moment will be eternal and eternity a moment."

So the Bible states. Each galaxy has its own secret motions. We are nothing. Our world, our troubles, our wars, our camps, and our split-second death . . . We formulate laws, but they only debase nature. Just try to apply them to the physics of high-speed processes. You'll find yourself laughing at the laws you blindly believed in. You'll only discover your own worthlessness. Only by chance, blind chance unaffected by any laws, will you be able to discover anything about physics. Common sense is of no use in understanding high-speed subatomic movements. That's what Harrie Massey wrote.[23] A new age in physics has been born. Our current social development is like a high-speed nuclear reaction. There's no point in formulating hypotheses for it or trying to establish its parameters. This will lead only to anachronistic discoveries. You must shatter your preconceived notions.

And then there is Messing and the secret of clairvoyance.[24] World and anti-world cancel each other at their point of contact. In the world a human life proceeds from conception to death. In the anti-world the order is reversed: from death to conception. We worry, suffer torments, and murder one another in order to reach our goals, disregarding everything for their sake. Yet our future has already occurred in the anti-world, and the ending to our goals has long been predetermined. If we were all clairvoyants like Messing and could see what lies in store for us, we'd drop our hands in bewilderment or return to the state of primitive man. But a zek cuts through all this nonsense. He realizes that if everyone were a clairvoyant, there would certainly never be prisoners, prisons, or our beloved Soviet labor camps.

A zek is not an abstract concept. He is very real, as real and tangible as his bunk and latrine. As substantial, too, as the workshops, the gruel he's fed, the library, and the political indoctrination sessions he's forced to attend. Or as palpable as the foremen, the supervisors, the brigade leaders, and the "educators" from the Republican KGB organs. This very, very real whirlpool swallows the poor zek as he rushes to and fro, holding on to his spoon, his lathe, his broom, or the safety valve of his curses. It all passes before his eyes like an unending funeral procession, and the poor zek reaches out for varnish or *chefir*. But these distractions are only momentary, and the funeral procession continues to loom incomprehensibly. Conversations with friends are also temporary and do not provide rescue. Out there are the watchtowers and the police dogs, who yearn for freedom as much as the prisoners. At such times the zek fully realizes the absurdity of his miserable existence. Nothing has really happened. He can survive, in fact, if only he can find a niche for himself.

You write poetry. So go on writing. But your lines are drab, and they make everything around you seem even drabber. The grayness makes you lose all sense of color, and even red looks gray to you. A black abyss. Beyond the barbed wire is the swampy ravine. Its foul odor hits you in the nostrils and follows you everywhere you go. You yourself seem to be rotting. Why? What was your crime? Senseless idealism and power pitted against each other. The power of the inept. They'll wipe you out, bury you in that swampy ravine beyond the barbed wire. Behind the ravine is the burial ground. Graves marked by numbers. Barbed wire and more barbed wire. Hey, you dead prisoner! You don't eat your gruel and you don't produce even a quarter of your work quota. Chairs, sofas, wardrobes . . . damnation! Evil! Why? What was your crime? Did you rob or murder anyone? You yourself were robbed, and now they're killing you. Aha! I can just see the innocent eyes, my foot, of our "rehabilitators":

"How dare you, bastard?"

"What?"

"You ought to be shot!"

"What?"

Beyond the assembly shops is a blind alley, a tiny strip of open ground near the barbed wire. Sometimes zeks climb to the top of the fence, and from there they dare to ridicule the world. The world is of a serious turn of mind and shoots one of them. It shoots him in the eyes, the face, and the chest. The zek falls headlong over the fence. Finally! They drag him back by the feet. His head bounces on the rocks.

"You communist beasts, the man's still alive!" someone screams.

A dog runs alongside, snapping at the body. Too bad, the poor animal missed its chance. They taught it to savage human flesh, and now they won't let it touch it. It's a dog's life.

"What are you doing, you fascists? The man's still alive!"

"Get away, you shithead, or I'll shoot!"

"Yes, of course, your excellency!"

Later the zek tries to hang himself. He is beyond all hope. They find him near the washbasins. He seems to be washing himself, but in fact there is a gray rope twined around his gray neck. They drag him out. By the feet again.

"Well, you bastard, why aren't you screaming that the man's still alive?"[25]

They say that feather-brained Shved with the itchy trigger finger is a Ukrainian.[26] He wanted to work his way up to a general's rank. His specialty was shooting prisoners at point-blank range. He'd lead a man out into the woods and say, "Here's to your fucking Ukraine, you goddamn Banderite!" That was how Shved amused himself through the drab camp days. He was color-blind as well. Couldn't distinguish any colors except the red of blood on the ground. Later his skillful sadism made the brass a bit edgy, and they busted him to the ranks. That was in Khrushchev's time, I think. After that Shved went around heaping curses on the Premier's bald head.

Zeks can find a thousand hiding places for a steel blade. They slice their veins as if cutting paper. So what! They saved one, and then he grew even grayer. He dreamt of freedom— not of eating his bread in the outside world, but of swallowing cyanide. Gold? Shit! Rat poison is what he wants.

He stealthily gets up during the night and makes his way

to the latrine. He knows what he's after. Suddenly he turns around and runs back. He can't do it. Someone's feet are sticking out, and there's blood all over the floor. The blade was dull. It is midwinter. The guard rubs his sleepy eyes: "What a bastard that zek is, pulling a joke like that. Won't let a man get some sleep. Keeps a sliver of glass hidden for months, and then you can't get a good night's rest."

In the winter the ravine closes in on you. Grayness. A search. An odor that makes you sick. Give back the papers. Then someone says, "Spit!"

"Where are you spitting, shithead? Do you want to make the cooler?"

"Hell!" The zek welcomes it.

The mess hall serves as our auditorium. Gruel, line-ups, and representatives from the outside—writers, artists, or scientists. Well-fed, well-starched, and self-satisfied. But they feel ill at ease: official business, you see . . . two sixty per. They rise from . . . They speak of . . . The zeks are not idiots. They open their eyes wide and clench the benches they are sitting on. They become rooted to the spot and sleep brazenly. One zek hangs a moon toward the stage. Chess. Checkmate. "Let's shoot some craps, we've heard that shit before." Somewhere on stage, they . . .

Quotas exceeded. Everything is flowering. Buildings now stand where once there were vacant lots. We are expanding. The five-year plan. Ever closer. Trees for the hangmen.

A young zek makes his way to the stage and extends to the speaker a bouquet tightly wrapped in newspaper. "Permit me, in the name of all my countrymen, to present to our Homeland these flowers, which grow here so far away from her."

The zek offers his bouquet to the speaker. The latter shakes the zek's hand in gratitude and grasps the bouquet. At that moment the zek tears the paper off: it's a bouquet of barbed wire!

The barbed bouquet is hurled to the floor. Someone kicks it

under the table. Someone else rushes to the door but stops dead in his tracks when the zek shouts, "Long live free Estonia!"

Then everyone knows that the zek is an Estonian. There are shouts and whistles of encouragement for him, and a riot almost breaks out. Someone is still shooting craps. Suddenly the guards. The representative: "As long as I get paid for this." Pandemonium. The zek is dragged off to the cooler. Another zek leaps to his feet. What a . . . ! The commandant reaches for his . . . The prisoner ought to get it in the . . . Could use a shot of varnish. What an occasion! Now the zeks can shake off their tedium for a day or two. Four days later they're still talking about it. In the old days you'd get a bullet in the brain for a joke like that.[27]

A zek runs to the library and strains his weakened eyes over books. Then he crawls back to his corner. He sees a shadow. "It's only me," the zek whispers. He has just learned that a Soviet police dog is fed a more nourishing diet than a prisoner. The allotment for a dog is forty rubles a month; for a zek—thirteen rubles and eighty kopecks.

Zek Arutiunian is from Armenia, far to the south of here. He is still a young man, going into his fifth year at the camp. He submits a petition: "In light of the fact that dogs are fed a more nutritious diet than prisoners, I urgently request that I be granted canine status. I take it upon myself to wear a muzzle and even to bark a great deal. I sincerely hope that you will not deny my last request as a human being."

The dogs are angry at Arutiunian. He gets his answer: "We regret to inform you that due to the anti-Soviet spirit in which your request was submitted we are unable to take it into consideration." Now Arutiunian is angry at the dogs.

"I would have kicked the bucket long ago," says zek Yevgrafov, who is serving ten for the Chinese, "but I still have hopes." What hopes, no one except zek Yevgrafov knows. He knows everything. Ask him anything you like about Monte Carlo. The only thing he doesn't know is how much a fifth of whiskey cost before the war.

Yevgrafov buys an accordion. But the music just won't come. He has heard too much misery in his life for his fingers to find a gay melody. "But I still have my hopes," he declares. What hopes, no one except zek Yevgrafov knows.

The zek turns to poetry. He is one of those poets who write a petition every day. "Please review my case. . . ." Around all the departments. He has submitted close to three thousand petitions. They laugh at him; he's not your ordinary zek, but Yevgrafov replies, "I have to fight back in some way. Do you know any other way?"

Zek Osadchy must fight back, too. He's no worse than zek Yevgrafov. In any case, his penmanship is better. Calligraphically, tactfully, he writes: "I should like to ask . . ." Zek Osadchy is ready to write six thousand petitions. But he receives a reply before he can write a second petition: "Please inform zek Osadchy that his petition has been reviewed by the Office of the Public Prosecutor of the Ukrainian SSR, which has come to the conclusion that his sentence should be upheld."

Then zek Osadchy slowly drags his feet. He sees zek Yevgrafov and the last Procurator of Judaea waving at him from a barracks roof.[28] They're standing side by side, gazing out at the Yavas River. The Procurator of Judaea rubs his hands impatiently. Out on the river he sees women bathing. They are huge, fat women, as big around as sewer pipes. "Oh, if only I could get a piece of that fat ass," the last Procurator of Judaea exclaims.

At this point, trying to save himself from total despair, the zek clutches at anything that comes to hand: flowers, sunflowers, Hyde Park, or the library. Some zeks spend all their free time reading at a table in the library. Whenever someone approaches them, they put their books aside and begin to spout wisdom. They may have not got past fifth grade, but even a university professor had better not tangle with them. These zeks are wise men, although their hair hasn't turned gray yet. But then, they can't grow gray hair because their heads are always shaved.

The zek may be the writer Sinyavsky. You can see him making notes. His shoulders are hunched, and he casts squint-eyed glances in all directions. No guard can sneak up on him unexpectedly. His apostolic beard grazes the book he is reading. Zeks Sinyavsky, Skujenieks, and Karavansky are all book-worms. Zek Karavansky specializes in writing petitions—against a journalist for writing an article about him, against the minister of higher and special secondary education of the Ukrainian SSR for Russifying Ukrainian schools, and against the judge who unlawfully deprived him of his freedom. The journalist was paid a fee for his efforts. Zek Karavansky will get three years in Vladimir Prison for his petitions.[29]

A commission arrives at the camp one day. "Who are they? From where? What are they after? A COMMISSION is here!"

The visitors look through the books in the library. "What, these men are reading Dostoevsky? And Tolstoy, Chekhov, Flaubert? Zeks who are here to suffer want aesthetic pleasure from good books?"

The commission takes these books away. And others, too. Instead the zeks may read Kozachenko, Korniychuk, Sobko, Dmyterko, or Zbanatsky.[30]

The zek can't stand it. He runs to the latrine and vomits. "You rats!" he screams. "Goddamn queers! I hope your hands fall off with leprosy! I might not be very well educated, you bastards, but even I can write better than that! Those writers are nothing but a bunch of drill sergeants!"

The zek isn't at all educated and doesn't read critics. His curses are wasted. Because of his attitude he'll never publish anything or enjoy the cognac, the cars, and the weekends in the country that royalties bring. Read our wise and benevolent critics, zek!

But the zek hasn't been completely isolated. He does maintain ties with the outside world: printed matter comes in the mail for him. Incredible! For the first time in the entire history of the labor camps zeks are receiving books and letters. They come to Panas Zalyvakha,[31] Oleksandr Martynenko, Yaroslav Hevrych, Mykhaylo Masyutko, Mykhaylo Horyn, and Yuliy Daniel. They come from Kiev, Lviv, Odessa, Lutsk, Kharkiv, and Moscow. Absolutely incredible: scores of packages and letters!

The camp administration is confused. "What's this? Who are the people sending this?"

"Friends."

"Friends? Who are these friends who think they can shit all over us like this?"

There is no camp regulation about withholding of packages. On the contrary, there is a regulation that packages must be delivered. But this would be a show of support for the prisoners! Give those books to the zeks and they'll "take heart." "Do they think we're running a vacation resort for them?"

So the powers that be begin to keep five packages for every one they give out, and they even go over this one with a fine-tooth comb. "Maybe it contains some seditious material. Or maybe they've found some clever way of concealing money."

But the parcels demonstratively continue to arrive at the camp. They come from Ivan and Nadia Svitlychny, Ivan Dzyuba, Vyacheslav Chornovil, Lyudmyla Sheremetyeva, Halyna Sevruk, and Halyna and Venyamin Kushnir.[32] This listing could go on and on, so many people are sending parcels. In the meantime, in Lviv, Kiev, and Moscow, parcels are being returned to the senders: "Undeliverable"; "Embargo to This Destination"; "Refused by Addressee." (Of course, it wasn't the addressee, but the post office at Yavas.)

· Letters to zeks are of two kinds: those with encouragement for them, and those that "say nothing." The latter are delivered in a few days. The former arrive in a month or two, or not at all. Letters to zeks should be short and mostly about the weather. A good letter, if it gets through, is an event, and everyone gets to read it if it is not too personal. The best letters are written by Valeriy Shevchuk, Vasyl Stus, and Daniel's wife, Larissa Bogoraz.[33] They contain news of public life, literary gossip, and similar things. Valeriy Shevchuk's letters are like polished short stories. They are read to pieces.

Zek Osadchy receives a letter too: "Court Summons No. II–B, 1784. The People's Court of the Lenin District of the City of Lviv summons you to appear in court at 10:30 A.M. on 4 August 1966 as defendant on the motion of eviction." The letter is signed by the court clerk and delivered in two days. Zek Osadchy's wife is being evicted from her apartment in Lviv. The zek suffers and walks about as if possessed.

"Hey, shithead," one of the pigs calls out, "why aren't you jumping up and down any more?"

But zeks are not doomed creatures. They may write letters, too—one every fortnight. The zeks' letters are censored, as is all Soviet literature. If a zek writes that the going is difficult for him and the food is bad, the censor admonishes him, "This won't do," and refuses to pass the letter.

A zek is supposed to write: "Dear Mother (Sister, Wife): I have received your letter. I am living well. The administration is pleased with my work. I am involved in socially useful labor at the camp. I am making every effort to get the authorities to look into the possibility of letting me out on probation. Yours with love . . ."

The zeks are furious with such sample letters. "That's no letter! That's pure bullshit!"

"Fuck off, you sonofabitch, you didn't come here to write novels!"

Dozens of the prisoners in the camp want to be writers and to lead a literary life.

"We could put together an anthology of poems by our writers, poets of various nationalities," says Daniel. "We must show the world that those who are imprisoned here are not 'bandits' or 'anti-Soviets.' There are talented, gifted people here, and the world must know about them. Our anthology will be in all the languages of the camp poets: Zaura Kabali will be writing in Georgian, Ali Khashagulgov in Ingush, Knuts Skujenieks in Latvian, and Valdur in Estonian. We'll get Panas Zalyvakha and our other artists to design it. We've got to tell the world we're not bandits."

"Today we're going to start celebrating the dates of important writers and artists," announces Knuts Skujenieks. "We can't just live the life of zeks: gruel, barracks, and chair legs."

Our programs are held on Sundays over a cup of tea. August 1966: we commemorate Ivan Franko and Shota Rustaveli.[34] Early September: we celebrate the Estonian artist Kristjan Raud.[35] The writer's compatriots prepare the program. We translate literature into various languages. Then we read our translations. There are many willing listeners and also many who want to read.

I particularly recall the evening of Jānis Rainis.[36] We read him in Ukrainian, Ingush, Georgian, Estonian, and Russian. Coffee is served.

"What's this, a meeting?" asks one of the pigs. He sees our books and flips through the pages. "Rainis. Who is this foreigner? Some sort of nationalist traitor?"

"No, the national poet of Latvia."

"Then why are you honoring him?"

More pigs arrive and look through the books as well. "There's nothing seditious here," one of us explains. "These are all Soviet publications."

"I've got my own eyes, so I don't need you to tell me. Everybody break it up!"

"We won't leave!" we insist.

The guards drag off the man sitting at the end of the table.

"Let him go! We won't let you take him!" we all shout. "We're quietly having a cup of coffee and talking about a writer who has the full approval of UNESCO." There are two guards and about twenty zeks.

"Too bad we don't have more men here," one of the pigs

says, "or you'd get what's coming to you. Daniel, I know your type. You'll be personally held responsible for disturbing the camp regime."

"All right, you can hold me responsible. I'll answer when the time comes," Daniel replies.

You can survive here better than anywhere else. If ever there was a fully democratic country, it must have been a labor camp. Think anything you please here, say whatever you like. You can even preach the wisdom of a bird brain. No one cares. A man who has been punished cannot be punished more.

Take Knuts Skujenieks, for example. Latvia does not have her own camps; she must rent them from the Mordovians. The Russians are the rental agents. Knuts strokes his red beard. He raises his arm calmly and asks, "What's your hurry?" His foot wrappings are always protruding from his shoes. He carries dry crusts of bread in his pocket. "They taste good," he says. He toasts his bread on the radiators in the workshop and laughs when no one can bite through it. "You've gone bad in the teeth," he says. "I'll have problems holding a discussion with you."

Knuts has led a remarkable life. After graduating from the Gorky Literary Institute in Moscow he worked for a Riga youth newspaper. He wrote poetry. Then he was sentenced to seven years for anti-Soviet propaganda and Latvian nationalism. "That's very funny," Knuts laughs at the word "propaganda." It's not propaganda the authorities are afraid of; it's the artist. An artist rejects evil and strives for good which exceeds the demagogic promises. But he is not understood. Instead of being appreciated, he gets a label pinned on him and is sent off to a "resort." Then it's Hyde Park and gruel for him. It will be a miracle if he survives this "vacation."

Knuts strokes his red beard. This is not skepticism. Man is a fighter by nature. The writer is his voice. Who wants to write about a streetcar that goes back and forth on its route without derailing even on the iciest days? There must be another world, created independently, which bears a message and tells you something, a personally conceived model of the world. But the artist's model, his paradigm of the new world, is not understood. He's put away as quickly as possible, and his lid is welded back on posthaste because he wants to replace "the best of all possible models" with a new one, which he believes to be even better.

What is an artist? When he was given the Nobel Prize, Camus said that the artist is an oarsman. The steering may be badly handled, but the oarsman bends to his oar. His strength has not failed yet, and he knows where he must bring the galley—to his own coast. That coast is his new model of the world. The storm on the high seas is the old one.[37]

The artist does not faithfully reproduce nature, depicting beautiful sunsets and people silhouetted against them. That's the artisan's job. The real artist leads man through nature, through the sunsets to what lies beyond. In his own world the artist is a dictator, absolutely certain of his vision. The artist can understand life only if he tries to escape it. He has to avoid the daily nuisances of existence, or else they will destroy him. Like Democritus, he must gouge out his eyes in order to gain an insight into the very essence of being. If he wishes to glimpse the horizon of what may prove to be his new world, the artist must surmount the squalls and storms of life.

Our society is afraid of such artists and considers them dangerous. Yet they are essential to society. A decade or two later such men are brought into the public arena to be admired as heroes. Kafka, Joyce, Dostoevsky, Bulgakov, Golding—none of them were understood in their lifetimes because they cut themselves off from the world like that oddball Demosthenes who crawled into a barrel to contemplate his supreme realities. These men did not merely reject the existing models of the world; they also created new models which society now grasps at feverishly the way a drowning man catches at straws. Here we are talking not about a social model, but a spiritual model, one that begins to inspire people several centuries before it is implemented.

Knuts strokes his red beard and says that the Ukrainian poet Kalynets also has a new model. His world is remarkably serene and profound Go in and you will come out disturbed. You may not understand the model Kalynets proposes, but you will be disturbed nonetheless. It will make you look for something. If you succeed in finding it, you'll be in luck. If not, you'll reject the poet's new world from your pithecanthropoid perspective and call him an anachronism. You may even banish him from society, but years later your grandchildren will embrace this new world, and you'll be forced to stand by and helplessly look on. Art must be created by artists, and they must be the masters of their creations. Art dies when it is appropriated by a different master, a dogmatic one. Art cannot stand meddling by know-nothings. It belongs to artists, not artisans.

"Wipe your feet when you enter literature," Ostap Vyshnya said. And Knuts says: "Art can be created only by a free mind. Once it is enslaved, the most the mind can do is to reproduce a brilliant model of its enslavement with all its limitations and barred windows. But it will never be capable of creating a progressive model of the world, one that future generations will come to comprehend."

"A poet must walk the path of freedom; he must follow the dictates of a free mind," Pushkin said in the nineteenth century. The Upanishad of Brahmabinda stated thousands of years ago that the mind is the cause of both bondage and freedom. Enthralled by the objects of perception, man can free himself only by systematically purging his mind of perceived reality.

Rafalovich points to the sky and says that it can be as interesting to read as any science fiction. Mars is yellow, but not because it has jaundice. Venus is greenish, but not because of jealousy. She is good-natured, like a lazy cat. And there's the constellation of Pisces in the sea of heavens, but it's no place for fishermen.

Knuts strokes his red beard in the darkness. "Well, boys, it may be the moon or Venus for you, but for me it's time to get back to gluing plywood."

Our society is lazy and refuses to think. It did not understand Herzen.[38] The new world announced by the tolling of his bell was taken as an insult and a senseless challenge. A duel? Ha! Today the tsars themselves would concede that the tocsin should have been heeded because the great Herzen said so a hundred years ago. If Knuts starts a new bell tolling, he'll be cutting plywood for another seven years. Someday they'll say that Knuts not only cut plywood for society, but also constructed a new and much more interesting model. This will be a new *De rerum natura.*

But while Knuts is fashioning this new model, he must live far from Latvia, gluing plywood and abusing the cooks for serving rotten cabbage again. Knuts must survive for the sake of his model. In order to do so, he has created a Eurydice for himself. He leaps out of bed at night and rushes into the compound. He thinks she is standing out there, incomparably beautiful. This is not the Eurydice that mythical Orpheus, lyre in hand, went to fetch from the underworld. This is a new Eurydice, one who is looking for her Orpheus. He is lost somewhere on earth, busy gluing plywood and eating rotten cabbage. Betrayed, Knuts comes back to the barracks. He is confused. He may not survive after all. Then clever Knut tries to outwit himself. He writes an unusual poem about the Eurydice who searches for her Orpheus:

> I do not see you, I do not hear you, Eurydice!
> But I sense you out there, Eurydice!
> Always and always out there, Eurydice!
> Forever and ever, Eurydice!
> My speech, my eyes, my lyre, Eurydice!
> Your glance was the beginning,

> Your glance will be the end,
> Eu-ry-y-di-ce-e!

A dim light glows in the night. Long legs hang down from an upper bunk. That's Knuts. A guard's black shadow looms in the doorway. His evil eyes burn bright. The guard is waiting. He is tired of waiting and turns away. Knuts stretches forth. He will fool everyone. No Eurydice will ever find him. Knuts simply wants to survive.

For the Ingush, the word for wolf is feminine in gender.[39] The wolf is the symbol and flag of their homeland. When the Ingush were deported to Northern Kazakhstan during the war, the wolves disappeared from their mountainous homeland. The wolves could not live without the Ingush; they did not want to become a flag symbol for foreigners. The wolves disappeared from the mountains. They did not go north with their Ingush into the bitter cold and the blizzards. The mountain people were left lying on the roads, cold and lifeless corpses. The Ingush were not used to such cold. It decimated them. The wolves abandoned their warm homeland. A new master ruled there while the Ingush died like flies in exile.

Ali Khashagulgov did not witness any of this. His father would say, "Ali, Ali." He would stare ahead with a stony gaze and intone, "Ali, Ali, our wolves are gone." He said no more.

And who was the old crone whose mouth always hung open? She would bring a thick darkness into the room with her. For twenty years she could not close her mouth. It gaped like a huge, mute hole.

"Ali," his father would say, "Ali, our wolves are gone. Our wolves are gone, Ali."

"If they had sent away as many of our intelligentsia as they did in Ukraine in 1965, no one would have been left," Ali says. Most of his people's intelligentsia was "done away with" not in the thirties, but a little later, Ali explains.

In 1960 the Ingush were permitted to return to their mountain homeland. But the highlanders burrowed deeper into their frozen hovels and refused to go. They were afraid of being deceived again. Then those who wanted to see the wolves come back went around exhorting their compatriots, "Go home, the wolves are waiting for you."

"Our wolves are gone, Ali," his father would repeat, "all gone, Ali."

The agitators were imprisoned and disappeared for good. But the mountain people had already changed their minds, and they did return to their homeland. Then, they say, the wolves reappeared in the mountains. They came back to the Ingush.

"Our wolves are gone, Ali," the old man would say. "All gone." Even when Ali was studying at the Teachers' College in Grozny, he could hear his father's words, "Our wolves are gone, Ali, all gone."

Later Ali was arrested with another teacher twice his age. They were accused of anti-Soviet, nationalist (pro-Ingush) activity. Ali was told that he had exhibited anti-Soviet tendencies at the age of thirteen when he had written a "nationalist" poem. Ali and the other teacher were accused of having formed a clandestine organization of two. The older man was supposedly the leader and had influenced Ali.

"He didn't influence me," Ali told his interrogators. "I influenced him." Both men were given four years.

Our wolves are gone, Ali, all gone.

"We can't get into the university," Ali says. "They're afraid to teach us. They're afraid that we shall begin to understand. A nation lives in ignorance and fear if it has no intelligentsia. Our language is short on many words: freedom, work, even intelligentsia. There are 250,000 of us. A 250,000 herd of men. I think Kafka talks about a herd that has no leader. When our nation disappears from the face of the earth, high up in the mountains the skeleton of a giant wolf will freeze in its place forever. It will be the last wolf on earth. That will be the revenge of the mountain people."

Our wolves are gone, Ali, all gone.

"If I knew that my language would die tomorrow, I would kill myself today. I bear no malice toward any people or its tongue, but we have been much abused.[40] I can point my finger at those who committed these deeds. They walk among us. We see their smiling faces. They suffer no remorse for having destroyed thousands."

Our wolves are gone, Ali, all gone.

"I was nineteen when I was arrested. I was proud and had nothing except my pride. I didn't know how to conduct myself. Only later did a prosecutor come up to me and say, 'You act like a spy, snotnose.'"

" 'Do you mean I stand firm?' "

"That anonymous old poet spent his entire life in prisons, exiled from his native highlands. He came home as weak as his nation, and he never did write anything of significance for his people. When he was dying, the old poet said, 'I wanted so much to tell you something, my people; I had so much to tell you.' He died with these words on his lips, 'Our wolves are gone, Ali, all gone.' "

Ali's skin, as dark as the soil of the hills he comes from, is dripping with sweat. He has the finisher's job, and he is feeding parts through the planer.

"Do you see these veins? Do you think mountain blood can flow in them? Let it flow in the mountains. It has no place in an ocean, an ocean of foreigners."

"Zek, come here!"

Ali steps up. He has a dignified face and wise eyes. This zek is from the mountains.

"Why don't you salute your superior?" Two narrow red eyes bore into Ali. The whites have blue veins in them, probably from drink. The face is grotesquely distorted into a mask of obesity and malice.

Our wolves are gone, Ali, all gone.

Running. Stumbling. "Your *brod* . . . your *brod* . . ." Gasping . . . wheezing . . . "Co—Com . . ." Gasping, "Comrade . . ."

Wheezing, "Comrade Commandant of Dubrovlag, Colonel Gromov . . ." He stumbled, he fell, he can't move. His eyes plead, his eyes are full of fear, he gasps. "Into the BUR with you!" "What for, Comrade Co—Comman . . . ?"[41]

"You prisoner, what's your name?" *Our wolves are gone, Ali, all gone.* "Do you see these veins? Do you think mountain blood can flow in them? Let it flow in the mountains. It has no place in an ocean, an ocean of foreigners." "My name? Ali Khashagulgov." "Not Ali, but zek Khashagulgov. Five days in the cooler for you!" "What for, Commander?" "Next time you greet your superiors." "But in the mountains where I come from to salute a person is to wish him good health, and I do not want to see you in good health."

The basest, most criminal people in the world are the Ukrainians. Walk up to any one of them, peer into his eyes, and you will see the glint of treachery. There's something so piercing in that look that you know you must put up your guard. If you don't, he will play you for such a fool that the devil himself won't be able to make head or tail of it. Do you know why? It's because Ukrainians are nationalists to the very core. You just can't help noticing this when you're around them. And they're very tenacious of life, too. Step on their tail and they'll run off without it and later grow another tail.

These Ukrainians feel perfectly at home in the camps. They even hang their smelly foot wrappings on the birch trees to air out. It is not fitting to hang foot wrappings on the trees; there's no beauty in it. But just try to tell them that! They'll sidle up and stare at you with their criminal eyes. Oh, these Ukrainians! There are more of them here than of any other nationality. That's why they have such terribly insolent manners.

But that's only the half of it. They are also inveterate nationalists. They make no bones about it: they speak their own language whenever and wherever they can. A zek may be a Russian or a Lithuanian, and here he's gibbering in Ukrainian.

It's not just the zeks. Even the pigs use Ukrainian phrases: *harazd*—"all right," *pohano*—"bad," *lykho*—"bad luck," and *dobre*—"good." At this rate the entire camp may be speaking Ukrainian in a few years. Knuts knows Ukrainian, so does Daniel. Then there's that Finn, and he never even set foot in Ukraine.[42] Call it what you will, but I say that's not merely nationalism. That's outright chauvinism.

The fact is, these Ukrainians have never been just nationalists. They are chauvinists and don't even bother to conceal it. But they are imprisoned for nationalism because the powers that be haven't got around to chauvinism yet. There is no article in the Criminal Code to deal with it. But don't worry, once we get such a law the word "nationalism" will no doubt go out of use. The Ukrainians are hiding behind this word, you know. It's very convenient for them.

What do the Ukrainians actually want? They want Ukraine to be independent. All right, give them their independence and stand back. In a few years they will assimilate every other language and anybody who objects will be dispatched to the camps of Mordovia. It's just as well that society understands this and does not let it happen. And anybody who goes against the will of the people is thrown into the calaboose. Let them proclaim their independence there. These Ukrainians have really got out of hand. How can they bring down shame on their people like that? Why bother inspecting them closely the way they do here—you can smell those curs a mile away.

And they're all such smart alecks, too. The brass tells the guy to go to a political lecture so that he can be reformed and made into a human being. After all, the authorities only want what's best for him. Instead he runs from the barracks to the stadium to play a little soccer. What a bunch of bigots! The machines stand ready, and there's a mountain of back legs waiting to be jointed, and he's flopped out on his belly in Hyde Park, trying to draw some strength from the sunshine. You throw the dog in the cooler for fifteen days, and he comes out with color in his cheeks. "Where in hell's name did you get color in the cooler, man, sleeping on your concrete bed?"

And these Ukrainians just can't get used to discipline. The camp has a collective council with committees for internal order, culture, sanitation and hygiene, and sports. He'll run his legs off during a soccer game, but just try and get him to hustle for the council. Catching the wind in a net would be easier.

The CO calls him in, talks to him man to man, equal to equal. Asks the prisoner to rehabilitate himself and to condemn his past actions. What's in it for him? He could write four letters a month and have an extra two rubles to spend at the commissary. Once half his term is up, he'd be permitted to receive a parcel every four months. The brass would respect him, and he might even get time off for good behavior. But he says no, he can't do it. He digs his feet in and stands there like a mule. But you can bet that when he should be quiet, he's out yelling his head off enough to make you go deaf.

And then there are the old fossils who have never held on to a piece of ass. Any self-respecting man could get out, find a wife, move to the Donbas to work as a miner or to Kazakhstan to run a threshing machine. But no, none of them will repent. And if one does happen to express contrition, do you think he can be released when it's plain as daylight that he's shamming? Let him sit it out if he's so smart! And the guy's got nine lives! There he is, serving his twenty-five. Anyone else would have kicked the bucket long ago, but he's still holding out. Holding out, hell! He's even got expectations.

He was such a sweet old man, so quiet and timid, always skirted the walls and stepped out of the way and respectfully said hello whenever he saw someone approaching. He was such a good old man that he signed up for all the committees. I remember him well, so gentle and peaceful. He told me one day that he used to be stubborn like the others, but then he rehabilitated himself and repented. He could have received parcels from home, but there was no one left in his family. He had permission to write four letters a month, but he had no one to write to. He could have bought all of seven rubles' worth of food at the commissary, but he was too old to work and had no money. The camp brass respected him greatly. They even reviewed his case. He told me that he would be released soon. I was happy for him. "Yes," I said, "you'll soon be a free man."

But then one day he up and died. I was so sorry for him. He was such a sweet and meek old man who understood life so well. But he died as soon as he repented. I was taken aback by this. As long as he held out, he stayed alive. But when he gave in, he died. Something was fishy here. He couldn't have died a natural death. I knew that something was wrong because when the old man was being buried no one came to pay his last respects. I walked alone at a distance from the coffin so that I wouldn't be noticed. Because if I was, who knows what might happen to me the next day?

Laughter in paradise! There's Daniel sitting beside a zek who is talking to him about something. Daniel is nodding his head and listening. His lips twitch and his eyes are veiled. His joy might give him away and make the zek feel sad. Laughter in paradise. Daniel sees a small room, a study. He sees a window and looks for new faces in it. Daniel is listening to the zek and thinking about laughter in paradise. Why look for characters on the streetcar when they're sitting right beside you and talking to you? You can write a whole novel on the basis of just one phrase of theirs. The zek is chary of words, but his body is eloquent. He is very sincere and doesn't realize that he is being used. Yuliy is robbing him of everything that a novelist who loves to write about people will steal from a man. He notes, for example, which words make the zek move his lips the most and why the zek says he doesn't care about freedom when in fact he dreams about it in his sleep. Why are the zeks so stubborn and yet let themselves be robbed so easily?

The zek reaches for his cup and asks Daniel to recite poetry.

Why does the zek want to hear poetry when he can barely read? The zek leans against the doorpost and appears to doze. But if Daniel stops, the zek opens his eyes in dismay and turns his head. Why does a zek need poetry when he is dozing off? Zeks let themselves be robbed. Images, characters. This is not a camp of criminals, but a cage filled with assorted characters and types. Describe it in a few terse words and you'll create an entire world, one that will both entice and repel you. Dostoevsky's world, profound and true.

But zek Daniel has no time to ponder any of this. He strips to the waist and feeds rungs into the jointer. Daniel has to produce his quota and earn his gruel. There's an uproar if he doesn't, and the threat of the cooler hangs in the air. Daniel is singled out.

A narrow aisle leads between the workbenches in the shop. When the men meet, one has to step aside. Chief Kravchenko is slowly walking down this aisle. His head is held high, and his face is blank and self-assured. The very machines and stacks of parts would move aside for him if he turned left or right.

But look! Daniel is walking toward him along the aisle. Three steps. Two. "Daniel, don't step in the shit!" someone calls out. Kravchenko halts. He raises his colorless eyes in astonishment and steps aside. "You want the cooler, you bastard?" But Daniel has already walked past him. Laughter in paradise. One foot after the other. Very slowly. You can shoot a zek, but you can't make him walk any faster. The zek is going to work.

You can read the posters, Daniel says: DOG-HANDLERS, BE AN EXAMPLE OF MILITARY AND POLITICAL PREPAREDNESS! Or the sign at the entrance to the work zone: THE EDUCATION OF A NEW MAN IS THE MOST IMPORTANT TASK IN THE TRANSITION FROM SOCIALISM TO COMMUNISM.

"Daniel, why haven't you met your work quota?"

Yuliy is silent.

"Daniel, why haven't you met your quota?" Kravchenko turns red in the face and raises his arm. "Daniel!"

"I told you a week ago that I won't speak to you unless you address me decently, using the formal 'you.'"

One foot after the other. You can shoot a zek, but you can't make him walk any faster. The zek is going to work. The free laborers who pass by on the other side of the barbed wire have sad, expressionless faces. The face of a free man, that's an abstraction that can't easily be deciphered. But the zek's face is an exposed nerve. Touch him but lightly and he will turn around. He will turn around very slowly, as he is expected to, but half an hour later he will start to scream. Laughter in paradise. It can kill you.

"Daniel, why do you get so involved with those filthy crooks? You're a decent chap, a writer. Why get mixed up with criminals?"

"I seem to like them." Daniel's tunic is carelessly slung over his left shoulder. He is in good spirits because he has washed up and is heading for the mess hall. The guards call him over.

"Do you recognize this?" one of them asks, showing him his portrait sketched by Roman Duzhynsky.[43] "Watch!" The pig shreds the picture into tiny strips.

Daniel's lips twitch. He hides his hands in his pockets so that they won't give him away and starts to walk off.

"Looking for trouble, Daniel?" the pig calls after him. Oh, yes.

An hour later Daniel explains: "Every nerve in my body was quivering. I felt they were grinding me into minced meat. I almost started to scream. It was all I could do not to lunge at the pig. I'm really surprised that I was able to control myself. I wasn't myself at all."

Daniel cannot work the rest of the shift. He sits in the drying room, saying over and over, "I felt they were quartering me but deliberately forgetting to cut off my head."

Daniel, did you ever receive any royalties for your writings other than the camp uniform you're wearing?

"Jewish and Russian blood flows in my veins, and I am standing on foreign soil. Oh, yes. . . ."

Laughter in paradise. Yesterday's truth won't even get you a bowl of gruel. You can die of hunger.

"Daniel, why are you reading a newspaper when you should be working?"

"We've run out of parts."

"Is that any reason to read the paper? Get going into the shop and have the foreman assign you to another job!"

One foot after the other. You can shoot a zek, but you can't make him walk any faster. The zek is going to work.

Slogans blaze from the walls: SOCIALIST DEMOCRACY IS THE HIGHEST FORM OF DEMOCRACY and TO FREEDOM WITH A CLEAR CONSCIENCE.

"Knuts, the happiness of the Latvian people depends on their friendship with the great Russian nation. Please forgive me that half of my blood . . ."

"Who is Yaroslav Stupak?"[44]

"I don't know. I only remember that he studied journalism in my department, wore glasses, and looked to be about seventeen."

"You'd never guess that from 'Pride.' I'd like to translate it into Russian, but the zeks have carried the magazine off, and I can't find it anywhere," says Daniel.

"Don't give those zeks any food," says Knuts. "I want to translate that brave lad too. The Latvians should be able to enjoy his writing also."

"I'm not interested in what it's about," continues Daniel. "What I'm interested in is—how? You feel that he's destroyed everything. Things that were petrified have suddenly exploded, and you see the universal wasteland."

"He's shattered the old model of the world," Knuts explains. "I thought I knew Ukrainian, but this boy has caught me completely off guard. His language is so powerful you can make pork chops out of the pigs with it. We've got to find that damn magazine."

The zeks forget all about food when they come to life.

We gather one evening at the second assembly shop. Daniel arrives last. The northern twilight sky glows red in the window. There is madness in this beauty.

"How about a drink, Yuliy?"

Daniel turns his head. "Oh, yes."

Varnish is the true zek's soul. *Chefir* is his art. The zek looks for himself in them and then can't get free of them. "Yuliy, there's enough for another round."

"Disgusting zeks!" But the guards sleep at night. Even trees get tired sometimes.

The zeks drink up and begin to talk. That's when Daniel is silent. He pretends to be watching the red glow of the sky through the window.

"You're lucky, Yuliy, you can fight the pigs with your verse. I'm a dumb sonofabitch. The only way I can get back at them is by shooting my foul mouth off. No way will you see me making verse. You're a real devil, Yuliy, the guards are afraid of you."

Guards break in on us. "Prisoner Daniel, what are you smearing yourself with?"

"It's insect repellent—Taiga."

"Let me have a look!"

The midges bite unmercifully. That's part of a zek's lot.

"Prisoner, hand it over!"

Give it to the guard and you'll never see it again. Daniel gets up on a table. More guards come running with an officer behind them.

"Give it here, I'll see if it's Taiga. I'll give it back."

Daniel gets down. The guards knock him off his feet, and one of them ferociously kicks him in the head. Another hits him with something heavy.

"Here, you bastard, here's your formal 'you'! Here's for Mykhaylo Soroka's coronary! Here's for interceding for him! Here's for his cure! Here's for playing the hero!"[45]

Daniel does not cry out or fight back. He only shields his face from the blows. When the guards let him go, he walks away smiling like an idiot.

"They're afraid I'll complain and they'll get hell. They think I'll complain." Daniel is cradling his injured hand on his breast. "Those cowards are afraid. They couldn't control the animal that's inside them. It would be ridiculous to go and complain. I have suffered, but I will bear my pain alone. I don't want to lessen it with a pitiful gesture of revenge. The pain will go away the way your love for a woman goes away when you find her in bed with another man. I need this pain as much as I need those odd zeks who ask me to recite poetry and who doze off when I begin to read. Laughter in paradise. I'll be free someday, and I don't want to come out empty-handed. I'd rather be carrying two bucketfuls of experience when I meet people. You know the old Ukrainian superstition that says there's bad luck in empty buckets."

Later we talk about Ivan Drach.

"Drach writes good poetry," Daniel says, "but I don't sense a human being behind it. His poetry doesn't reveal him as a man. When he was throwing flowers at your trial he was the greatest poet in the world. But when he wrote that article, the man disappeared for me and only his poetry remained. And his poetry doesn't convince me that he's a human being. I don't know, maybe if he's going to the UN General Assembly as an adviser for the Ukrainian delegation, he'll turn out all right. If he doesn't raise the question of releasing his peers and colleagues, releasing Daniel, the translator of his poetry into Russian, then I'll kill my memory of all the Drach poems that I've managed to learn by heart. But I have faith in Drach. He will at least speak up about this as a legal mistake."[46]

Sometimes one of the bed frames begins to collapse, and the zek slips from the upper bunk to the floor, where he continues to sleep, his head nestled in a dirty arm. Later he opens his eyes and drowsily looks around. He says something, but you will not hear anything even if you listen hard. It's a mirage on the wall. The zek has not really fallen out of bed. He is still sleeping in the twisted upper bunk. But something is bothering him. There's the backdrop of the red sky. The zek crawls to the very edge of his bed and stares at the ceiling. The lamp glows dimly. These are the colors of loss and separation.

"Where am I?" the zek asks, rubbing his eyes with his fist. He stands up on feeble legs and feels them tremble. His knees seem to be bending back, and he goes numb. How can knees bend back? Why isn't anything holding them in place? Then he realizes that his legs are lifeless. They can be twisted into thin ropes and tied into knots. The zek won't be able to go out to work in the morning, and he'll die. "But I don't want to die," he whispers. "I'll get well. It's just these damn treacherous knees."

Seven zeks are stoking a fire with newspapers in the center of the room and pouring water into a bowl. The zek suddenly crawls up to the lamp and bites into the bulb. Darkness. "I'll die in this darkness," the zek whispers. The bunk seems to be twisting out of shape again. The zek begins to cry. Through the barred window he sees the red sky descending on the barracks. Three of the zeks are cutting chunks of flesh from their calves and throwing them into the bowl. The newspapers flame high, and the doomed zek writhes with the pain of an ulcer.

"You're going to die tomorrow anyway, and they'll bury your body. Give us some meat, eh? It's all the same to you whether they bury you with flesh on your legs or not, isn't it?"

"But will you give me some?"

"What for, so you can go on living?"

The clubfooted zek falls to the floor and crawls toward the fire. "I want a piece of meat, too!"

The other zeks kick him in the teeth and pummel him on the head because he doesn't feel pain anywhere else. The zek turns his head up and howls bitterly.

"I know why we're beating him up," one of the seven shouts. "He swallowed my spoon!"

The zeks drag their victim to the door. He is an epileptic and goes into convulsions. His head bounces loudly on the floor.

"What are you doing to him?" someone shouts.

A zek holds a spoon up. "See," he says with a smile, "he didn't have time to digest it." Then he go s up to the window and starts to howl.

The fire goes out because it has not been   A feeling of loss comes over the zeks, the kind of feeling you g t when you anticipate the tightening of the hangman's noose around your neck.

A zek spots a guard through the window. The pig is running and pulling a sled loaded with newspapers.

"We have to kill the pig," says the zek, biting his lips until they bleed. "He's got newspapers."

"You can't kill a pig. They'll hang you for it."

"Well, then how are we going to cook our meat?" The zek falls silent. Two eyes speed out from the corner. They are the eyes of a small, tortured animal that has been brought to bay but continues to resist. They are the eyes of a small animal— zek Daniel, smaller than the rusty latrine bucket.

Our tea freezes solid in half an hour. The little stove seems to be giving off more cold than heat. Oleksandr Martynenko jumps up from his bunk and walks to the door.[47] He pounds on the door and curses as only a zek at the brink of despair can curse.

"You rats! Do you want us to freeze to death in here?"

I get down from my bare bunk, and we hammer on the door together as only zeks know how to hammer when they want to warm themselves a bit.

A sleepy-eyed guard walks up. "What is it? Why are you making such a racket?"

"Martynenko has an ulcer," I call to him. "He needs a doctor. He's in pain!"

131

"Cool it, don't worry," the guard mumbles and walks away.

Our situation becomes even grimmer when Oleksandr starts to writhe on the bunk in agony. An ulcer in freezing weather is unbearable. At times he staggers up and stares around with sightless eyes. Fear grips me—night, suffering, freezing cold, the ulcer. How lucky we are that our heads have been shaved. Otherwise our hair would freeze to the bunks. We manage to get up and pound on the door again. We want to stay alive till daybreak.

"Give us a mattress, you slimy beasts!"

"Cool it, cool it," the guard grumbles. We can hear his slow shuffling resounding in the empty corridor.

Toward morning a Security officer from the Kiev KGB arrives. "Do you know why we transferred you from the camp regime to the prison?"

Martynenko looks up with reddened, sleepless eyes.

"We've been informed that you haven't repented in the least. You got your three years, and you seem to like it here so much that you want to stay for the rest of your life."

Martynenko leans back in his chair. The KGB officer rivets narrowed eyes on him.

"Deny what you will, but we know for a fact that you still subscribe to your nationalist views and share them with your friends."

'What are you talking about?" Martynenko retorts. "I realize that you're as omnipotent as mannequins in a shop window, but I don't give a damn about that. All I want to know is why we are being left to freeze to death in the cell. Why am I not allowed to receive medicine? You know I have a stomach ulcer. Do you know what it means to have an ulcer in freezing weather?"

"Take it easy! Take it easy! Everything will be cleared up."

While things are being cleared up, we are issued two mattresses. We lie on one and cover ourselves with the other. Martynenko says that we can survive this way, that "nationalists" are not all that hopelessly doomed. He can hardly be seen underneath the mattress. Only his nose protrudes as he recites Pushkin's *Eugene Onegin* from memory the rest of the night. He knows all three variants of some of the chapters. Impressive, I think as I fall asleep.

"The North is baneful to me," Pushkin wrote. He was some talent. So is Martynenko with such a memory. He knows all of Lermontov and all the Ukrainian poets by heart. Sleep soundly, Oleksandr, you man of great memory.

Captain Marusenko, the Security officer from Lviv, has a pleasant, clean-shaven face.

"You say you find it a little chilly here?" he asks me with a smile. "I've had a chance to look over your dossier. I found a lot of misunderstandings, a good deal of confusion in it. The fact is, your whole case was legally unsubstantiated."

"Then why are you keeping me here?" I ask. "And why didn't you send Novychenko here? He got up at the Ukrainian writers' congress with a speech that would have earned me at least seven years.[48] You have a strange way of deciding what's going to happen to whom."

"All sorts of things can happen, you know. But don't assume that all these writers are so brave. Maybe one was, but all the others are peering out of their burrows to see which way the wind blows."

This man from Lviv isn't so bad, I think, then add aloud: "You know that Novychenko can afford a speech like that after all his swaggering about. He wiped out whole generations of Ukrainian writers. Now he can afford this bit of amusement. The old fellow's just flirting a little with the young crop of readers."

Captain Marusenko slides a sheet of paper toward me. "Sign it."

The deposition reads: "He continues to subscribe to his nationalist convictions, which he expresses. . . ." It is signed by the commandant of Dubrovlag and one other person.

"The mill is at it again," I remark.

"Well, if you insist, I'll delete this." Marusenko crosses out the part about my opinions and beliefs. Instead he writes, "Osadchy was summoned here at his own request," and hands the paper back to me to sign.

"This is the same sort of fabrication as my Case No. 107," I write on it.

You can't catch a zek off guard. Tell him that a revolution has broken out in America, and he'll say, "Okay, I'm on my way now." Tell him that someone swallowed two sets of chessmen and washed them down with two spoons, and he'll raise his eyes to you. "Were the spoons wooden?" Tell the zek that someone fell into the boiling water used for soaking logs, and he'll say, "Finally; now they'll put up a guardrail."

You can't catch him off guard. The zek stands firm and knows his worth. He is a skeptic and likes a good joke. But tell the zek that someone has told you that he has heard somewhere about a new amnesty, and the zek's hands will begin to shake. He'll corner you and make you tell him everything you know. "There will be an amnesty in honor of the fiftieth anniversary of the October Revolution," says the rumor. Someone has supposedly read this in *Neues Deutschland,* the East German Party daily, or heard it from a relative who's high up in the government.

When this happens, the zek forgets about everything else: he can't eat, he can't work. He is very quiet and trusting. Even the skinflint takes his store of tea from its hiding place and pulls you into a supply room.

"Listen, what have you heard about the amnesty? They've been saying . . . But I know . . . Have a drink. Listen, it's the fiftieth anniversary and they have to mark it somehow, don't they?"

Some zeks are skeptical. "Don't let them sell you any fried ice cream," they caution.

"Shut up, you nut! Don't you trust your own bones? That's not any old thing, that's the fiftieth anniversary."

Then the skeptics are ready to believe, and the shaken believers begin to doubt. Topsy-turvy. Inasmuch as there is talk of an amnesty, there naturally must be one.

"Well, take the rumor about Stalin's daughter Alliluyeva escaping. Nobody knew about that, but we zeks knew. What do you say to that? It wasn't just a rumor, was it?"

Somewhere someone told someone the truth. You get the hatchet for that sort of thing.

The zeks want an amnesty. They long for freedom so desperately that they can practically smell it. They can barely walk straight. One foot after the other. They have gone completely soft.

Someone comes up with the date when the announcement will be broadcast: May nineteenth. Now everything is hushed with anticipation, and no one asks any more questions.

On the morning of the nineteenth everyone runs to the "Liars," as the zeks call the camp loudspeakers, for the news broadcast at 0600. "The Chairman of the Committee for State Security at the Council of Ministers of the USSR, Comrade Semichastny, has been relieved of his official duties."

A zek knows no greater joy than seeing his family. When he hears they're coming to visit him, he diligently shaves his hollow cheeks and brushes his teeth. He goes to the tailor shop and presses his tunic. He asks Ivan Hereha to give him some flowers. Then he sits down and tries to decide what part of his clothes he'll sew the money into. Everyone gives him advice because money means tea, coffee, and sugar. At these times everyone respects the zek, while he simply can't contain his excitement. That's the camp tradition.

The visitor arrives. Ivan Svitlychny has come from Kiev—to see not just one zek, but all of them. The camp bustles. Zeks scurry around asking questions about him. Some have heard of Svitlychny and ask for something of his to read. He's brave and talented, they say, but the place he lives in is practically a doghouse. He's out of work and survives on stale bread. That's worse than the hard-labor camps!

"I've seen him!" someone exclaims. "He's the one in the cap, standing by the guardhouse and looking in!"

The prisoners are in an uproar: for the first time in fifty years a Ukrainian writer has come to see them. And not like Taras Myhal once came.[49]

The zeks go out to work. One foot after the other. You can shoot a zek, but you can't make him walk any faster. He has a visitor!

Svitlychny is standing beyond the barbed-wire fence. Daniel and I approach him. We begin to call back and forth.

"Get away, you bastards, or you'll be thrown in the cooler!" a pig screams.

We move away after a moment. Svitlychny continues to stand on the other side of the barbed wire.

"Svitlychny, come join us!" zeks call to him. "It's better in here!"

"I'd like to, but they won't let me!"

Then a zek remarks, "You shout and the barbed wire vanishe before your eyes."

"You've shattered the old model of the world from joy," explains Knuts.

The zeks are thoroughly confused when another visitor arrives from Kiev—Venyamin Kushnir, the artist. The authorities are provoked. Kushnir is taken to the guardhouse, searched, and told, "Get back to your Kiev immediately!"

Hardly has Kushnir departed when Nadia Svitlychny arrives. The zeks forget all about their rumors and amnesties. They live for freedom.

Finally, flowers in hand, the zek goes to the guardhouse. His wife has come to see him. The guards frisk him and poke through his bouquet. "You behave yourself, Osadchy!" they caution him.

You forget everything when you see a person you love. The barbed-wire fences vanish before your eyes. As Knuts says, you've shattered the old model of the world from joy.

The zek absorbs everything he is told like a sponge and

promptly forgets it. He remembers it in a week or so when his happiness has subsided and the old world is again resting firmly on its foundations. His wife would rather not talk; she just wants to look at him, but the zek is made happy with words. He is not used to silence.

"A funny thing happened in the geography department at the university," his wife relates. "During a lecture on Party history the students asked the lecturer about the arrests in Lviv in 1965. 'Those people were confined, and rightly so,' the lecturer replied. 'They wanted to separate Ukraine from the USSR.' The lecturer continued with his presentation and told the class about the territorial and administrative divisions in the Soviet Union and about Article 17 of the Soviet Constitution, according to which every republic has the right freely to secede. The students howled with laughter when they heard this, but the lecturer couldn't see what was so funny and just stood there blinking his eyes."

I recall this story later, when Harashchenko, the representative of the Ukrainian KGB, comes in.[50]

"Why does your husband so stubbornly refuse to go home?" he asks my wife. "We keep trying to get him to go home to his family, but he just says no."

My wife stares at me in astonishment.

"There's just one small condition," I explain. "I have to confess to a crime I never committed." I was never very tactful, and now I'm about to get myself into hot water again.

"All he has to do is sign this piece of paper, and he walks out a free man."

"No matter, I'll wait," my wife replies.

She must wait, and the zek must wait. Who suffers more? He lives for a spiritual ideal. She lives for his return.

"Well, do you want me to tell the guards to let your husband have the parcel you brought?" Harashchenko asks from the doorway.

The zek has his self-respect. He may be hungry, but he still has his self-respect. He is only afraid of looking foolish to his wife, and he lowers his head. He explains to her that the authorities are dishonest. Even if a prisoner confesses to a crime, they review his case and extend his sentence for confessing. Thus far the zek has denied everything, and his conscience is clear. The authorities like to play on a wife's naïve sentiments. A woman is a creature of instinct, and her lack of understanding sometimes unnerves the zek. He may be hungry, but he still has his self-respect and lowers his head.

Zek Suknovalenko hasn't thrown himself on the barbed wire yet, but he's not far from it. The Security officer was counting on female instinct when he told Suknovalenko's wife that her husband would be released if he asked for a pardon.

"Why should I bother?" responded Suknovalenko. "I'm not guilty. I got six years for proposing how to improve the disastrous state of our agriculture. I can stay here and do the same. The conditions are even worse here."

Suknovalenko's wife broke off her visit and left him. He hasn't thrown himself on the barbed wire yet, but he's not far from it: his wife disowned him and has refused to answer his letters for three years.

"Well, shall I tell the guards to forward your parcel?"

Do not degrade the zek! He may be naked, but he still has his self-respect. His eyes are wise and deeply set. You must reckon with him. The zek draws his worn fatigues around his shoulders and proudly walks out of the guardhouse. He can manage without the parcel. Even gruel can be savored if it is eaten by choice.

The vault and the graveyard, the graveyard and its vault, they are to the left of the narrow road. The road leads up to the grass, where it stops and turns back on itself. Commotion in the crypt. Entrapped silence. A darkness so complete that it cannot be distinguished from the silence. The dead man rises from the coffin. "Accursed life," he says. To lie there so long and suddenly to have a thought! He sits up on the coffin and looks around. The gravedigger knows: the road leads to the grass and has to turn back there, because the vault is on the left. The dead man puts his hands behind his head. He takes a deep breath. Holds it in and fumes at the gravedigger. A whirlwind rushes around in his breast. He can feel the uneasiness surfacing. The dead man is bustling about the coffin—someone has driven him out. Then he begins to run about in the vault. Something's happening, he thinks. The road can be heard turning back on itself outside. Someone is to blame: is it the gravedigger or the grass? Someone is bustling about the coffin. Who is it? It is I, the dead man thinks. He moves away hastily. He feels uneasy: a clean shroud, spotted on one side, and bread. Then—a rising agitation. The dead man scrambles back into the coffin, slams the lid down, and plays dead. A finger of sunlight pries its way through a crack in the lid. It lights on the floor and creeps over it. The snaking sunlight...

The lid inches up and two squashed little eyes peer out. The dead man forgot about them. A strange epiphany: two blue streaks that lead nowhere. A spot without meaning. But just scrape away the surface and the rest slithers away. Then the crypt ... The zek falls to his knees and tries to capture the snaking sunlight. He pounces on it and then realizes: he is very weak and is in fact trying to get away from the wall. Show him against a bell tower that has no bells. Let him appear as a minuscule apostle off to one side, and he shall be the bell. Let them strike him, or perhaps he'll ring himself. Then the bell tower stands for the crypt, where you cannot distinguish silence from darkness. There is only one world, but it is conceived of in many ways. Perhaps what is needed is a new model. Let its forerunner be that hand cautiously raised to the chest. Then Knuts will crawl off somewhere to the side if he is cut off from the bell tower by the two blue streaks that lead nowhere, but simply hover stubbornly before his eyes.

Let a horse run behind the zek. He will hear it and hastily jump to the left. He remembers the story about the reins and the hill. The horse will be mine, he thinks. He runs up to the horse, but St. George the Conqueror is seated on it, and he is holding a spear. The zek cannot dismount such a rider and use the animal to get away. The zek turns his head and sees the crypt. Who is bustling about the coffin? It is I, the dead man thinks. Should he tell Vasyl Pidhorodetsky that he is mortal too? That these two streaks, as pale a blue as the oneness of silence and darkness in the crypt, have cut him off from the horse? The streaks that lead nowhere, focusing only on the meadow and the grass? Then capture the snaking sunlight. It has no right to slink across the crypt. Pounce on it. The zek realizes that he is in fact trying to get away from the wall. Show it as black, blacker than the silence. Show nothing on it except a tiny barred window. Let there be a small face by the wall, a face that will help him. Let the zek think that he is on the other side of the wall, that the beyond starts just outside the window.

Then a happy face: Mykhaylo Soroka's bright eyes. "Don't paint me wearing my camp uniform. I am not the eternal prisoner." He takes two steps forward and goes down the stairs. Let there be a river below. But when he looks more closely he sees that two blue streaks have cut him off from it. The streaks that lead nowhere. Who has been bustling about the coffin all this time? It was I, the dead man thinks. Then zek Soroka sees the small barred window. It is at the back, the front, the side. He raises his head and sees the road that runs into the bed of grass and then turns back on itself. No need to paint the zek with hands then, he'd cover his face with them.

"You're a young man, Panas Zalyvakha. Your youth will destroy you just as it destroyed many others. In time your paintings will be turned to the wall. You are forbidden to paint!" The censor and the Security officer. Paint them very small so that they can chase the snaking sunlight? So that you can see how they try to get away from the wall? "I'll let it pass this time. I'll simply throw your daubings into the fire.

But maybe I shouldn't destroy this painting. Maybe it belongs in the Tretyakov Gallery."

A guard with legs instead of arms? Drive the pushcart into the boiler room, crawl into the corner, so that the foreman will shout, "Zalyvakha, you scoundrel!"

Carve on linoleum the white figure of a woman dressed in black? You can get the cooler for that, but so what? Who is bustling about in the coffin? It is I, the dead man thinks. The zek looks at the picture and sits down. You shouldn't look at pictures standing up. You have to sit down so that the two blue streaks rest on the crypt wall.

Then you can clearly sense a strange uneasiness surfacing within you, and the snaking sunlight appears again. I must capture it, the dead man thinks. It will be simple, just sit on the floor and everything will be clear. Only don't scare it away. Come up on it from the wall and chase it into the coffin with its nooks and crannies where it can finally be cornered. Or what about approaching it from the coffin? No, then there's the risk of stepping on it. Who is bustling about the coffin? It is I, the dead man thinks. The snaking sunlight seems to be dozing now, but where is that damn crack it crawled in through? If he can reach it, then that's the place to keep a watch. It won't slip through his fingers this time: it has to leave the same way it came in. But who's there mumbling something? It is I, the dead man thinks. I am awfully tired and cannot do a thing. I can't even think things out properly. That snaking sunlight! I can take a rest, I've tired myself out, the dead man thinks. He leans against the coffin, then crawls inside. The second his back touches the bottom, the lid slams shut. The dead man raises his head with suspicion. That noise reminds him of something. It cannot be. He touches the lid with his hand and presses. A breeze wafts by. It is somewhere outside the coffin, the dead man thinks. And then the dead man realizes that he is doomed. He sees where he went wrong: at the spot where the road ended at the grass and began to turn back on itself. That moment was enough for the sunlight to snake away and the lid to slip in place. And then with all his remaining strength the dead man presses his eyelids shut.

A zek stops being a zek when he loses his head. Without it he can neither eat his gruel nor work and is fit to be carried out to the graveyard. When a zek is missing an arm or a leg, he still remains a criminal. Let him go home, and he'll climb on a balcony railing and stage revolutions from there. No, a zek must serve his full sentence and think about the graveyard. The old fart must entrust himself to the graveyard. The old fart . . .

Everyone perks up when spring arrives. The old farts stop sitting on their committees and smelling the place up. The guards go by and pretend that they don't see the missile squad quarreling, brawling, or dragging their mattresses outside. "Oh, rot! The jet-propelled zeks are blasting off from their pads again."

The old fart is seventy or more and sleeps with his eyes wide open because he's afraid of being strangled in his sleep. He closes his eyes when he curses to give his voice more power. Sometimes when the sun gets very hot, the zek crawls away from his mattress like a lizard. He loses his sense of direction and is surprised when he finds himself back at his mattress. He'd try to make a break for it, but what about his damn mattress?

The birch trees put forth buds in the spring, and the zeks festoon them with cans to collect the sap, making the trees look like queer storks. When the cans fill up, the zeks get drunk. This sort of "alcohol" is permitted. The birches are rotten inside, but their sap is potable.

Anatoliy Shevchuk is particularly fond of birch sap.[51] He's a real wise guy. One day he brings us a fresh cucumber. Where in hell's name did he get it? Pulled out a board in the hothouse where vegetables are grown for the camp brass and stole it. He'd get the cooler if he were caught, but he's lucky. Later he and Ivashchenko dig a vegetable patch behind the plywood shop and plant radishes.[52] Shevchuk's some farmer. When his brother Valeriy sends us a packet of Golden Fleece tobacco, we're in seventh heaven. Everyone takes a puff on the fragrant cigarette whether he's a smoker or not.

Thus the days and weeks pass in this Ukrainian outpost. Most of the men were drafted in 1965 and are serving from one to six. Mainly on account of "The Trial of Pogruzhalsky." They come from Lviv, Kiev, Ivano-Frankivsk, Lutsk, and Zhytomyr. They are engineers, teachers, university lecturers, scientists, researchers, writers, workers, and doctors. That's our outpost—without a commander, but each man with a tour of duty.

Consider this: the zeks gravitate toward the Ukrainians. Their number is the greatest, and almost all of them are intellectuals. Intellectuals are liked if they haven't turned stoolie. The camp is plastered with posters calling for the friendship of peoples. They help zeks from different backgrounds to make friends. The zeks all stick together. They share the same life, the same hardships. They have the same commitment— to survive. At any price.

There are about fifteen nationalities here, including Chinese, Georgians, Armenians, Tatars, Lithuanians, Estonians, and Jews.[53] You can take each other by the arm just like on the outside and go for a coffee. There is about the same number of nationalities among the guards. They read the posters and diligently put the slogans into practice.

Then there's the Leningrad group of Marxists.[54] Several of them are serving their time at Camp No. 11: Ronkin, Smolkin, Yoffe, and Gvenko. They were either engineers or research assistants at the Institute of Technology and published a magazine titled *Kolokol* [The Bell]. They're disciples of Herzen, pure Marxians with their own program: a perfect application of Marxian theory to praxis. They spoke out against the bureaucratic leadership, and now they're serving from two to ten. Captain Yoffe, the Deputy CO of Camp Detachment

No. 2, rubs his forehead: he simply can't fathom these young Leningrad Jews.

"Listen," he says to them, "didn't you have good jobs and good salaries? Didn't you have food to put in your stomachs?" He comes up closer. "Look at me, an ordinary Jew. Would I have ever been promoted to Deputy CO if it hadn't been for the Soviet regime?"

I can see the madman.[55] Wiping the sweat from his brow. Not looking away when his eyes soar above the courtroom. Brushing back his shock of hair. Smalltime painter, tramp, or professor, leaning on the table and calming us down when there's no reason to get upset. Standing up to people and saying "No!" to them. Honesty is not outmoded. Saying "No!" and looking people in the eye. Let *them* look away if there's so little ability to reason outside the courtroom, if there's no difference between the belly and the brain.

A complete turnabout: throwing off the mask and saying "No!" Let them foam at the mouth. Let them eat more, a full stomach calms the nerves. Here, stand beside me, don't be afraid, never mind the years. We shall survive no matter what —behind, beneath, and beyond these walls. Mental nurture is mental torment. The turnabout brings out two drops of sweat. With your leave, comrade prosecutor: No! Judges, behind, beneath, and beyond, with your leave: No! And you, my attorney friends, don't get angry, you'll all get your fees, though you've somehow managed to reach out for truth and honor. They gave you a tongue-lashing, threatened to throw you to the mob. I thank you for your defense, I'll remember my debt to you for the full six years. And you, the witnesses, you were a bit intimidated. Would you be willing to shoulder another man's unnecessary misfortune, a man's misfortune, not society's? And yet a man's misfortune is society's. No need. I have the honor to bear it alone, however small I may be.

"No!" The judges have a new problem—the obstinacy of the accused. "No!" His head thrown back, his eyes penetrating and feverish with illness. "No!" A true demon. A Shevchenko or a mother who hammers at the prison gate. How hard it must be for him to stand so long with head held high. And suddenly: a warm and unimposing person. You can chat with him about the birds and delight in his innocence. He is both Demon and Innocence. Uncompromising in the face of evil, compassionate with the prisoner who stands beside him. Judges, prosecutors, and interrogators hate such men. And they get their revenge. "Here's the cooler for you, Mykhaylo Masyutko! Look through the bars and enjoy that patch of light on the wall."

When Mykhaylo Masyutko develops an ulcer, everyone contributes a few grams of sugar from his rations, and we send one of our guys to smuggle it into the cooler. "Hey, let me see that!" a pig screams. The sugar is dumped into the garbage. The zek's face is very red.

"Never mind," says Masyutko. "I'll get by without glucose. You know who needs glucose—athletes who run around with a ball. They're the ones who need the strength. What does a prisoner need strength for anyway? To keep him from sleeping? I am completely innocent and I cry No!"

Six years of labor camps? For saying "No"? Then the prosecutor, the judge, and the guard rear back: "No?"

"No!" Zek Masyutko throws his head back and roars: "No!" He is in a deep pit, and his "No!" bounces back from the walls; his "No!" veers off; his "No!" returns; his "No!" reverberates, a grim cat's cradle of echoing "No!" He sees it flying straight at him. He backs away and all at once feels the walls pressing in on him from front and back. His legs, arms, and head are flattened against the wall. In front of him, flying, rebounding, and hurtling on, comes his huge, devastating, shrapnel-shelling "No!"

Two months left now till freedom. These days pass in a kind of numbness. Two more months, and then Lviv and wife and son. The zek sleeps poorly at this time. Everything inside him is topsy-turvy, and he becomes as soft as a jellyfish. You have to ask him a question three times before he hears it. The

145

zek grows apart from the others. He is turning toward a different world, the world of freedom.

I am summoned and told to pack my gear. So soon? I haven't served my time yet. But nobody ever explains anything to the zek. He is simply told to get ready to move out. Someone ventures a guess: my term is coming to an end, so my case will be reviewed in Kiev, and I shall get another sentence. Two years is much too little for a political. But I won't get more than five. Comforting knowledge.

I say good-by to my friends. I feel very ill at ease, knowing that they are all staying behind in the camp. I feel it's my fault that I am leaving and they are staying. Vasyl Levkovych runs up and presses a bag of candy into my hand, five rubles' worth.[56] A zek could live for a month on that. But the zeks are a generous lot; they never think about themselves. After twenty-five years in camps, they are very sensitive men. Besides, there's the slogan: TO FREEDOM WITH A CLEAR CONSCIENCE!

The narrow-gauge railroad again. The same cell in the transit prison at Potma, but filled with new zeks—professional thieves and suckers. They ransack my suitcase the first time I go to the toilet, but they are disappointed: this zek is carrying nothing but books. Later I am locked into a separate compartment for the long trip. Ruzayevka, Kharkiv—I absorb only the place names as everything sails past. I spend twenty days on the train and almost go crazy with loneliness: I'm the only political prisoner in the entire railroad car. Everyone is curious about me.

"Hey, buddy, don't walk so fast when you're headed for the toilet," the other zeks call out. "Let us get a good look at you. You political types are kind of interesting. Khrushchev, our great corn-planter, told us there are no political prisoners any more, and here they're riding the trains."

The escort guards are all youngsters of about twenty. "Are you really one of those politicals?" they ask after staring at me for twenty minutes. "What are you in for? Did you really want to overthrow the government?"

"Sure, I wanted to be minister of sewers." We politicals don't talk much.

"Yes, that must be it. I just knew they don't put you guys away for nothing." They continue to stand by the door, staring at me and coughing.

At last there's Kharkiv. Here's the same old corridor and its familiar smell. "I've been through the whole of Russia, and I've never seen such godawful transit prisons."

I remember the police dogs, the professional thief, and the big-bellied warden whose jaded eyes perched on massive cheeks. The one who said, "These millions." You can't expect such a creature to remember.

The major in charge calls me in.

"I have no questions. I just looked at your dossier and noticed how young you are. And then those two years. What was accomplished in those two years?"

I tell him. He listens attentively and nods his head. I see a sly grin appear on his face.

"Yes," he says, "it's just your life they've ruined. I understand everything. But you see this uniform?" he crushes the fabric of his tunic between his fingers. "You can never go against its honor. Remember that. . . . Yes, but I do think that *you will find justice* in the Soviet Union."

Later I think about the way he drawled that out: "You will find justice."

The major summons a guard. "Give Osadchy"—I think he actually says "Comrade Osadchy"—"a better cell on the third floor and issue him bedding."[57]

In transit prisons zeks are never issued bedding, but I get it.

The cell is dry. I can sit and read. They don't give zeks any books in transit, but this major did. What a strange world! You can never fully fathom it. Sometimes you pretend that you do understand it, but you're only fooling yourself. It's all so very primitive.

The wooden awning on my cell window must have been designed by an artist. It is no ordinary awning, meant simply to shelter from wind and rain, but rather like one of those crooked mirrors you see in fun houses. This is particularly evident when the rays of the setting sun penetrate the awning and project the bars onto the plaster walls. The bars appear to be red, like a mangled carcass. I can't stand to look at them. I think I see blood trickling down the bars. Drop by drop. "Where should it drip?" I ask. "The bars are crying." I burst out laughing. I can't stop laughing until midnight, long after the sun has set.

Kiev, the capital, with blustery winds, greening chestnut trees, and a surprisingly intact Saint Volodymyr with his cross on the hill.[58] He gazes at what's left of the Dnieper these days. How good it is that he is holding a cross: it lends itself to peace and contemplation. The cross is necessary to understand the Eucharist, to repent the sins for which He died. Hook the fish, then throw it back into the water so that it can go on living. What happens after the hook? Can one survive after a million communions? Always!

"How are you, friend?" the dove asks.[59]

"I'm fine."

"You'll be receiving a letter with news in it."

"Thank you. Is it morning outside?"

In the morning the zek is brought into the interrogator's office. He can sit down, cross his legs, and not budge from the spot. He can even doze with his eyes open. When a zek is called in and told to sit down but not asked any questions, he might assume that he's been summoned to test the strength of the chair, which is firmly chained to the floor. A golden torpor. The zek dozes with his eyes open. Major Lytvyn clasps his hands behind his back and turns his head.

"I am not dozing. I am merely keeping still for lack of anything to say."

Half an hour passes. For the zek it seems like an hour because he has lost his sense of time. A zek is space without time. The zek yawns impudently without closing his eyes, then takes out his makings and rolls himself a cigarette two fingers thick. Flecks of coarse *makhorka* shower on his fatigues. He collects them assiduously and puts them back on the newspaper. The zek is a cautious man.

Major Lytvyn comes closer. "You've done time in prison."

The zek takes a drag on his cigarette and disappears in a cloud of smoke. Cold eyes suddenly bore into him. The zek is a specter and must be destroyed. His life isn't even worth a shot of varnish.

"Please," he says.

"I am not joking. You've spent time in prison," the major continues. "You pick up the bits of tobacco from your lap, and that means prison. Prison is a two-year university course. After five years they pick up the tobacco a little differently. After five years their minds are different, too. These homemade cigarettes—ha, ha!"

The zek puffs on his cigarette.

"Well, well, friend," Major Lytvyn says. "In a few days your sentence will be up, and you naturally want to go home very much. We have news for you. You're not about to go home. A new charge has been brought against you, and you'll be getting another sentence."

The zek disappears in a cloud of smoke.

"You wrote a petition to the Presidium of the Supreme Soviet of the Ukrainian SSR in which you slandered Major Halski."

"He tried to hit me!"

"Ha, ha! Do you know that Major Halski is our best man here?"

A stout man waddles in. His name is Harbuz, and he is a Senior Interrogator of the Ukrainian KGB. What a name: Major Harbuz—Major Pumpkin!

"You wrote that in 1965 the Ukrainian intelligentsia was supposedly subjected to repressions. Do you consider yourself a member of the intelligentsia? Our intelligentsia is people like Honchar,[60] myself, Major Lytvyn, and Major Halski. Were any of us ever repressed?"

The zek takes a drag on his cigarette. If you pick the tobacco off your clothing after two years, what do you do after five? The zek can smell another stretch coming as clearly as he can smell his cigarette. The zek is used to everything except rumors about amnesty.

Major Harbuz is in the prosecutor's office. He is short and has a funny potbelly. Peter, Peter, pumpkin eater, had a wife and couldn't keep her. How the women must ooh and aah over those cute little dimples in his cheeks.

"Please take a look, are these your poems?" Major Harbuz asks.

"Yes, they are."

"You can read them typed out. How did you get them out of the camp?"

The zek collects the bits of *makhorka* in his lap. He has done time.

"Those are my poems, and I'm pleased to see them typed out." The interrogator must know without asking to whom the poems were sent.

"Do you know that your poems were used by Vyacheslav Chornovil in his letter to Shelest?"[61]

How can a zek know such fine details about life on the outside? He collects the flecks of *makhorka* in his lap.

"You've been in prison, haven't you? Do you know Chornovil?"

"Oh, yes, he's a man who . . ." The zek takes a deep drag on his cigarette.

What a busy Tuesday! If it could be depicted in a painting, it would be composed like a collage of many small parts. Each part would be separate: a nose here, eyes there, a mouth, ears, and arms over there.

"Sorry, we're in a hurry," the Eyes say.

"We'll see you again," the Ears promise.

"There are some pressing matters," the Nose intones.

They're all so very clever. The Nose is really cleverest, but the Eyes manage to hold their own. You merely have to say something that hurts the Lips, and they begin to pout, and the Mustache swells up, ready for a fight. "Don't insult my brother!"

Vyacheslav and his beautiful wife Olena are neck-deep in a field of wild flowers, the kind that grow in mountain meadows.

What a busy Tuesday it is! "Sorry," say the Eyes, "we aren't very pretty, but you should see us laugh."

"My, my, aren't you witty," the Nose jokes. Oh, that Nose! And the Blond Hair is not far behind. "This Nose is an important person, mind you."

"Accused Chornovil, what was your purpose in using in your petition the poem by Osadchy titled 'Memorial Inscription on a Cross'?[62] What did you have in mind? How did you interpret this poem? Didn't you take it to refer to Osadchy's interrogators?"

"No," Chornovil replies. "I think Osadchy was speaking of West German imperialists."

"How can you prove that?"

"Well, in our country nobody puts crosses on graves. We put up posts with stars. Crosses are used only abroad."

"Oh, how clever that Nose is!" the Eyes whisper.

"Accused Chornovil, how did you manage to write five volumes of seditious material in such a short time?"

"That's my hobby, you know," the Nose replies.

The prosecutor profits from an adjournment to consult a dictionary.

"You aren't going to fool me the way you fooled the prosecutor in Ivano-Frankivsk with the word '*vatra*.'[63] I know that 'hobby' is a foreign word meaning a 'favorite occupation.'"

The Eyelids slyly veil the Eyes, which gleam with laughter.

Chornovil's Hand pitches in: "Having thoroughly analyzed the graphic distribution of the texts that were passed from hand to hand, and also of some literary works by Mykhaylo Masyutko, the panel of experts, which was composed of such learned authorities as Zdoroveha, Makhovsky, Yashchuk, and Kybalchych, has established that in both the former and the latter writings each sentence begins with a capital and ends with a period. The conclusion is obvious and incontrovertible: all the above-mentioned writings were composed by the same person, Mykhaylo Masyutko."[64]

Oh, those coquettish Lips! They really think they're something special. And the Hair is pushed back angrily from the Forehead. The Eyebrows slide up in surprise: "His Lordship, the Prosecutor, is telling us something."

Chornovil stands up to deliver his closing speech: "Lenin wrote that in our country every cook, every housewife should be able to run the State. I wanted to convince myself of this. The Comrade Judges will shortly inform us what resulted from my investigations."[65]

The Mustache twitches with a furtive smile. So smiled our Ukrainian Cossacks in their cups. Then an elderly pensioner, who has been ordered to attend the trial on pain of losing his Social Security benefits, cannot restrain himself any longer: "Shame, shame, Chornovil! You've argued yourself into a corner."

After the closing statements, the pensioner approaches the bench. "Say what you will, but this man Chornovil should be working for the Council of Ministers."

"Aren't you ashamed of yourself for saying that?" voices call from the back of the courtroom.

"No, not at all," the old man replies. "After what I've heard, I tell you that this man Chornovil should be working for the Council of Ministers."

What a busy Tuesday it is! If it could be depicted in a painting, it would be composed of many small parts: nose, lips, mustache, eyebrows, and hands. They would all exist separately and self-sufficiently, but in each one of them you would recognize Vyacheslav Chornovil.

The zek is permitted to go home. At last he can breathe freely again. He drags his shabby suitcase, full of books, toward the exit. He hears the door slam behind him and feels hasty, furtive glances follow him.

Remember the narrow-gauge railroad to Yavas. "These fences—they crushed the wide railroad tracks and made them so narrow."

The zek feels something pushing at his back and propelling him through the door.

"God grant you health." The sound is stealthy, almost not a voice at all. It must be footsteps. Whose are they? They're mine, the prisoner thinks. They're in front and in back of me. If I don't hurry, the sheer bulk of the front door will push me back. Then I won't be released, and no one will believe that I was pushed back by the door. They'll throw me back inside and sentence me again. "He left the cell with an insolent manner," they'll say, or something similar.

The zek hastily steps out into the street and suddenly feels very unsure of himself: the paving is dissolving from underfoot. After two years the world seems to have become as stately and fecund as a bulging-bellied woman. It sways from side to side as streetcars scud by, and the buildings sway restlessly to and fro.

This is freedom, the prisoner thinks. He cannot speak. He remembers the crypt at the graveyard, the stray graveyard squeezed out beyond the city limits by the buildings. The zek takes a step, then another. He is used to walking—he walked more than he stood—but again the cobbles are dissolving underfoot. The camps are behind him; his friends wait ahead; everywhere are people. But why are the ordinary cobblestones no longer underfoot?

Lviv, March–May 1968

THE AFTERMATH

1
Vyacheslav Chornovil's View of the Trial

On 15 August 1965, when the arrests in Ukraine were cresting, Vyacheslav Chornovil dispatched a protest to Komsomol and Party authorities.[1] Two weeks later Security agents appeared at his flat and conducted a nine-hour search. The books they confiscated, like those taken from Osadchy, were published outside the Soviet Union and dealt with Ukrainian history and culture.

While Osadchy was being held under investigation, Chornovil was brought in for a "confrontation" with him. Perhaps Osadchy does not mention this episode in his account because of regret for momentarily giving in to the interrogator's bullying.

When the trial of Osadchy, the Horyn brothers, and Myroslava Zvarychevska opened in April 1966, Chornovil was summoned as a witness. Osadchy has already described for us the scene in the Lviv courtroom when Chornovil refused to give evidence at a trial held behind closed doors. He was immediately assailed by the prosecutor as an "enemy who has no right to speak about socialist legality"; his brief was rejected, and Chornovil was charged, under Article 179 of the Code of Criminal Procedure, with refusal to testify.

Three days later the prosecutor, Borys Antonenko, and the judge, S. I. Rudyk, decided to prosecute Chornovil under the much harsher—and more flexible—Article 62, which had been used for indictment in the previous political cases. But on 17 May the Supreme Court of the Republic reversed the lower court's decision, and on 8 July Chornovil was brought before the bench on the original charge. The people's court issued a summary verdict of guilty and awarded him the maximum penalty: three months of "correctional labor" with a twenty percent deduction from his wages.

Additional details of Osadchy's case and a clear picture of the dissidents' principled stand emerge from Chornovil's brief and from his closing statement at his trial.[2] Soviet law explicitly gives the accused the right to make a final speech without any interruptions, even by the presiding judge. However, the transcript indicates that Chornovil was hectored by the judge after almost every sentence: "Why are you telling us these legal axioms? This is beside the point! Don't concern yourself with the case that was heard in the provincial court. How much longer will you talk? This has no bearing on the case. You are trying to use your closing statement for agitation." The passages that Chornovil was not permitted to read to the court are set off here in italics.

A COMPLAINT
TO THE LVIV PROVINCIAL COURT
FROM CITIZEN V. M. CHORNOVIL

17 April 1966

The Lviv Provincial Court is now hearing the case of B. Horyn, M. Horyn, M. Zvarychevska, and M. Osadchy, who have been charged with anti-Soviet propaganda and agitation. I am involved in this case as a witness.

Please have the court hearing take into account the gross violations of procedural norms that were committed by the

KGB investigators during the preliminary investigation, and please punish those responsible.

1. By order of the Lviv KGB and the Lviv Province prosecutor, a search was conducted at my flat "for the purpose of confiscating anti-Soviet documents manifolded by [me]." No such documents were found because I never "manifolded" anything of the sort. Nevertheless, going against both the search order and plain common sense, Lieutenant Berestovsky, an investigator for the Kiev KGB, took to the KGB a large portion of my scholarly library (190 books and sets of old publications). I sent two complaints to the Kiev Province KGB and wrote to Republic KGB Chairman Nikitchenko, but never received an answer (in violation of Articles 234 and 235 of the Ukrainian Code of Criminal Procedure). The books confiscated from me were old editions "manifolded" in Austro-Hungary and pre-war Poland. I need them for my scholarly research and have never used them for "agitation and propaganda."

Hence I request the court to issue an order to return those fifty-five books that are still held by the KGB and to punish those who were responsible for confiscating them.

2. When I was being interrogated as a witness in Lviv, KGB interrogator Klymenko behaved very brutally. He addressed me with the familiar form and made such threats as, "Why are you lying and trying to wriggle your way out of this? We don't have to let you out of here." Conducting the confrontation, Captain Klymenko violated Article 173 of the Ukrainian Code of Criminal Procedure, which states clearly: "Evidence given by the participants in a confrontation during the preliminary investigation can be made public only after it has been *entered into the record*." When Osadchy declared that it was not I who had given him "Eisenhower's Speech at the Unveiling of the Shevchenko Monument," Captain Klymenko failed to enter this doubt into the record, but shouted instead at Osadchy, "Then why did you testify before that you took it from Chornovil?" Osadchy immediately told Captain Klymenko what he wanted to hear, and this statement was

entered into the record. The facts cited indicate that the charges presented in court are based on illegally obtained evidence and therefore must be considered invalid.

V. M. Chornovil

VYACHESLAV CHORNOVIL'S FINAL SPEECH AT HIS TRIAL ON 8 AUGUST 1966

I made an unexpected discovery in my encounters during the last year with judges, prosecutors, and KGB interrogators: despite their lack of professional training, defendants and witnesses frequently have a more profound understanding of the spirit of Soviet law than legal experts. Is this possibly caused by a difference in age? The accused and witnesses at this year's closed trials are for the most part young people whose minds were shaped after the Twentieth Party Congress. The people trying them are somewhat older and are obviously unable to overcome in themselves the inertia of the Stalinist style.

Let me get to the point. Soviet law does not simply recommend, but actually demands that a convicted person be punished for his crime and that the reason for it be established and the conditions that bred the crime be determined. Article 23 of the Ukrainian Code of Criminal Procedure states: "During the investigation and legal examination of a criminal case, the organ of investigation, the investigator, the prosecutor, and the court are required to determine the circumstances that contributed to the commission of the crime and to take measures through the appropriate organs to eliminate them." A complete and objective examination of the circumstances of the case is also required by Article 22 of the Code.

Unfortunately, the court sometimes forgets these legal axioms. For example, when Tom attacks Dick with a knife, and Dick, misjudging the strength of his blow, cripples or kills his assailant, the judges do not rush to pronounce the death sen-

tence on Dick. Instead they carefully investigate the danger
that Tom posed and the way that both Tom and Dick behaved. If they find justification, they exonerate Dick or let him
off with a light punishment.

When Candidate of Sciences Osadchy, who only yesterday
was an instructor in the ideological department of the Lviv
Province Party Committee and a lecturer at the university,
read one or two anonymous articles about the nationalities
situation in Ukraine and without an ulterior motive gave them
to read to one of his closest friends, he was promptly sent to
a strict-regime camp *as an anti-Soviet and attempts were made
to evict his wife and three-month-old baby from their apartment. The confused defendant was helped neither by his flaw-
less record nor by his excessive repentance. The question why
did such a person, a Party instructor and a university lecturer
whose behavior had been entirely proper until then, develop
an interest (if only a passing one) in these articles—that question remains unanswered.*

I tried to raise such questions when I was being interrogated
at the Kiev and Lviv KGB. But every time the interrogators'
eyes went blank. Instead of rebutting my claims that Leninist
norms in the nationalities policy were being violated, leading
to "indictable" attitudes, they monotonously repeated to me:
"Article 62, violation of the law, crime. . . ."

Let's take today's trial. If you approach it formally—as this
court is doing—the man standing before you is a criminal. He
was involved as a witness in the case of Osadchy. As we
learned from the documents in today's case, the KGB at one
point even brought up the question of indicting him under
Article 62 of the Ukrainian Criminal Code, thus raising the
possibility of prison, a closed trial, and the development of
the national economy of the Mordovian ASSR. Finally, the
man standing before you committed a crime when he refused
to testify at a political trial. If Article 62 does not apply to
him, then Article 179 certainly does. He should accept his
three months of compulsory labor, bear the burden of his
criminal record, which will keep him from finding any work in

his field, and thank God and the Lviv court that he got off so easily.

But why don't you want to conduct a psychological examination of the criminal? Why don't you try to see what led him to crime?

Eleven years ago the present criminal graduated with a gold medal from a Soviet school. Six years ago he graduated with honors from Kiev University. He was secretary of Komsomol branches at school, in his university group, and at the Lviv television studio. He was a member of regional and city Komsomol committees. He worked on two Komsomol shock-brigade construction sites: a blast furnace in the Donbas and the hydroelectric station near Kiev. At the newspaper offices and television studios where he worked you will not hear a single bad word about him as a journalist (unless, of course, there are instructions from above). And then unexpectedly he appears in the dock. How do you explain this: as a typical phenomenon or as an exceptional one?

If this is an exceptional case, then what explains the fact that a score of people, mostly young with exemplary records, were convicted under Article 62?

If this is a typical phenomenon, however, then the situation is very frightening indeed. One simply refuses to believe that intelligence, curiosity, and a concern for social justice produced anti-Soviet attitudes in these young people. *But perhaps what is labeled anti-Soviet is simply a concern for the purity and irreproachability of the Soviet way?*

I personally knew some of those arrested in August and September of last year. That is why I anxiously waited for their trial and why several dozen colleagues and I even wrote to the Prosecutor and the Chairman of the KGB of the Ukrainian Republic, requesting that we be allowed to attend their trials. The petition was signed by writers, scientists, scholars, students, and workers.

I believed that everything would be cleared up in court. Either the actions these people were accused of would prove to be not anti-Soviet, but rather concern for the moral well-being of the Soviet regime, or my colleagues and I would be shown the duplicity in the actions of Zalyvakha, an artist of great talent, and the scholars Mykhaylo Horyn and Mykhaylo Osadchy, and I would be able to eliminate them from my mind forever without any pangs of conscience.

The first closed trials were like a bolt from the blue for me (and not only for me). Why don't they want to expose the crime, why don't they trust the ability of people to sort things out for themselves? Why, for example, is the fate of the artist Panas Zalyvakha being decided by a few people quite removed from art while his professional colleagues can't even attend his trial?

I went to legal experts for an explanation. They shrugged their shoulders: according to the Code the trial in this case should apparently be open to the public, but the court itself decides in each case whether the trial is to be open or closed. This answer did not satisfy me. How can it be that the law says one thing, but the court can decide otherwise? Then I turned to the law myself.

Article 20 of the Code of Criminal Procedure is formulated the way every law should be: clearly and unambiguously. I did not find any other laws about the holding of trials in public. If there are some secret instructions, then why are they secret? Article 20 states that a trial can be held in camera only when sexual crimes, intimate affairs of the accused, state secrets, or crimes committed by minors are involved.

Can the reading of an article or a book, and one published abroad at that, be termed a state secret? I am well acquainted with Panas Zalyvakha, Mykhaylo Osadchy, and some of the other defendants, and I can verify that they did not collect or transmit any strategic secrets to foreign intelligence services. Furthermore, I remember that when the traitor Penkovsky, who had in fact conveyed state secrets to foreign intelligence services, was being tried, his trial was open to the public and the trial transcript was published as a book.³ Only the session *where experts evaluated the information passed abroad was held* in camera, *after the permission of the accused himself was obtained.*

My attention was also drawn to the Universal Declaration of Human Rights in the journal Mezhdunarodnaya zhizn' [*International Life*]. *We not only voted for the Declaration at the UN, but even insisted that it be incorporated in the legislation of all countries. My incomprehension increased even more because Article 11 of the Declaration clearly speaks about the right of every individual accused of a crime to a defense and a public investigation.*

I came to the conclusion that the closed trials of the Horyns, Zalyvakha, and the others are a violation of the letter and spirit of Soviet law and that as a Soviet citizen I am obliged to state my attitude toward this phenomenon.

*My decision was not caused by a nervous breakdown or an unstable character, as Bohdan Horyn's testimony implies. I came to the trial with a firm intention: to take no part in a crude violation of socialist legality. I acquainted myself beforehand with Article 179 of the Ukrainian Criminal Code and found in it a passage that justifies my action: a person is brought up before the court for refusing to give evidence with-*out grave reasons. *I regarded a violation of socialist legality as a sufficiently grave reason to justify my decision.*

During the interrogation by the KGB (and also here in court) I was asked: Who do you think you are, Chornovil, that you take upon yourself the right to decide whether the law was violated? The court was wrong; the Supreme Court of the Ukrainian SSR was wrong when it upheld the decision of the lower court; only you think and act correctly. I shall try once more to answer this question.

First of all, as a Soviet citizen who is guided by the Moral Code of a Builder of Communism, I have the full right and indeed the obligation to speak out forcefully whenever I notice a violation that may be causing damage to the Soviet system. If I am wrong, my mistake should be explained to me in a reasoned way. I did not receive a cogent answer as to why people were being tried in secret session either from the KGB or here in court. To say that "the court decided that way" is to make a lame excuse, not give an answer.

Second, by telling the story of Stalin's crimes at the Twentieth and Twenty-second Congresses, the Party taught us not to take anything on faith and to examine everything with our own minds. When a large group of Soviet Ukrainian writers— now rehabilitated—were executed as terrorists immediately after Kirov's provocative murder, they were shot by Soviet NKVD agents and the murders were sanctioned by Soviet Prosecutor-General Ulrikh. I won't even go into the terrible times of Yezhov and Beria.⁴ If somebody decided to put the criminals of those years before people's courts the way we are still trying fascist criminals, there would be a terrible judgment lasting a thousand and two nights.

When my uncle, a dedicated communist and a builder of the new Soviet school in the Cherkasy region, was being tortured, later to be secretly condemned by the NKVD in Uman, he could not believe that this was being done in the name of the Soviet regime and Soviet law. In a note which he miraculously managed to pass out of the prison, he wrote with his blood, "Tell me, what regime is in power now?"

All this was perpetrated by the Soviet NKVD and the Soviet courts, and Soviet prosecutor Vyshinsky laid down the thesis that the accused himself must prove his innocence and that the testimony of an arrested person is sufficient proof of his guilt.⁵

Understand me correctly: I am not establishing a direct analogy with those terrible years, but if you permit illegal closed trials today—even if the people being tried have committed real crimes—you are paving the way for a return of the Stalin-Beria troykas.⁶ Only the fullest public control, only the further consistent democratization begun by the Twentieth Party Congress can prevent the return of arbitrary rule and lawlessness.

These were the thoughts I had when I decided not to appear at the closed trial, which I considered illegal. By refusing to testify I deliberately placed myself in an awkward position because I deprived myself of the opportunity to correct Osadchy's testimony against me, for the most part groundless and not corroborated by any other witness or legal expert. I mention this now because the evidence at today's trial includes an excerpt from the record of the Horyn and Osadchy trial which states that I gave Osadchy Eisenhower's speech at the unveiling of the Shevchenko monument in Washington and an anonymous article about the burning of the library of the Ukrainian Academy of Sciences. I have read the latter article. It was of only passing interest for me. To ease Osadchy's situation I admitted that I may have shown him this article. I admitted the possibility but did not confirm it. These are quite different things. As for the Eisenhower speech, I never gave Osadchy such a document and read it only when Osadchy was in prison and I was called in for interrogation. I read it to see what I was being accused of. Isn't it strange that the KGB and the court were satisfied with just Osadchy's testimony, exactly as in the times of Beria and Vyshinsky? The verdict stated that I had given this material to Osadchy. Later this completely unfounded assertion cropped up in the circular from the Central Committee of the Communist Party of Ukraine.

My refusal to testify also made my situation awkward because it kept me from presenting in court my opinion of the material that had been labeled anti-Soviet. Knocked together from vague generalities, Eisenhower's speech is to my mind no more anti-Soviet than the speeches that French President de Gaulle made in Moscow. According to the Constitution, each Soviet nationality is sovereign, but de Gaulle repeatedly referred to the Soviet Union as Russia and lumped all the nationalities together as Russians, thus unintentionally bringing grist to the mill of Great-Russian chauvinism, which V. I. Lenin condemned so sharply.

As for the anonymous article, "The Trial of Pogruzhalsky," it is not at all anti-Soviet, at least in the version that I read, because it criticizes not the power of the Soviets nor of the

Soviet regime as such, but rather individual defects which have survived since the days of Stalin's despotism, particularly in the nationalities policy. Government and Party bodies are themselves responsible for the appearance of this article. The burning of the national library was the crime of the century. The trial of the new Herostratos should have received complete coverage in the press. Why was this cannibalistic act wrapped in a deadly silence?

I wanted very badly to say all this at the trial, but by saying anything at all I would have recognized the legality of the court. And this I could not allow.

The "witnesses" here—the prison warden and the chief of guards—have even charged me with giving flowers to the defendants. It was for these flowers, as witness Ivanov [the chief of guards] has confirmed, that Judge Rudyk called me an enemy. I have not been able to find in the Criminal Code any article that prohibits giving flowers. By presenting the defendants with flowers on 15 April I was expressing my solidarity with them for being tried by a court that blatantly violated the law. The details of many of the closed trials have now become known because nothing comes sooner to light than that which has been hid. Mykhaylo Horyn's closing statement, the transcript of Masyutko's trial, and his closing statement are passing from hand to hand. Now I would give these people flowers not only for being tried in violation of the law, but also for being unjustly punished.

A few last words about today's trial. I am not a lawyer, but I think that an unbiased lawyer would be very surprised by some of the incidents in today's hearing. First of all, I was muzzled every time I tried to present my opinion of the closed trials. And then let us look at the witnesses. Two of them [Osadchy and Bohdan Horyn] have been convicted and disfranchised, and they are in a camp thousands of kilometers from here and cannot be questioned, so that one has to rely on testimony taken down inside KGB walls and written in a KGB hand.

The two other witnesses are the KGB prison warden and

the chief of guards—those very same people who expelled me from the courtroom. Thus it is entirely understandable that they noticed such minor details as what I held in my hands and what I said, but failed to hear how the prosecutor usurped the right to speak about socialist legality, losing his magisterial composure and hurling my brief to the floor. Migalyov [the prison warden] noticed my "categorical tone," but did not notice how the judge pounded his fists on the table and tried to shut me up or how he screamed "Enemy!" at me. These are not unimportant details. Experts in law with many years of experience suddenly lost their professional self-control. Doesn't this indicate that deep down they knew they were involved in an illegal matter and that they were so upset because they were being reminded of this?

I do not have any illusions about the verdict. You will, of course, award me the maximum penalty permitted by the law. But even if I were threatened not merely with compulsory labor and all the ensuing administrative misfortunes, but even with prison and forced labor, I would still say the same things here. There is no more terrible punishment than the agonies of a guilty conscience, no higher court of law than truth itself.

I have finished.

2
Letters from Yavas

Excerpts from the letters Mykhaylo Osadchy wrote
while he was confined at Camp No. 11 were obtained
by Vyacheslav Chornovil and included, together with
a bibliography of Osadchy's publications, examples of
his poetry, and his free renditions of Garcia Lorca,
in *The Misfortune of Intellect*. The letters are here
retranslated from the original Ukrainian.[7] Bracketed
notes signed with the initials "V. C." are Chornovil's.

[October 1966]
Volodya, my big request to you: do not write anything and
do not go to anyone with humble petitions because—apart
from your humiliation and my own—this does as much good
as last year's snow could do for the development of jet technology. Volodya, I said at [our?] confrontation and I wrote
that the court trial did not reveal any criminal intent in my
actions because even the most terrifying moral and psychological pressure cannot disclose something that never really was.
Thoroughly confused by my attorney, who was three times as
scared as I was and who was afraid to touch even slightly
upon the gist of the case, deprived of the basic documents
of Soviet legislation and juridical sources, in which I had never
taken an interest and which were simply denied to me here,
I found myself in a difficult situation, although my intuition
kept telling me: Something is wrong here, something is very

wrong; and I decided, therefore, no matter what sentence I might be handed, to deny in court everything that had been fabricated during the pre-trial interrogation. My truth was so convincing that even the Supreme Court withdrew practically all the charges, leaving only two incidents, which were not proven in any way either. In future letters I will possibly try to write you the contents of my statement to the Central Committee, which unfortunately hasn't been read by anyone because the time that it took for the reply to get to me and the time that my statement was en route to its destination were equal, ten days each way.[8] So if it spent ten days getting there, it must have taken ten days getting back, and who could have had the opportunity to learn what was in it?

Thus there isn't even any "formal" crime in my actions, Volodya, not to mention the question whether reading any kind of literature is a "crime." To give an example, I quote Article 19 of the Declaration of Human Rights, which I read for the first time here in camp:

Everyone has the right to freedom of opinion and expression; this right includes freedom to hold opinions without interference and to seek, receive and impart information and ideas through any media and regardless of frontiers.

The fact that my convictions did not clash with the official ones—this was not disputed even by the investigation, nor was I accused of this. The fact that I did not collect or impart any information except of a literary and artistic nature—this, too, was established by the investigation, and beyond this—nothing more. The fact that my trial was a whim of the small toe on the left foot of the powers that be—but what have I to do with that?

Volodya, please write to me, maybe you've learned more in Freedom, what am I supposed to confess? Something that I have not committed? If you have already sent that kind of letter, I think a way must be found to get it back.

Volodya, death, in this case my own, may be twenty or so

years nearer or farther away, but my life, even if I should be released at this very moment, has been cut short—so what does it matter? Volodya, I want you to understand that, in spite of all the trials and tribulations of fate, I shall be led by, my guiding star will be, my desire to be of service to my people. Ivan Franko wrote this once, and I shall repeat it to my dying day.

Yes, Volodya, my health has been seriously undermined. I think that in this respect even worse results must be expected. My prospects in life, which have already been curtailed, do not worry me much, because even if, through no fault of mine, I leave nothing behind in the way of lasting literature or literary criticism, still if my suffering should inspire at least the people who are close to me to greater flights of fantasy and urge them on to work—then I will know that my life has not been wasted.

The roar, the howling, and the grinding of machinery and lumber are affecting the state of my nerves and causing complications in both the new diseases and the old ones that I brought here with me. But I manage somehow to hold out and trust that I'll survive to cure my frail body at some later date. . . . By the way, the quote above is from the Declaration of Human Rights, which was promulgated by the United Nations General Assembly in 1948. Our government has ratified it. It goes without saying that having read here the comments on the Criminal Code, particularly on Article 62, I was even more astonished: what a tragic judicial error was deliberately made in deciding my fate; I don't mean the trial, because the honor of the uniform compelled them to act as they did, but the arrest itself and the difficult interrogation.

Everything passes, everything goes by when there is assured faith—I wrote that in some poem when I was nineteen or twenty. We've already had a few snow flurries, soon it will be winter, then spring and summer—that is the only pardon I shall have, the only truth I shall know, for no other comes to hand.

[14 February 1967]

. . . Lately I've been reading a lot of Goethe's poems about love. The old German obviously knew how to fall in love and how to live by the body and spirit of a woman. . . .

I've also read some very interesting articles in [the literary journals] *Novy mir,* No. 10, and *Neva,* No. 12. The article in the latter is titled "America and the Americans" and deals with intriguing aspects of urban-rural relations, intellectual trends, and popular customs and traditions. This was an essay, a new genre in our literature. I've also read Gatuyev's *Zelim-khan,* about the ruler of Ingushetiya and Chechniya, somewhat similar in style to Ivan Olbracht's *Nikola Šuhay—Robber.*[9] I felt a breeze of fresh mountain air, a sense of the human spirit's unlimited reach, and a longing to see unfettered action. What sweet joy—to feel spaciousness in your hands, your body, and above all your spirit—that sweet and fresh feeling of spaciousness that we value so little in our mindless childhood and squander so heedlessly.

Right now I want to learn as much as I can about Eastern literature. I have before me a small volume of poems by Makhtum-Kuli translated from the Turkmen.[10] How pleasant to feel embraced by his wisdom, experience, and insight into things. This feeling of mastery exalts a man and makes him more noble. . . .

[3 March 1967]

. . . I told them here how little Taras would catch reflections of sunbeams on the floor. Funny. . . . You know, no matter how I strain my memory, I just can't picture in my mind's eye what he looks like or how he takes his first stumbling steps. . . . Write to me in detail about everything the child does. . . .

I have selected *Snow-Gone Road* [a collection of poems by V. Mysyk—V.C.] as one of our best books of poetry in the last year, and Pluzhnyk gave me a sea of delight.[11]

[10 March 1967]

. . . I wondered today how the intellectuals—softhearted rabbits, stepchildren of society that they are—will look me in the eye?

. . . Were you surprised to receive the map of the ethnic composition of the Republic?[12] Let it wait at home for me until I return. Friends sent it to me, but such things are *verboten* here. . . .

There are complications with his [Bohdan Horyn's—V.C.] eyes, and the diagnoses are for the worst—total blindness. We don't tell him about this, but he's figured it out himself because he's educated.

. . . Spiritually I feel well, better, perhaps, than ever before.

. . . Read two very interesting articles in *Voprosy filosofii* [Problems of Philosophy], one about freedom of intellectual activity, the other about existentialism. This modern philosophical trend gives a man in my situation a great deal of moral satisfaction and lifts his spirits because it becomes the advocate of many strange and, at first glance, irrational human actions. I absorbed all of it with the greatest of pleasure.

[18 March 1967]

. . . Some of your letters, the tenth, the fifteenth, and the twentieth, are still wandering in the mail. High mountain passes. . . .

Have just finished reading Andriyashyk's novel *People of Fear*, and it left me dissatisfied.[13] The author's efforts to show the historical background of Western-Ukrainian life and customs before and after 1917 are so feeble that they actually burst the seams of his inadequate preparation and his hazy understanding of the true situation toward the end of the 1910's and the beginning of the 1920's. He himself has no clear knowledge of it, so what can be expected from the heroes he has released into the world? It's true that in places he attempts to get away from literary conjecture, and then some of his monologues and observations, though somewhat unnatural in

173

the mouths of characters of 1919, sound fresh, timely, and stirring in this day and age. These droplets of fresh dew on the hard-baked surface of the novel arouse in the reader a few thoughts of his own to compensate him for the time wasted on reading.

Roman Ivanychuk's novel *Thirst* in the first issue of *Dnipro* is likable in places, and some episodes are handled skillfully and with a knowledge of the subject and compassion for social ills.[14] But the composition is very shaky, and the ending is false, with the result that the heights the author rises to prove to be only snowmen, which quickly melt and collapse.

Korney Chukovsky's *My Whitman* is quite interesting,[15] and there's a very attractive article by one Shenkman in *Voprosy filosofii*, No. 12 for 1966, about freedom of intellectual endeavors, including writing, not as an expression of a social assignment, but as a gain for men's humanistic ideals, which connect their past with their present and intertwine their present with their future. A writer stands above the social demands of the day and hence is often ostracized or even worse. Such, approximately, are the thoughts of the article.

As you see, I'm stuffing my battered head and dreaming of doing independent literary work in translations, poetry, and literary criticism, but my wings have been clipped. It doesn't matter, however. The last issue of *Literaturna Ukrayina* brings Kozlanyuk's letters,[16] and in one of them—to a sweetheart—Kozlanyuk asks her to reassure his mother with these words: Tell her that even Napoleon had to endure prison. With the same thought I console you, too, my beloved Oksana. . . .

[April 1967]

. . . Guillaume Apollinaire is now settling on the "solid-gold" shelves of my memory. As morning separates day from night, so he has clarified for me many questions about the sources of Mieželaitis, the greatest contemporary poet of the Soviet Union.[17] His poetry is not merely an echo of Apollinaire's experiences, moods, thoughts, and rhythmic structure, but whole handfuls of images that Mieželaitis took from Apollinaire the way I stuffed inside my shirt front the sweet pears I stole from old Stepanyda. For example, Mieželaitis's collection *Man* has a poem titled "Hands" with this line: "My days are dying like people, how sad it is to bury them. . . ." Apollinaire writes: "J'ai eu le courage de regarder en arrière / Les cadavres de mes jours / Marquent ma route. . . ."[18] I can't make any more comparisons because I don't have *Man* at hand, nor do I reproach Mieželaitis; I only say how late poetic revelations reach the consciousness and imagination of naïve poets. . . .

Strange dreams possess my mind: I'm either in a library or in the cooler. This is probably because I've developed an adult longing for a well-furnished library. The kind the Romans said that the dead speak in. I can smell at a distance the paper pollen of libraries and anticipate the wise tranquility and the sweet moments of discovering spiritual truths that they bring. . . .

My dear, it's not my fault at all that the telegram I dispatched on 30 March was delivered only on 3 April. O mighty gods, what are you doing to us mortals?

3
The Persecuted of the Regime

Political prisoners who emerge from the labor camps are usually unable to get any but the most unskilled jobs, even if they have higher degrees, and a secret part of the "Identity-Card Regulations" prevents them from settling within a hundred kilometers of big cities or in ports and border areas. Mykhaylo Osadchy was no exception: he was not given a permit to live in Lviv for quite some time after his release, which meant that the police could detain him when he tried to visit his wife and son, and when he finally did find work, it was in a factory and then a newspaper archive.

A vivid picture of the demi-monde that ex-convicts inhabit emerges from "The Persecuted of the Regime." Signed with the initials "P. Ts." and presumably written in Lviv in the spring of 1968, the document circulated as bootleg literature before reaching the West.[19]

The iron-curtain policy entirely suited both Soviet State and Party leaders and Great Russian chauvinists. Behind such a curtain they could, during the thirties, commit with impunity acts of lawlessness not merely against groups or individuals, but also against entire nations. In the forties and early fifties, Stalin's arbitrariness reached an apogee. Even without Party directives, judges and people's assessors knew in advance that whoever came before the court was an enemy of the people and could not be awarded less than twenty-five years of strict-regime camps.

Stalin had reasons for such forms of punishment: he must have realized that he would not manage to build a happy socialist society—which he had so readily promised the world after Lenin's death—with bare ideas and Party resolutions. Needing a material basis to compete with capitalism, Stalin tried to build one as quickly as possible and at minimum cost: in the conditions of the Soviet Union, using the manpower of innocently convicted people. But these convictions were only for "foreign consumption," and those sentenced seldom returned from the camps.

Khrushchev and today's Party leaders have, in this respect, been compelled by pressure from the whole world to show greater honesty. When even the most closed trials are powerless to keep the regime's lawlessness secret, when messages reach the outside even from the most remote camps, the lackeys of the regime resort to other methods of destroying their opponents and subduing sound thought.

Let us demonstrate the "humaneness" of the autocratic regime's lackeys by the example of Mykhaylo Osadchy. Born in 1936, Mykhaylo Osadchy was a Ukrainian journalist and Senior Lecturer in the Department of Journalism at Lviv State University. He was arrested unjustifiably in August 1965 and held in prison until April 1966, although the Code of Criminal Procedure of the Ukrainian SSR now in force permits preliminary detention for no more than two months. On 18 April 1966 Osadchy was sentenced by the Lviv Provincial Court at a judicial session held *in camera* to two years' deprivation of liberty in strict-regime camps for "anti-Soviet agitation and propaganda" (meaning: for reading a few sheets of "bootleg literature").

Inhuman conditions in the political camps undermined the young man's health, while the guards managed to confiscate from him translations done in the camp and his own poetry. After serving his term, Osadchy returned to life with bright hopes of making up for the time which had been forcibly taken from him. But he was due for a greater disappointment than he had expected. Immediately after his return from the camp, in November 1967, he was "put to the test" as a witness in the trial of Vyacheslav Chornovil (the author of *The Misfortune of Intellect*).

Osadchy's truthful testimony did little to satisfy the stage managers of the trial and earned him no concessions. His right to reside in Lviv, where his wife lives with their young son, was not restored to him after his release from prison. Osadchy is still not registered anywhere for permanent residence, and those who are not registered are not accepted anywhere for work.

The KGB keeps a careful watch on his wife's flat in Lviv. As soon as Osadchy dares to come home in order to visit Tarasyk, his small son, the KGB men burst into the flat, levy a fine on his wife, and throw him out. Similarly, they fine and threaten those of his acquaintances who receive him in their homes.

Thieves and swindlers who find themselves in a similar situation after serving their terms of punishment commit new crimes in order to get to prison where they can receive some sort of rations and stave off death by starvation. But Mykhaylo Osadchy is no enemy, no murderer, no criminal—he is an honest worker, an able journalist, and a man of intelligence, and so he has to suffer the fate of an exile in his own country and be a beggar among those poor people on behalf of whom he raised his voice.

4

In Defense of
Svyatoslav Karavansky

More brushstrokes were added to the picture by Osadchy's spirited letters to the authorities. In September 1969 Svyatoslav Karavansky, a linguist and translator who had served time with Osadchy in the Mordovian camps, was transferred from Vladimir Prison to the KGB prison in Kiev and charged under Article 62 with having smuggled out of Vladimir petitions to the authorities. In Soviet law, prisoners may be investigated without being released at the end of their old terms. This provision is used as a selective, sometimes bewilderingly arbitrary weapon against political dissenters. The trials are conducted without a defense attorney or courtroom spectators, and the witnesses are usually camp guards and other prisoners.

When news of Karavansky's plight reached the outside in December 1969, Osadchy joined his colleagues from the prisoners' dock and the camp barracks in writing a forceful—and in the circumstances, foolhardy —protest. Its text was made public by the *Ukrainian Herald* in January 1970 under the expressive title " 'Prison-Cell' Trials Again?"[20]

Comrade [Oleksandr] Lyashko,
Chairman of the Presidium,
Supreme Soviet of the Ukrainian SSR,
and Comrade [Fedir] Hlukh,
Public Prosecutor of the Ukrainian SSR

We, former political prisoners, are disturbed that in recent months repressions of people for their convictions have again intensified in Ukraine. We have in mind the trial in January 1969 of three workers at the Kiev Hydroelectric Station, the conviction in May of M. Beryslavsky for attempting to immolate himself, the arrests by the Lviv KGB of the scholars V. Ryvak and S. Bedrylo,[21] and other politically motivated arrests in Kiev, Lviv, Dnipropetrovsk, Novomoskovsk, and Kolomiya.

We are particularly disturbed that a new investigation was recently begun by the Republican KGB in the case of political prisoner S. Karavansky, accused of conducting "anti-Soviet agitation and propaganda" at Vladimir Prison.

After a respite of many years we are again witnessing the so-called "camp" (or "prison-cell") trial, that ugly offspring of Stalinist legality which condemns an already condemned man, without regard to his first sentence, to life imprisonment. We know from our own experience that practically every inmate in a prison or camp can be condemned for oral or written "agitation." We also know the legal value of such secret trials where the witnesses are prison guards and camp informers or where there are no witnesses and evidence at all.

Anticipating the stock accusations, we declare that we are not concerned with justifying or presenting our own evaluation of S. Karavansky's actions in 1944; nor are we speaking about the sentence he received then. We only note in passing the cruelty of a twenty-five-year sentence for a person who had not turned twenty-five himself, wisely nullified by Soviet law after Stalin's death. But no matter how official and un-official—backstage—propaganda attempts to defame S. Karavansky as it prepares a moral justification for a new reprisal against him, we still fail to understand what new crimes S. Karavansky committed after he became a free man in 1960, why his amnesty was annulled, or why he was forced in November 1965 to serve out the remainder of his illegal twenty-five-year sentence. We know that while he was a free man S. Karavansky worked productively as a translator and linguist and compiled a fundamental *Ukrainian Rhyming Dictionary.* His critical articles about language policies in Ukraine cannot in any way be termed anti-Soviet. Therefore, if S. Karavansky in camp or at the Vladimir Prison said or wrote something that the KGB considers to be "anti-Soviet," then the responsibility for such a Karavansky must be placed on the abnormal conditions of camp and prison confinement of a man who is capable of doing intellectual work. Hence the responsibility for the present Karavansky rests with those who treated him self-willedly (S. Karavansky's amnesty was annulled by the Public Prosecutor's Office at the request of the KGB). Can it be humane or just to demand in prison "correctness" and loyalty from a person subjected to such cruel injustice? And can the indisputable fact that the man was traumatized by lengthy imprisonment (twenty years!) be discarded from the scales of justice?

At present, a man who has almost five years left to serve of a twenty-five-year sentence is being threatened with a new sentence of indeterminate length. This is therefore not a matter of reeducating a man, but of physically destroying him. This will not be difficult to achieve. But do the initiators of this case concern themselves with the purely moral and human aspect of their actions?

On the basis of our own bitter experiences in camps and prisons (regardless of the fact that some of us have since been rehabilitated) and out of concern for the establishment of normal living conditions, which would be possible with a true renewal of socialist legality and socialist democracy, we consider it our moral right and civic obligation to raise before the highest governmental and judicial bodies the following questions:

1. Annulling statutes (particularly Article 2 of the Law of the Ukrainian SSR of 28 December 1960) which contradict the principle, accepted by Soviet jurisprudence, of retro-actively eliminating or mitigating punishment (Article 6 of the Criminal Code of the Ukrainian SSR), and thus make possible the imprisonment for twenty-five years of people convicted during the personality cult;

2. Releasing all those condemned to twenty-five years after they have served the present maximum of fifteen years, including political prisoner S. Karavansky, who spent more than twenty years in imprisonment after his first trial;

3. Prohibiting so-called "prison-cell" or "camp" trials as a possible regression to Stalin-Beria despotism;

4. Full publicity for all political trials as an important condition for maintaining legality and justice.

Iv[an] Hel—Sambir; Mykhaylo Osadchy, Vyacheslav Chornovil, Yaroslava Menkush, Olha Horyn, [Myroslava] Zvarychevska, B. Shastkiv—Lviv; Valentyn Moroz, Iryna Senyk, Oksana Popovych, Lyubov Lesnyk—Ivano-Frankivsk; B[ohdan] Horyn—Khodoriv; O[ksana] Meshko, B. Khudenko, Iv[an] Rusyn —Kiev; V[olodymyr] Ivanyshyn—Irkutsk.

5

Continuing Persecution

In 1970 the *Ukrainian Herald* brought even more frightening news: not only was Osadchy himself being harassed, but his name was being used to intimidate those who might be starting to question the order of things.[22]

Illegal questionings—without presentation of a summons or an official deposition—have frequently occurred in Lviv throughout 1969 and early 1970. Termed "conversations," these questionings are carried out by employees of the Provincial KGB, particularly by one Security officer who calls himself Borys Ivanovych. As a rule, the KGB has no factual basis to question the people it calls in. The KGB is obviously interested in intimidating a certain group of people and hopes that in the course of such a "fishing expedition" the questioned person will say something of interest. The people who are summoned do not know that the questioning is illegal and that they have a right not to take part. Here is a list of the questions asked: "Who are your friends and acquaintances? Where are you planning to spend your summer vacation? Have you read Honchar's *The Cathedral* or Ivanychuk's *The Hollyhocks?* Do you have these books, and what is your opinion of them? With whom is your wife or daughter on friendly terms? Are you acquainted with Osadchy (Chornovil, B. Horyn)? Why are you on intimate terms with them? Don't you have anyone else to be friends with? Have you collected any money and for whom? Has anyone given you rubbish to read?" (The reference, of course, is to *samvydav*.)

Some people are blackmailed with questions about intimate affairs, although this is against the law. Some have been called in two or three times, and some are very intimidated by such unexpected summonses. There is precise information about the summoning of more than ten people. We cannot disclose their names because they have been cautioned not to tell anyone about being questioned.

> Six months later, the possibility of renewed KGB thuggery added a black tone to the already gloomy prospects.[23]

As we have reported in the past, the Lviv KGB continues to conduct illegal questionings, which it calls "conversations." Not having the right to name those who have been interrogated, we can mention the type of questions, which almost never change: "Who are your friends and acquaintances? What do you read? What do you talk about at the writers' workshop? Why are you friendly with Osadchy, Chornovil (sometimes B. Horyn or [Hryhoriy] Chubay[24])? What do they say to you, and what do they give you to read?"

Such questionings, which are not authorized by an official summons or deposition, are frequently accompanied by threats: "Do you know what we can do to you if we like?" Recent questioning of several students, engineers, and researchers is known about. Those questioned are warned not to tell anyone about being summoned to the KGB. Because of the serious nature of the incident, however, we must name one person. Lida Lanko, a correspondence-course student in her fourth or fifth year at the Literature Department [of Lviv University], told friends that the KGB man who questioned her was very insolent and hit her when she refused to confirm that she was friendly with someone (possibly H. Chubay). If the girl did not make this up to reinforce the effect of her story about the KGB, then this is the second incident in recent years after Major Halski beat Osadchy in 1965, when the Lviv KGB used physical force at an interrogation.

6

In Defense of Valentyn Moroz

When it was Valentyn Moroz's turn to face a second trial—after he had been a free man for all of nine months—Osadchy was prompted to a touching, but even more foolhardy, act of solidarity: he wrote a personal letter to the eminent writer Oles Honchar, asking him to use his authority to intercede on behalf of the young historian.[25] Then shortly before Moroz's trial, which was held on 17–18 November 1970, Osadchy joined Ihor Kalynets, Iryna Stasiv-Kalynets, Hryhoriy Chubay, Stefania Shabatura, Olha Horyn, and others in firing off a telegram to the Public Prosecutor's Office and to the Ivano-Frankivsk Provincial Court, demanding to be informed of the date of the trial— Soviet law requires that such trials be held in public— and to be given permission to attend it. The very next day, reports the *Ukrainian Herald*, those who had signed the telegram were summoned by their bosses and warned that a trip to Ivano-Frankivsk would mean summary dismissal from their jobs.[26]

———————

Lviv
7 July 1970

Comrade Oles Terentiyovych Honchar,
Chairman of the Writers' Union of Ukraine,
Deputy to the Supreme Soviet of the USSR

Dear Oles Terentiyovych:

Valentyn Moroz was arrested on 1 June 1970 in Ivano-Frankivsk, a city bearing the name of Ivan Franko, one of the most freedom-loving representatives of Ukrainian culture. I was informed of this sad event by the victim's wife. Preliminary queries indicate that Valentyn Moroz is accused of having been motivated by anti-Soviet feelings in his sharply controversial and well-written articles. These writings reflect like a kaleidoscope the urgent issues of contemporary Soviet life in the areas of national relations, education, morality, honor, and the pride that our citizens feel for their national and cultural heritage, and for the artistic traditions of the great and talented Ukrainian people.

Those members of the intelligentsia who have, in one way or another, become acquainted with Valentyn Moroz's writings have been roused by the diversity of his subject matter, its topical and controversial nature, and its fiery style to heated discussions on the need to carry on the glorious traditions in the arts and in the social actions of the industrious and freedom-loving Ukrainian people.

These very themes, Oles Terentiyovych, ring clearly in your own recent works, particularly in your novels *The Cathedral* and *The Cyclone*. Even such alarming problems as the scattering and huckstering of Hutsul folk art resound in both your own fiction and the articles of Valentyn Moroz. This is the most eloquent proof that Valentyn Moroz is a young, socially sensitive writer who confronts the important problems of today—those very same problems that bring pain and concern to

187

you, a talented writer respected and honored by our people, our teacher and mentor.

Dear Oles Terentiyovych!

I am not a personal friend of Valentyn Moroz. I even disagree with some of his controversial ideas and rash generalizations. But I am above all Valentyn Moroz's peer. I am hurt by the low moral prestige that our country—yours and mine—presents to the world when it isolates from society people for whom courage and the expression of their individuality have become guarantees of honesty in social involvement.

I appeal to you, a Deputy to the Supreme Soviet of the USSR, to do everything possible to assure that Valentyn Moroz's case will be placed under the effective control and protection of our citizens. Moral authority and power must be used to demand that:

1. Valentyn Moroz publicly declare that he is not being beaten or subjected to psychological pressure;

2. The texts of Valentyn Moroz's articles, which have been declared anti-Soviet, be made public;

3. An objective and unbiased commission of the most qualified writers be formed and that this commission provide a true, and not pre-paid, analysis and evaluaton of the writings of Valentyn Moroz;

4. The case of Valentyn Moroz be made a matter of public record.

I appeal to you in the name of humanism, of our native Ukrainian culture and literature, and of socialist legality.

Yours,

Mykhaylo Osadchy

7
More Harassment

The picture of cat-and-mouse freedom and unremitting surveillance was further delineated by the *Ukrainian Herald* in January 1971.[27]

More than three years after his return from imprisonment the writer and journalist Mykhaylo Osadchy is still suffering persecution. At first he was not permitted to live with his family in his Lviv flat. The militia would catch him at night, and he was even arrested for several days for "breaking identity-card regulations." In recent months he has been persecuted for signing protests against the "prison-cell" trial of S. Karavansky and the arrest of V. Moroz. M. Osadchy was called in to the Provincial Party Committee, where he was brutally dressed down and threatened.

In August 1970, Osadchy's sister-in-law was not admitted to the Lviv Printing Trade School even though she had passed her exams and had sufficiently high marks. She was told that she had not been admitted because of her brother-in-law and also because her mother's first husband (not her father) had been a Banderite. The rector of the institute failed to obey instructions from the Ministry to admit the girl. When Osadchy wrote a statement about this shocking incident to the Party Provincial Committee, he was called in, told that his statement was written in the spirit of BBC broadcasts, and threatened with a new arrest.

When M. Osadchy was taking a bus to visit his wife's relatives in the country, a KGB man was assigned to follow him. The agent at first tried to strike up provocative "anti-Soviet" conversations, then right on the bus, having polished off two bottles of wine, confessed to Osadchy who he was and why he had been sent to follow him, and in the presence of the other passengers repented that he was doing such dirty work. When Osadchy was returning from the village the next day, the KGB man, who had obviously sobered up and come to regret his frankness, set the militia on Osadchy. M. Osadchy was dragged by force from the bus at the town of Radekhiv, detained for some time at the district militia station, although no complaint had been lodged against him, and threatened with punishment for unknown crimes.

8
And Rearrest

So the actual arrest, reported by the *Ukrainian Herald* in March 1972, was no surprise. On 12 January, a "wave of arrests and house searches," surpassed only by the one of 1965 and apparently intended by the KGB to wipe out bootleg literature, had caught up an unusually large number of writers and university staff. In Kiev, thirteen people were arrested and eight had their flats searched. In Lviv, nine people were subjected to searches and five were arrested. Among them was Mykhaylo Osadchy.[28]

Only the scantiest details of Osadchy's second trial, held on 4–5 September 1972, have reached the West. The publication of *Cataract* in West Germany the previous year and the adoption of Osadchy as a prisoner of conscience by Amnesty International would have probably annoyed the authorities. Unable to prove that he had transmitted his manuscript abroad, the court (meeting again in closed session) found Osadchy guilty of writing "nationalist" poetry, some of which had been confiscated in a search at his flat. The sentence, in any case, was maximal: seven years of strict-regime camps, to be followed by three (some sources say five) years of exile.

As this book goes to press, in the summer of 1975, there has been a report that several prominent prisoners—including Osadchy, Svitlychny, and Chornovil—have been brought back from the Mordovian camps to KGB prisons in Ukraine.[29] Osadchy, the report goes,

is being held at the Lviv prison where he is being subjected to intensive interrogation as part of a plan to
extract a repentance from him (obtaining an admission
of guilt from a sentenced prisoner is one of the KGB's
primary objectives) or to file a new charge against him
while at the same time creating the impression that
he will soon be released. Also, the *Ukrainian Herald,*
which has managed to surface after two years' sub-
mersion, disclosed that in the spring of 1973 Osadchy's
name was placed on a KGB blacklist of writers who
may not be mentioned in the Soviet press.[30]

The picture is not complete, but the outline is clear
enough: Mykhaylo Osadchy's education is still not
finished. There will yet be laughter in paradise.

NOTES

Notes to Introduction

1. Ivan Dzyuba, *Internationalism or Russification? A Study in the Soviet Nationalities Policy*, 2nd ed. (London: Weidenfeld and Nicolson, 1970; New York: Monad Press reprint, 1974), p. 5.

2. Victor Swoboda, "The Ukraine," in George Schöpflin, ed., *The Soviet Union and Eastern Europe: A Handbook* (New York: Praeger Publishers, 1970), pp. 213–214. Much of the available material on the 1961 and 1965 arrests is analyzed and translated in Michael Browne, ed., *Ferment in the Ukraine* (New York: Praeger Publishers, 1971; New York: Crisis Press reprint, 1973).

3. *Ferment in the Ukraine*, p. 145. An example of growing public opinion was an appeal to Brezhnev, Kosygin, and Podgorny in April 1968 signed by 139 citizens of Kiev from all walks of life, including prominent writers and intellectuals. The letter expressed alarm about violations of the law during political trials. "An ominous circumstance," said the letter, "is that in many cases the defendant is charged with views . . . which are in no way anti-Soviet in character, but are merely critical of certain manifestations in our public life. . . . The political trials held in recent years are becoming a form of suppression of those who do not conform in their thinking. . . . In the Ukraine, where violations of democracy are magnified and aggravated by distortions in [the field of] the nationality question, the symptoms of Stalinism are manifested even more overtly and grossly." For the complete text, see *Ferment in the Ukraine*, pp. 191–196.

The disturbance of somnolent public opinion has also led to the phenomenal growth of uncensored literature. The Russian *Chronicle of Current Events* began to appear in Moscow in 1968. Its Ukrainian counterpart, the *Ukrainian Herald*, was founded in 1970. These two publications represent the first known efforts at a free press in the Soviet Union since the last few independent papers were suppressed on Lenin's order in 1918. Limiting themselves to a sober record of what was happening to dissidents at the hands of the KGB, these two journals were both an expression of awakening public protest against arbitrary repressions and a stimulus to its further development. The first eleven issues of the *Chronicle* are available in Peter Reddaway, ed., *Uncensored Russia: Protest and Dissent in the Soviet Union* (New York: Heritage Press, 1972). Only fragments from the *Ukrainian Herald* have so far appeared in English.

4. The two dossiers circulated widely among Ukrainian intellectuals and then were smuggled to the West a few pages at a time. The first dossier appeared as *Ya nichoho u vas ne proshu* [I Ask for Nothing from You] (Toronto: 1968); the second as *Lykho z rozumu* [The Misfortune of Intellect] (Paris: P.I.U.F., 1967). The two appeared in English (with some omissions and in a rather inexpert translation) as *The Chornovil Papers* (New York, Toronto, London: McGraw-Hill, 1968). Most of my quotations from Chornovil are retranslated from the original. Details of Chornovil's trial in November 1967 and several additional documents by him are in *Ferment in the Ukraine*, pp. 157–171.

5. The memorandum was sent to twenty-five regional Party secretaries for comment, and copies soon began to circulate among Ukrainian intellectuals. When one of these reached the West it was published as *Internationalism or Russification?*; see note 1 above.

6. Bohdan Stanchuk, *What I. Dzyuba Stands For, and How He Does It* (Kiev: 1970). Stanchuk's attack is subjected to a thorough analysis in a postscript to the second edition of *Internationalism or Russification?*

7. After *Literaturna Ukrayina* (9 November 1973) carried a recantation by Dzyuba (somewhat ambiguously worded: he did not actually condemn his book), the Presidium of the Supreme Soviet of the Ukrainian SSR found it possible to grant him a pardon and to permit him to work on an

"extended critical analysis of *Internationalism or Russification?*"

8. "Report from the Beria Reserve" was smuggled out of the camps, typed out by Chornovil, and forwarded by him to four deputies of the Ukrainian Supreme Soviet before reaching the West. A translation is available in *Ferment in the Ukraine,* pp. 119–153. There are also two book editions which include Moroz's other essays: John Kolasky, ed., *Report from the Beria Reserve* (Toronto: Peter Martin Associates; Chicago: Cataract Press, 1974); and Yaroslav Bihun, ed., *Boomerang* (Baltimore: Smoloskyp Publishers, 1974). None of the translations is entirely satisfactory, and my quotations from Moroz are usually retranslated from the original.

9. *Report from the Beria Reserve,* p. 25; *Boomerang,* pp. 31–32. "Totalizator" was a KGB officer's way of telling Moroz that he was opposed to totalitarianism.

10. *Report from the Beria Reserve,* pp. 116–120; *Boomerang,* pp. 1–4.

11. For an eye-witness report of the Kiev fire, see *Problems of Communism,* July–August 1968, p. 15. The text of the Pogruzhalsky article is in *Suchasnist',* 1965, no. 2, pp. 78–84. An abridged translation is in *Atlas,* January 1966, pp. 36–38.

Two further library fires on 26 November 1968 strengthened suspicions about the role played by the authorities in the Academy Library fire. In the Vydubetsky Monastery in Kiev 150,000 volumes of a Hebraic collection, as well as Ukrainian archives saved from the 1964 fire, were destroyed. The other fire gutted the Great Synagogue in Odessa with its library of Jewish documents. See P. Grose, "Archive Fires in Ukraine Stirring Suspicions of a Plot," *New York Times,* 20 February 1969.

Prolog Research Institute in New York has reported that there were another three fires in the Vydubetsky Monastery, two in mid-December 1968 and one in January 1969. There are also reports that Pogruzhalsky, sentenced for arson to five years in prison and five years in a labor camp, did not in fact serve his sentence.

12. *Ferment in the Ukraine,* p. 164.

13. This was my own understanding until Wolfram Burghardt, of the University of Western Ontario, found the key to these passages. Osadchy may have taken the basic idea for the crypt scene from Taras Shevchenko's dramatic poem, *Velyky Lyokh* [The Great Grave], in which Ukrainian freedom lies buried in a vault.

Notes to Part One

1. Panteleymon Kulish (1819–1897): prolific writer, scholar, and translator. Soviet orthodoxy often castigates him as a "reactionary Romantic" and a "founder of Ukrainian bourgeois nationalism," and his historical researches are not available in the USSR. But *The Black Council* (1857), a novel in the manner of Sir Walter Scott, has been held up to Soviet readers for its "exposition of class conflicts" among Ukrainian Cossacks in the 1650's, and it was included in his *Vybrani Tvory* [Selected Writings] (Kiev: Dnipro, 1969). There is an English translation by George S. N. and Moira Luckyj, with an introduction by Romana Bahrij Pikulyk (Littleton, Colorado: Ukrainian Academic Press, 1973).

2. Mykhaylo Hrushevsky (1866–1934): eminent Ukrainian statesman and historian. Deported from Ukraine in 1931, Hrushevsky died in circumstances suggesting murder. He was partially "rehabilitated" in 1966, but his *History of Ukrainian Literature* (five vols., 1923–1927), his monumental *History of Ukraine-Rus'*, and his many shorter treatments are officially condemned for not interpreting history as a class struggle and for "attempting to deny that the Ukrainian and Russian peoples struggled jointly against tsarism and capitalism."

3. Bohdan Lepky (1872–1941): Western Ukrainian poet, short-story writer, and novelist, best known for his historical novel *Mazepa* (1926), which is proscribed in the USSR for "showing Ukraine's past in a nationalist perspective."

4. The Lviv KGB headquarters and "isolator"—the special prison for political detainees and espionage suspects—are located at One Peace Street in a former Polish jail.

5. Valentyn Malanchuk (b. 1928): seasoned Party historian and ideologist, hard-line promoter of "internationalism"—that is, Russification—in Ukraine; since October 1972 Third Secretary of the Central Committee of the Communist Party of Ukraine, in charge of "agitation and propaganda."

6. Ostap Vyshnya (pen name of Pavlo Hubenko, 1889–1956): extraordinarily popular Ukrainian satirist and humorist. In the Party drives against "bourgeois nationalism" and indigenous traditions in Ukrainian literature in the early 1930's, Vyshnya was labeled, among other things, a "kulak jester" whose "fame was artificially inflated by the nationalists." On 26 December 1933 Vyshnya was arrested on a trumped-up charge of terrorist activities and sentenced to death, but this was commuted to ten years in a labor camp. In 1943 Vyshnya was brought back to Kiev to help with his writings in the war effort and forced to deny publicly that he had ever been imprisoned.

7. Ivan Svitlychny (b. 1929): one of the most influential of the younger critics, Svitlychny became widely known in the early 1960's for his translations of French poetry and his spirited articles on the poetry of the Sixtiers. Arrested for protesting against the arrests of 1965, Svitlychny was detained by the KGB for eight months but released without trial. Remaining under police surveillance, he nevertheless managed to obtain and to forward to the West a collection of letters and petitions smuggled out of the Mordovian camps: *Ukrayins'ka inteligentsia pid sudom KGB* [Ukrainian Intellectuals on Trial by the KGB] (Munich: Suchasnist', 1970).

These documents revealed for the first time the details of several waves of arrests and trials in Western Ukraine. The most significant of these was the case of a group of lawyers who had discussed the possibility of conducting peaceful propaganda in favor of Ukraine's secession from the USSR. Although their aim was implicitly constitutional, the lawyers were indicted for treason, tried in 1961 in total secrecy, and sentenced to long terms in prison camps. In March 1972 Svitlychny himself was rearrested, tried on charges of anti-Soviet agitation and propaganda, and given the maximum sentence: seven years in labor camps and five years in exile.

Bohdan Horyn (b. 1936): literary and art critic, professor of design, research worker at the Lviv Museum of Ukrainian Art. Horyn was arrested, like his brother Mykhaylo and Osadchy, on 26 August 1965. On 18 April 1966 he was sentenced to three or four years in strict-regime camps. Released in 1968, he was not permitted to return to his former employment or to live in Lviv.

8. Oleksa Novakivsky (1872–1935): Western Ukrainian painter with a leaning toward impressionism. The book Osadchy borrowed was most likely V. Ostrovsky's *Oleksa Novakivsky* (Kiev: 1964).

9. Probably Elie Borschak's *Napoleon i Ukrayina* (Lviv: 1937), which details French plans for an independent Ukrainian state (*Napoleonida*).

10. Looking for an ally in his struggle against Polish rule, Bohdan Khmelnytsky, leader of the Ukrainian Cossacks, signed in 1654 the Treaty of Pereyaslav, under which Ukraine accepted the protection of the Muscovite tsar but remained a separate body politic. The treaty was vaguely formulated and led to considerable conflicts between Ukraine and Muscovy. Soviet historiography regards the treaty as a highly progressive act inaugurating the "reunification of Ukraine with Russia," and its tercentenary in 1954 was celebrated with a major propaganda campaign.

11. Vacation resorts at the height of the tourist season are one of the few places in the Soviet Union where people from different cities can meet without arousing suspicion. A group of Ukrainian activists, including Svitlychny, the Horyn brothers, and Mykhaylo Ozerny, planned a holiday trip to the Crimea to discuss the problems of the Ukrainian Movement. They were all arrested on the train before reaching Yevpatoria.

12. Article 62 of the Ukrainian Criminal Code states:

ANTI-SOVIET AGITATION AND PROPAGANDA. Agitation or propaganda carried on for the purpose of subverting or weakening Soviet authority or for the purpose of committing individual especially dangerous crimes against the State, or circulating for those purposes slanderous fabrications which defame the Soviet State and social system, or circulating, preparing or keeping for the same purpose literature of such content, is to be punished by deprivation of liberty for a term of from six months to seven years, with or without an additional period of exile for a term of from two to five years. The same acts committed by a person previously convicted of especially dangerous offenses against the State, or committed in wartime, are to be punished by deprivation of freedom for a term of from three to ten years, with or without an additional exile for a term of from two to five years. (E. L. Johnson, *An Introduction to the Soviet Legal System* [London: Methuen & Co., 1969], p. 154.)

It has not escaped the attention of the dissidents that Article 62 (and its equivalent in the Russian Code, Article 70) is worded so broadly that it contradicts Article 125 of the USSR Constitution, which guarantees freedom of speech and freedom of the press, and Article 19 of the Universal Declaration of Human Rights, which was ratified by the Soviet Union and the Ukrainian SSR and which states:

Everyone has the right to freedom of opinion and expression; this right includes freedom to hold opinions without interference and to seek, receive and impart information and ideas through any media and regardless of frontiers.

13. Ivan Michurin (1885–1935): Russian geneticist who adapted some three hundred species of plants to growth in colder climates.

14. The UHVR, or Ukrainian Supreme Liberation Council, was established in 1944 as the political arm of the Ukrainian Insurgent Army, which fought against both Nazi and Soviet encroachment.

15. Ivan Ostafiychuk (b. 1940): a painter and book

illustrator who studied at the Lviv Institute of Applied Arts, Ostafiychuk illustrated Osadchy's book, *A Moonlit Field*. After graduation Ostafiychuk was appointed an instructor at the Institute, but because of his involvement in Osadchy's case, the appointment was canceled and Ostafiychuk was sent to work in the Donbas region.

16. Petro Kalnyshevsky (1690–1803): commander of the Zaporozhian Cossacks in 1775 when their main encampment on an island in the Dnieper was sacked by a Russian army. Kalnyshevsky was exiled to solitary confinement in a monastery on the Solovetsky Islands in the White Sea, thus becoming a symbol of Ukrainian resistance. Pardoned by Tsar Alexander in 1801, Kalnyshevsky insisted on living out his days in the monastery.

17. Ivan Drach (b. 1936): one of the most gifted poets of the Sixtiers Group, he has also published translations and film scripts. For examples of his poetry in English, see Vladimir Ognev and Dorian Rottenberg (eds.), *Fifty Soviet Poets* (Moscow: Progress Publishers, 1969), pp. 170–173; *Four Ukrainian Poets: Drach, Korotych, Kostenko, Symonenko,* translated by Martha Bohachevsky-Chomiak and Danylo S. Struk, edited, with an introduction, by George S. N. Luckyj (New York: Quixote Press, 1969), pp. 1–21; and *Modern Poetry in Translation,* no. 9 (January 1971), pp. 1–3.

18. A running account of the bureaucrats' campaign against Dzyuba appears in the appendix to the second edition of *Internationalism or Russification?;* see p. 195.

19. Mykola Kholodny (b. 1939 or 1940): often regarded as the most popular poet of Ukrainian *samvydav*. His only legal publication was a small selection of poems (*Dnipro,* 1963, no. 3). He then ceased to be published because of his activity in the opposition movement, but two collections of his poetry have circulated privately. Kholodny was expelled in 1965 from Kiev University for his unorthodox poetry, and his protests thus effectively barred him from any occupation appropriate to his training and intellectual ability. In 1968 he was detained for two weeks for participating in a demonstration.

In March 1972 Kholodny was arrested and reportedly subjected to "psychiatric treatment" by the KGB. He was released after publishing a letter (*Literaturna Ukrayina,* 7 July 1972) in which he renounced his "politically erroneous" poems and named those who had exposed him to the "pernicious influence of bourgeois propaganda."

20. Mykola Khvylovy (pen name of Mykola Fitilov, 1893–1933): Ukrainian writer who achieved fame with stories about the Revolution. A communist by conviction, he satirized the ugly reality around him. This, and his pamphlets advocating cultural orientation toward Europe and away from Moscow, brought on a Party campaign against him and his numerous followers, culminating in the mass arrests and deportations of 1933, when, unrepentant, he committed suicide. Although many of his associates have been at least partly rehabilitated, Khvylovy remains firmly on the Soviet blacklist. See his *Stories from the Ukraine,* translated and with an introduction by George S. N. Luckyj (New York: Philosophical Library, 1960).

21. Azazello: a minor demon in Satan's retinue in Mikhail Bulgakov's novel *The Master and Margarita,* which satirizes the pharisaic mediocrities who dominate the Soviet literary world and whose chief official function is to discourage literary talent.

22. Simon Petlyura: leader of the Ukrainian Social-Democratic Workers' Party, prominent member of the Central Rada, the Ukrainian national government (1917–1918), chairman of the Directory (1919–1920), and commander in chief of the Ukrainian national armies from 1917 to 1920 against the Bolsheviks and White Guards. Assassinated in Paris by a Soviet agent.

Stepan Bandera (1909–1959): leader of a faction of the Organization of Ukrainian Nationalists (OUN), directed anti-Soviet forces in Ukraine in the late 1940s; assassinated in Munich by a Soviet agent. The term "Banderites" ("Banderovtsy" in translations of Solzhenitsyn) has become a Soviet pejorative for all Ukrainians suspected of nationalism.

Nestor Makhno (1884–1934): leader of an anarchist guerrilla

movement in southern Ukraine during the Civil War, emigrated to Paris in 1921.

23. The UPA, or Ukrainian Insurgent Army, was formed by the OUN in 1942 to fight for an independent Ukrainian state. It continued guerrilla actions against Polish communist and Soviet forces until the middle 1950's.

24. Yuliy Daniel and Andrey Sinyavsky, a critic (both born in 1925), identified as the authors of works published in the West since 1959 under the names of Nikolay Arzhak and Abram Tertz, were arrested in September 1965. They were tried before the Supreme Court of the RSFSR on 10–14 February 1966 under Article 70 of the Russian Criminal Code on charges of disseminating slanderous material defamatory of the Soviet State and social system. Daniel was sentenced to five years' deprivation of liberty and Sinyavsky to seven. They served parts of their sentences at Camp No. 11 in the Dubrovlag complex of "labor colonies" in the Mordovian "Autonomous Republic," where their fellow inmates were many of those sentenced in the Ukrainian trials, including Osadchy.

For a full account of the Sinyavsky/Daniel case see *On Trial: The Soviet State Versus "Abram Tertz" and "Nikolai Arzhak,"* translated, edited, and with an introduction by Max Hayward (New York: Harper & Row, 1966). The poetry Daniel wrote in confinement is in *Prison Poems by Yuli Daniel,* translated by David Burg and Arthur Boyars (London: Calder and Boyars, 1971). Sinyavsky's letters to his wife from the camp are in the forthcoming English translation of *Golos iz Khora* [A Voice from the Chorus]. For a description of Daniel at Camp No. 11 see Anatoly Marchenko, *My Testimony* (London: Pall Mall, 1969; Harmondsworth: Penguin, 1971), pp. 367–382 and 411–414.

25. Vitaliy F. Nikitchenko (b. 1908): Chairman of the Ukrainian KGB from 1954 until July 1970 when he was abruptly replaced by Vitaliy Fedorchuk (he had been elected a Deputy to the Supreme Soviet only a month before). Nikitchenko was officially given "responsible work" with the KGB in Moscow, but the fact that his successor replaced all the

provincial heads of the KGB in Ukraine indicates that the Moscow leadership was dissatisfied with Nikitchenko, possibly because his handling of the dissidents was excessively mild.

26. For the use of weeping and screaming (often recorded) as an instrument of psychological torture, see Aleksandr Solzhenitsyn, *The Gulag Archipelago, 1918–1956* (New York: Harper & Row, 1973), p. 107.

27. Drach is known to have personally applied to Party and State agencies for an explanation of the arrests in Ukraine in August–September 1965 and, as Osadchy and Chornovil (*The Chornovil Papers*, p. 72) testify, to have attempted to gain admission to the trials in Lviv in March–April 1966. Drach also signed three collective letters to the authorities, asking for an explanation of the arrests and appealing for publicity and fairness. For one of these, "The Appeal of the 139" (*Ferment in the Ukraine*, pp. 191–196), Drach was expelled from the Party, of which he had been a member since 1959.

Pressured to dissociate himself from "bourgeois nationalism," Drach finally published in *Literaturna Ukrayina* on 22 July 1966 a vituperative rebuttal to an émigré critic's interpretations of his poetry (Bohdan Kravtsiv, " 'Protuberantsi sertsya' i kredo Ivana Dracha" [*Protuberances of the Heart* and Ivan Drach's Credo], *Suchasnist'*, 1966, no. 1, pp. 5–25). Drach was then readmitted to the Party and took to writing versified lampoons against "bourgeois nationalists."

28. Taras Shevchenko (1814–1861): painter and poet, born a serf, whose work had an enormous effect upon the Ukrainian national movement. In 1845 Shevchenko joined with Kulish, the historian Mykola Kostomarov, and several others to form the radical Brotherhood of SS. Cyril and Methodius. Their program advocated the abolishment of serfdom, an end to religious and national hatred, and the establishment of a democratic union of Slavic peoples.

In 1847, after a denunciation by an informer, the Brotherhood was disbanded by the tsarist government. Kulish and the other members were punished by banishment to various cities within the empire. Shevchenko, whose manuscript poems had been found at the time of his arrest, was sentenced to penal army service in Central Asia, with a rider in the Tsar's own hand: "Under the strictest supervision and with a ban on writing and sketching."

29. Les Kurbas (1887–1942): leading Ukrainian stage producer, known for his expressionist experiments. He was deported to Siberia in 1933. He has since been rehabilitated, but a recent book on him—*Les' Kurbas: spohady suchasnykiv* [Les Kurbas: Recollections by Contemporaries] (Kiev: Mystetstvo, 1969)—manages to discuss Kurbas and even to include a detailed chronology of his life without once mentioning that he was arrested and died in a labor camp.

Mykhaylo Dray-Khmara (1889–1939?): poet, philologist, critic, and translator, member of the Neoclassic Group. Arrested and deported in 1935, he died in the Kolyma labor camps.

30. The twenty-five-year sentence was introduced in 1947 by Stalin to replace the death penalty, which had been abolished as a humane act. The present maximum is fifteen years.

31. Vasyl Kozachenko (b. 1913): Ukrainian prose writer and ideological boss of the Ukrainian Writers' Union. He was deputy chairman of the Union at the time of this account, now chairman. Kozachenko is also known for his vitriolic attacks on Ivan Svitlychny before the latter's arrest and on the signatories of the "Appeal of the 139."

32. The first of the series of trials of those arrested in 1965 was held late in January 1966 in the Volyn Provincial Court at Lutsk. The accused were two lecturers at the Lutsk Teachers' College: Dmytro Ivashchenko (b. 1920?), a lecturer in Ukrainian literature, and Valentyn Moroz (b. 1936), a historian. The indictment was for "propaganda directed at separating Ukraine from the USSR." Ivashchenko was sentenced to two years of labor camp, Moroz to four.

33. Whatever his role in Osadchy's case, Sandursky was himself subjected to repressions: in June 1966 he was dismissed from his post as lecturer in the social sciences at the

Lviv Agricultural Institute and remained for a time unemployed.

34. Mykhaylo Horyn (b. 1930): teacher of Ukrainian literature and school inspector, later industrial psychologist. Arrested on 26 August 1965, he was tried in Lviv with his brother Bohdan and with Osadchy under Article 62 (the actual charge was reading and passing on to one or two colleagues four Ukrainian books published abroad and possessing four manuscript articles). On 18 April 1966 Horyn was sentenced to six years in strict-regime camps. An abridged translation of his closing statement at his trial and excerpts from letters from camp are in *The Chornovil Papers,* pp. 105–116.

In December 1966 Horyn was put for six months into the camp prison for having Dzyuba's *Internationalism or Russification?,* although KGB agents in the camp admitted to his brother that it was not an anti-Soviet document. For writing a protest to the camp administration against ill-treatment of a prisoner's mother who came to the camp in June 1967, Horyn was transferred in July 1967 for three years to the Vladimir Prison, notorious for its appalling conditions (*Ferment in the Ukraine,* pp. 108–109: see p. 195 above). Horyn is also author of a letter to the Minister of Foreign Affairs of the Ukrainian SSR, protesting ill-treatment of Ukrainian political prisoners in the Mordovian camps and forced assimilation of Ukrainians living outside the Ukrainian SSR (*ibid.,* pp. 110–115), and of a letter to the UN Human Rights Commission, appealing to it to stop the drugging of prisoners' food (*ibid.,* p. 216).

35. Chornovil's description throws additional light on this incident: "I had a chance at the trial of the Horyn brothers, [Osadchy], and Zvarychevska to get acquainted with the public prosecutor of the Lviv Province, Antonenko. (He is also a writer and the author of a book about the valiant Cheka agents and the supreme justice of our courts.) I declared that I would not give any evidence at a *closed trial* because I did not wish to participate in a flagrant violation of socialist legality and at the same time presented flowers from their

friends to the people unlawfully condemned. Then the prosecutor jumped up and in a high-pitched voice called me an *enemy* who had no right to speak about socialist legality. Soldiers were ordered to remove me from the courtroom, and they performed their offensive operation with such lightning speed that I did not have enough time to open my mouth. But I had a great desire to ask the prosecutor, a writer, why it is that I, who was protesting against the revival of lawlessness similar to the cult-of-personality days—the closed tribunal—am branded an enemy, while he, who in his capacity as the provincial public prosecutor sanctioned this gross violation of the letter and spirit of our laws, claims to be a friend of the Soviet system." (*Ya nichoho u vas ne proshu*, p. 70; *The Chornovil Papers*, pp. 35–36.)

For the text of Chornovil's brief and the consequences of his refusal to testify against Osadchy, see p. 157.

36. Valentyn Moroz's account of this incident is worth quoting here: "A student of the Lutsk Teachers' College, Anatoliya Panas, who appeared as a witness at the trial, dared to describe the reign of chauvinism in the Crimea where she did her practice teaching in Ukrainian literature. Her colleagues called her a *Banderite* to her face and openly declared: 'If Lenin were still alive he would gag that national riffraff' and advised her not to speak Ukrainian, 'if you wish to be on good terms with us.' Article 66 of the Criminal Code of the Ukrainian SSR states:

Propaganda or agitation for the purpose of arousing hostility or dissension between races or nationalities, or the direct or indirect restriction of rights or the establishment of direct or indirect privileges for citizens depending on the races or nationalities to which they belong, shall be punished by deprivation of freedom for a term of six months to three years, or by exile for a term of two to five years.

"No one mentioned any punishment for the chauvinists in the Crimea, but the student who dared to testify on behalf of the law and her national dignity was failed in her state examinations." (*Report from the Beria Reserve*, p. 40; *Boomerang*, p. 46: see p. 197 above.)

37. Yaroslav Kendzyor, a Lviv trade union employee, is known as a signatory of the "Appeal of the 139." On 8 January 1968 the KGB searched his apartment and confiscated Kulish's *The Black Council* and an "Open Letter to the Editors of *Literaturna Ukrayina.*" Kendzyor is also reported to have protested to the Ukrainian Supreme Court the harsh punishment meted out to Moroz, demanding repeal of the sentence and immediate release of the condemned man. On 12 January 1972, at the time of Osadchy's second arrest, his apartment, as well as the apartments of his parents and parents-in-law, was searched again.

38. Myroslava Zvarychevska (b. 1936): after obtaining a degree in Ukrainian literature from Lviv University, Zvarychevska worked at the university library, as a newspaper proofreader, and as a copy editor at the Provincial Archives. She was arrested on 24 August 1965, tried together with Osadchy by the Lviv Provincial Court under Article 62, and sentenced on 18 April 1966 to eight months of imprisonment. Unemployed for a while after serving her term, she then began to teach school in Lviv.

39. From "To a Fellow Prisoner," written at the Fortress of Orsk in 1847. *The Poetical Works of Taras Shevchenko*, translated by C. H. Andrusyshen and Watson Kirkconnell (Toronto: University of Toronto Press, 1964), p. 318.

40. Lina Kostenko (b. 1930): poet, prominent member of the Sixtiers Group. Frequently charged by Soviet critics with "formalism" and "detachment from Soviet reality," she ceased to be published in the mid-sixties when she became active in the opposition movement, sought to gain admission to the closed trials in Kiev and Lviv and signed appeals for publicity and judicial fairness. Translations of her poetry are available in *Four Ukrainian Poets*, pp. 43–63.

41. Iryna Vilde (pseudonym of Daryna Polotnyuk, b. 1907): Western Ukrainian novelist and short-story writer, began publishing in 1927. Deputy to the Supreme Soviet of the

Notes

Ukrainian SSR and chairman of the Lviv branch of the Writers' Union, Vilde was awarded the Shevchenko Prize for her novel *Sestry Richyns'ki* [The Richynsky Sisters] (1958–1964).

42. Mykola Petrenko: poet and colleague of Osadchy at the Lviv television studio, editor of Osadchy's book, *A Moonlit Field*. Petrenko was severely reprimanded for mentioning in a broadcast Roman Kudlyk, who had asked a question about the arrests of 1965 at a Writers' Union meeting, and his own book of poetry was stricken from the list of the Kamenyar Publishing House.

Roman Kudlyk (b. 1941): gifted young poet who has been publishing since 1957. Early in 1966 he was dismissed from the staff of the literary monthly *Zhovten'* [October] for his question about the arrests.

Ihor Kalynets (b. 1939): one of the finest poets of the young generation in Ukraine. Only his first book, *Vohon' Kupala* [The Fire of St. John's Eve] (Kiev: 1966), was published in the Soviet Union. Subsequent ones have circulated as bootleg literature and then been published abroad.

Upon the second arrest of Valentyn Moroz on 1 June 1970 Kalynets, along with Iryna Stasiv (who later became his wife), Lyudmyla Sheremetyeva, Yaroslav Kendzyor, and Yuriy Shukhevych, wrote a statement to the authorities protesting the arrest. Then, together with Osadchy, Stasiv, the poet Hryhoriy Chubay, the artist Stefania Shabatura, and Mykhaylo Horyn, he sent a telegram to the prosecutor of the Ukrainian SSR and the Ivano-Frankivsk Regional Court, demanding the date of Moroz's trial and permission to attend it. On 29 November Kalynets and Stasiv wrote to the Supreme Court of the Ukrainian SSR, protesting the closed nature of Moroz's trial and the injustice that was perpetrated upon him. They deplored the "unprecedented fact" of a person's being sentenced to fourteen years "for thinking."

Iryna Stasiv-Kalynets was arrested in January 1972 and charged under Article 62. In late July or early August she was sentenced to six years' imprisonment and three years' exile.

Ihor Kalynets was arrested in July 1972 and sentenced in November to nine years' imprisonment and three years' exile.

43. Markian Shashkevych (1811–1843): member of the "Ruthenian Triad" in Galicia (then part of Austro-Hungary). His program of cultural Ukrainianism initiated a modern literature based on the vernacular in Western Ukraine, stressing pride in the national past, calling for the ethnic unity of the Ukrainian lands, and pointing to the peasantry as the most valuable element in the contemporary national community. Shashkevych's programmatic poem, "Rus'ka mova," criticized those Ukrainian aristocrats and clergymen who had become Polonized or Germanized.

44. Ivan Franko (1856–1916): leading Western Ukrainian prose writer, poet, scholar, and journalist. He failed to secure an appointment to the Chair of Ukrainian Literature at Lviv University, although he was the best-qualified candidate, because of his socialist and agnostic views.

45. Mykhaylo Kosiv (b. 1934): a lecturer in Ukrainian literature at Lviv University, Kosiv was arrested in August or September 1965, but released without trial after five months, possibly because of a severe coronary thrombosis attack in prison. Unemployed for six months after his release, Kosiv was not permitted to return to the university and took up teaching in a village school.

46. Mykhaylo Masyutko (b. 1918): a retired teacher, Masyutko was arrested on 4 September 1965 and sentenced on 23 March 1966 to three years of prison and three years of strict-regime camps (commuted to six years of camp). In December 1966, together with Mykhaylo Horyn, Valentyn Moroz, and Levko Lukyanenko, Masyutko was sentenced to six months in the camp prison. In August 1967, he was transferred to Vladimir Prison for three years. Masyutko is the author of a lengthy letter to the Supreme Soviet of the Ukrainian SSR (*Ferment in the Ukraine*, pp. 97–107), in which he sets out the details of many political cases.

47. Aleksey Svirsky (1865–1942): Russian novelist, author

of *The Slums of Rostov* (1893), *Rudko* (1901), *Black Men* (1931), and the autobiography *The Story of My Life* (1928–1938).

48. Oleksiy Poltoratsky (b. 1905): literary careerist notorious for his political and moral turpitude ever since he published denunciations of Ostap Vyshnya, declaring that the popular writer was a kulak and a fascist agent and demanding that he be dealt with physically.

In an echo of the terminology of the 1930's, Poltoratsky published in *Literaturna Ukrayina* on 16 July 1968 an article titled "Whom Do Certain 'Humanitarians' Protect?" (*Ferment in the Ukraine*, pp. 200–204), in which he scurrilously attacked Vyacheslav Chornovil and Svyatoslav Karavansky, calling them "enemies and ideological saboteurs."

Notes to Part Two

1. Hanna Sadovska: a design engineer, she was arrested in Lviv in August or September 1965 and released after five months in detention without trial.

Yaroslava Menkush (b. 1923): arrested on 25 August 1965, she was sentenced on 25 March 1966 to two and a half years' imprisonment (later commuted to one year). She was released in August 1966 but not allowed to return to Lviv or to her former employment.

2. Semen Shakhovsky (b. 1909): Ukrainian critic and literary historian of a rather orthodox bent who was prominent in the 1930's in attacks on "bourgeois nationalists" which led to the deportation or death of numerous writers.

At his trial on 21 March 1966, Masyutko was accused of having written some "anti-Soviet stories" (they were about camps in the Kalmyk Steppe, where he had been a prisoner under the Stalin regime) and several anonymous "anti-Soviet" articles, including "The Trial of Pogruzhalsky." As a member of one of two panels of experts, which included Borys (not

Volodymyr) Zdoroveha, Pavlo Yashchuk, and Kybalchych, Shakhovsky asserted that Masyutko was the author of the articles in question on the basis of such tenuous stylistic and lexical features as the use of antithesis, rhetorical questions, the words "chauvinism" and "imperialism" in "hostile" contexts, the colon, and the pluperfect. On appeal, the Supreme Court of the Ukrainian SSR dismissed the commissions' findings but upheld the other charges of writing "anti-Soviet stories" and possessing and circulating the anonymous articles.

3. Vladimir Soloukhin (b. 1924): Russian journalist and author of poetic sketches, including "Back Roads of Vladimir District" (1962), an account of a journey into the deep interior of central Russia.

4. Volodymyr Vynnychenko (1880–1951): socialist politician and popular writer. The basic theme of many of his novels is a conception of amorality according to which "honesty with oneself" permits a person to disregard conventional morality.

5. Anton Oliynyk, a member of the OUN, was arrested in 1947 and sentenced to twenty-five years in a Far North labor camp. He escaped in 1955 but was caught in Ukraine and given a second twenty-five-year sentence, the first three years of which he served at Vladimir Prison. In the summer of 1965 Oliynyk escaped again, this time with Roman Semenyuk, a member of the UPA who had been arrested in 1950 and also condemned to twenty-five years. They were captured four months later in Rivne in Western Ukraine. Oliynyk was sentenced to death on a fabricated charge of mass murder (serving in the Gestapo when he was sixteen years old) and executed in Rivne in June 1966. Semenyuk was sent to Vladimir Prison, where he has taken part in numerous hunger strikes and protests.

For an epitaph on Oliynyk by a group of prisoners in Mordovia see *Ukrayins'ky visnyk, VI* (Paris: P.I.U.F.; Baltimore: Smoloskyp, 1972), pp. 110–113. For information on Semenyuk see *Uncensored Russia*, pp. 220–221, and *Ukrayins'ke slovo,* 1 June 1975.

6. Volodymyr Samiylenko (1864–1925): Ukrainian poet, translator, and author of satires and feuilletons on problems of the day.

7. *Chefir* (or *chifir*) is a powerful stimulant brewed from tea by the zeks.

8. A prison sentence is a more severe punishment than a term in camp. The most notorious prison, reserved for particularly dangerous political prisoners, is in the historic city of Vladimir. For an account of conditions there see Marchenko, *My Testimony*, pp. 103–204.

9. Is this Ivan Hirchanovsky? Cf. Mykhaylo Horyn's account in a letter to his wife: ". . . since Kharkiv, three of us have been living and traveling together: myself, Osadchy, and an old man [illegible] years old, who comes from Berezhany—by the name of Ivan Vasylovych Hirchanovsky. He was convicted for collaborating with the Germans and for being a member of the OUN. It appears that old cases, covered by twenty or twenty-five years of historical dust, are being revived again. Doesn't it look like a repetition of the last days of Khvylovy?

"Night. I cannot sleep because it is terribly cold. Sleeping on just a mattress, without a blanket, in a cellar with a concrete floor, is unbelievably cold even in summer. I didn't know about this, nor about many other things.

"Morning. Everybody has influenza, especially Osadchy. . . ." (*Lykho z rozumu*, p. 45; *The Chornovil Papers*, p. 113.)

10. Yaroslav Hevrych (b. 1937): a medical student in Kiev, he was arrested in August 1965, charged under Article 62, and sentenced on 11 March 1966 by the Kiev Provincial Court to five years in strict-regime camps (reduced on appeal to three years). For details of his trial and letters from camp see *The Chornovil Papers*, pp. 39–40 and 97–100.

11. Mykhaylo Soroka (1911–1972): an architect by training and a high-ranking member of the OUN, he was first arrested in 1940 and sentenced to eight years' imprisonment. He was released in 1948 and returned to Lviv, but in 1949 was deported to the Krasnoyarsk Province. He was rearrested in

November 1951 for protesting against conditions in the camps and sentenced to death (commuted to twenty-five years). In 1957 his 1940 conviction was quashed as groundless, but his eight-year term was not deducted from the second one. Died in Dubrovlag. See *My Testimony,* p. 35.

12. Ivan Rusyn (b. 1937): a geodesist by training, Rusyn was arrested on 18 August 1965, tried the following March in Kiev, and sentenced to one year in strict-regime camps. In 1968 Rusyn signed the "Appeal of the 139" (*Ferment in the Ukraine,* pp. 191–196).

13. Babyn Yar (Babi Yar) is the ravine on the outskirts of Kiev where the Nazis massacred some 200,000 enemies of the Third Reich during their occupation of Ukraine. Drach's poem was published in *Poeziyi* [Poetry] (Kiev: Molod', 1967), p. 160.

14. Mykhaylo Kotsyubynsky (1864–1913): outstanding Ukrainian novelist and short-story writer in the impressionist manner, author of *Shadows of Forgotten Ancestors,* which was made into a remarkable film in 1964 by Sergei Paradzhanov.

15. Knuts Skujenieks: only scanty information is available about him. He was born in the late 1930's, his father a playwright who emigrated to the U.S.A. and died there in 1972. Moroz writes that at Yavas a portrait of Skujenieks was taken from the painter Panas Zalyvakha and the painter himself was forced to cut up his work (*Report from the Beria Reserve,* p. 47; *Boomerang,* p. 53). Skujenieks published one or two books of poetry before his arrest, and there are reports that he has been back in Riga since about 1973 and is publishing translations of Ukrainian poetry.

16. This may be the Mahmed Kulmagambetov whom Moroz describes in his essay "Report from the Beria Reserve": "In 1958 a lecturer of philosophy at the Frunze Medical Institute, Mahmed Kulmagambetov (at present in Camp No. 11), brought a request into the rector's office asking for release from his post. The reason? Disagreement with the program of studies. This created a sensation. A herd of careerists, each pushing his way to the trough and trampling his

own conscience, dignity, and convictions in order to climb higher and snatch the booty from his neighbor, was unable to understand how a person could reject 120 rubles simply because his outlook had changed. Kulmagambetov became a laborer. And then in 1962 he was arrested. The court in Kustanayi sentenced him to seven years' imprisonment and three years' exile for 'anti-Soviet activities. . . .' The case is typical in daily KGB practice, but unique in its undisguised arbitrariness. As a rule, the KGB tries to concoct at least a semblance of 'anti-Soviet' activity. But in this remote province it did not even deem this necessary and admitted that Kulmagambetov was *convicted for his views.*" (*Report from the Beria Reserve,* pp. 4–5; *Boomerang,* pp. 10–11.)

17.   Kateryna Zarytska (b. 1914): first imprisoned in Poland at the end of the thirties for her part in a Ukrainian nationalist attempt on the life of the Polish minister of the interior. During and immediately after World War II she was an organizer of the underground Ukrainian Red Cross and a courier for the OUN. She was arrested by the Soviet authorities in 1947 and sentenced to death (commuted to twenty-five years). After serving time in the Verkhne-Uralsk and Vladimir prisons, she was transferred to a strict-regime camp. Released in October 1972. Her son Bohdan Soroka was born in 1940 in Lviv Prison.

18.   Oleksander Oles (pen name of Oleksander Kandyba, 1878–1944): popular Ukrainian lyric and civic poet with a later leaning toward Symbolism. Often wrote on national liberation themes. Emigrated to Czechoslovakia in 1919.

19.   Oleksandr Korniychuk (b. 1905): Ukrainian novelist and dramatist. An adept exponent of socialist realism, he has held various high Party and government appointments and been awarded five Stalin Prizes for his plays.

20.   Vasyl Pidhorodetsky (b. 1925): an agent of the OUN Security Service, he was arrested in 1953 and sentenced to twenty-five years. For organizing a mass hunger strike at Tayshet in 1956 he was given a second twenty-five-year sentence.

21.   Volodymyr Drozd (b. 1939): popular Ukrainian

writer whose stories and novels deal largely with rural and small-town life.

22. Yuriy Shukhevych-Berezynsky (b. 1933): sentenced to ten years at the age of fifteen as the son of the commander in chief of the UPA. He was released in the spring of 1956 as one who had been arrested when a minor, but returned to confinement in the autumn of that year. On 21 August 1958, the day that he was due to be released, Shukhevych was re-arrested on a trumped-up charge and sentenced at a closed, illegal trial to an additional ten years.

The *Ukrainian Herald*, no. 6, reports that Shukhevych was approached after the trial by KGB officer Klymentiy Halski. Not denying that the charges had been completely false, Halski declared that Shukhevych would not have to serve his sentence if he would cooperate with the KGB by writing an article against Ukrainian nationalism and in particular against his father. Shukhevych refused the offer and was sent to a camp in the Mordovian ASSR. He is known to have taken part in a hunger strike there in February 1968.

Released later that year, Shukhevych was not allowed to live in Ukraine for fear that he might become a focus for national feelings. He settled in the north Caucasus, married, became the father of two children, and appeared to be far removed from the national movement in Ukraine. In February 1972, however, Shukhevych was arrested a third time, tried in September under Article 62, and sentenced to five years of prison, five years of strict-regime labor camp, and five years of exile.

23. Sir Harrie Massey (b. 1908): prominent British scientist, author of numerous books on mathematics and physics. Osadchy was apparently reading Massey's *The New Age in Physics* (London: Elek, rev. ed. 1966) because he uses a quotation from the book as the epigraph to "Elegies on the Theory of Relativity," a cycle of poems he wrote at Yavas.

24. Wolf Messing (b. 1899): Polish (now Soviet) telepathist and clairvoyant who frequently gave stage shows of his psychic abilities.

25. A very similar, possibly the same, suicide is described by Marchenko, *My Testimony,* pp. 298–304.

26. For corroborating details about Shved, see *ibid.,* p. 266, and Avraam Shifrin, *Chetverty vymir* [The Fourth Dimension] (Munich: Suchasnist', 1973), pp. 372, 374, 387.

27. The incident with the barbed-wire bouquet is also described by Marchenko, *op. cit.,* pp. 321–326.

28. Possibly another reference to Bulgakov's *The Master and Margarita,* in which Pontius Pilate figures prominently.

29. Svyatoslav Karavansky (b. 1920): writer and scholar, arrested in 1944 for membership in the OUN and sentenced to twenty-five years. Amnestied in 1960, Karavansky returned to his native Odessa and resumed his literary work: he completed a comprehensive *Ukrainian Rhyming Dictionary,* which he had begun in camp, published translations (Shakespeare, Byron, Shelley, and Kipling) and articles on linguistics, and undertook a translation of Charlotte Brontë's *Jane Eyre.*

Early in 1965 Karavansky wrote three articles which circulated among his friends. One was an appeal to the public prosecutor of the Ukrainian SSR to indict Yuriy Dadenkov, the minister of higher and special secondary education, on charges of violating the national rights of the Ukrainians by promoting the Russification of schools. The second protested against a 1959 law which abolished Ukrainian as a compulsory subject. The third, addressed to Wladyslaw Gomulka, then Poland's Party chief, called for a world communist conference to deal with the nationalities question. (See *The Chornovil Papers,* pp. 170–185.)

For these and other writings Karavansky was rearrested on 13 November 1965. His 1960 amnesty was revoked, and he was sentenced, without investigation or trial, to serve the remaining eight years of his twenty-five-year sentence. In 1967, for writing further protests from camp, Karavansky was transferred to the Vladimir Prison. From there he tried to smuggle out more petitions to the authorities, and in the autumn of 1969 he was charged with anti-Soviet agitation and propaganda and in 1970 sentenced to an additional five years in prison and three years in a strict-regime camp. (See p. 179 for Osadchy's protest.) Karavansky's wife, Nina Strokata, was cashiered from the Odessa Medical Institute in 1971 for defending her husband at his trial. In May 1972 she was herself charged with anti-Soviet agitation and sentenced to four years' imprisonment.

30. Vasyl Kozachenko, Oleksandr Korniychuk, Vadym Sobko (b. 1911), Lyubomyr Dmyterko (b. 1911), and Yuriy Zbanatsky (b. 1914): of these "official" writers, the last has some talent, but the others are hacks, and all of them are staunch pillars of neo-Stalinist orthodoxy. Dmyterko is a known police informer.

31. Panas (or Opanas) Zalyvakha (b. 1925): Ukrainian artist and art teacher, one of the creators of a Shevchenko stained-glass panel at Kiev University which was destroyed for "ideological reasons" on orders from the Party in 1964.

Zalyvakha was arrested at the end of August 1965 and sentenced on charges of anti-Soviet agitation and propaganda in Ivano-Frankivsk in March 1966 to five years in strict-regime camps. He served his sentence at Camp No. 11 at Yavas, where he worked as a stoker. His paintings were confiscated, and he was forbidden to paint in his spare time (cf. *The Chornovil Papers*, pp. 117–130).

32. Lyudmyla Sheremetyeva: apparently a journalist employed at the Lviv branch of the Academy of Sciences of the Ukrainian SSR, known as one of three authors of a letter in defense of Ivan Dzyuba (*Lykho z rozumu*, pp. 309–320; see p. 196 above). She is also author of a statement protesting the second arrest of Valentyn Moroz (*Boomerang*, pp. 187–188). Called in for questioning about this statement, she admitted that she was one of the authors and refused to answer further questions.

Halyna Sevruk, an artist, was one of the creators of the Shevchenko stained-glass panel and a signatory of the "Appeal of the 139."

Venyamin Kushnir (b. 1927): painter who studied in Lviv. No information is available about his wife.

33. Valeriy Shevchuk (b. 1939): excellent young short-story writer and novelist, signatory of the "Appeal of the 139."

Vasyl Stus (b. 1938): poet and critic who completed graduate studies at the Academy of Sciences of the Ukrainian SSR. Active in the opposition movement, Stus was unable to publish his poetry after he signed the "Appeal of the 139." He was attacked together with Dzyuba and Kostenko in 1966 by the Kiev Party committee chairman, who complained that they had "succumbed to nihilist moods, enthuse about formalist trends, and sometimes come out with ideologically harmful assertions (like the bourgeois slogan about some 'creative freedom' that transcends class)" (*Komunist Ukrayiny*, 1966, no. 6, p. 17). Stus is also the author of an open letter in defense of Chornovil to the Presidium of the Ukrainian Writers' Union (*Suchasnist'*, 1969, no. 4, pp. 76–81).

Larissa Bogoraz-Bruchman (b. 1929): active in the Moscow Civil Rights Movement since the early 1960's, Larissa Bogoraz was tried with Pavel Litvinov, Vladimir Dremlyuga, and others for their demonstration in Red Square on 25 August 1968 protesting the Soviet intervention in Czechoslovakia. She was sentenced to four years' exile in central Siberia. See Natalia Gorbanevskaya, *Red Square at Noon* (London: André Deutsch, 1972; Penguin Books, 1973).

34. Shota Rustaveli (late twelfth–early thirteenth centuries): great Georgian poet, author of the national epic, *The Knight in Panther Skin*. See note 44 on Franko, p. 211.

35. Kristjan Raud (1865–1943): Estonian educator, collector of folk art, and painter of a rather eclectic bent.

36. Jānis Rainis (1865–1929): Latvian poet, playwright, and revolutionary whose writings, frequently based on folklore themes, have strong nationalist overtones. Editor of the Social-Democratic newspaper *Dienas Lapa* [The Daily News] from 1891 to 1895, Rainis was arrested in 1897 and sent to prison and various places of exile. He took part in the 1905 Revolution, then emigrated to Switzerland, returning to Latvia in 1920. Although Rainis has been proclaimed in the Soviet Union

as a great Latvian poet, much of his nationalist poetry is suppressed.

37. In a lecture he gave at the University of Uppsala on 14 December 1957 Camus said in part: "Every artist today is embarked on the contemporary slave galley. He has to resign himself to this even if he considers that the galley reeks of its past, that the slavedrivers are really too numerous, and, in addition, that the steering is badly handled. We are on the high seas. The artist, like everyone else, must bend to his oar, without dying if possible—in other words, go on living and creating. . . . On occasion art may be a deceptive luxury. On the poop deck of slave galleys it is possible, at any time and place, as we know, to sing of the constellations while the convicts bend over the oars and exhaust themselves in the hold. . . . And it is very hard to make any objections to the art that has known such success in the past. But things have changed somewhat, and the number of convicts and martyrs has increased amazingly over the surface of the globe. In the face of so much suffering, if art insists on being a luxury, it will also be a lie." (*Resistance, Rebellion, and Death*, translated and with an introduction by Justin O'Brien [New York: Knopf, 1961; Vintage Books, 1974].)

38. Alexander Herzen (1812–1870): prominent Russian publicist and radical thinker, a founder of Populism. Living in emigration (chiefly in London) from 1847, he published *Kolokol* [The Bell], the first Russian émigré paper, which had much influence inside Russia.

39. The Ingush and the closely related Chechens formed the Chechen-Ingush ASSR in the northern Caucasus, with a population of half a million in 1939. In 1944, the Chechens, the Ingush, and six other small nations were rounded up by Soviet troops, loaded onto cattle trucks, and removed to eastern Siberia and the Sino-Soviet frontier. About one third of the million and a half people deported died during the first year. Stalin justified this genocide with accusations of pro-Nazi sympathies and even collaboration. For a detailed ac-

count based on Soviet sources, see Robert Conquest, *The Nation Killers* (London: Macmillan, 1970).

40. This sentence echoes the lines of a poem by the Ukrainian poet Mykola Vinhranovsky:

> I bear no malice toward any people,
> Toward no people on this earth do I bear malice.
> Why then is it ever more difficult
> To live on earth in spiritual plurality?

Mykola Vinhranovsky, *Poeziyi* [Poetry] (Kiev: Dnipro, 1971), p. 126. These lines are also quoted by Ivan Dzyuba with the comment that they express the "grief of many Ukrainians." (*Internationalism or Russification?*, second edition, p. 13.)

41. The paragraph may be a flashback to the time when Ali's father was deported, and *brod* is perhaps an Ingush word or syllable interjected into his broken Russian. For a description of Gromov, see Marchenko's *My Testimony*, pp. 261–265.

42. This seems to be Vilho Forsel, about whom Moroz writes in "Report from the Beria Reserve":

A Finn, Vilho Forsel (now in Vladimir Prison) graduated from Petrozavodsk University with distinction and worked in the Karelian National Economic Council. He accompanied a Canadian communist delegation touring Karelia as an interpreter. After the tour, the KGB men demanded that Forsel should report the contents of conversations carried on by the Canadians with individuals who had met them. Forsel refused, saying that the law did not give anyone the right to treat him in this way. "All right, a time will come when you will be begging to cooperate with us," the KGB replied. A few days later Forsel was dismissed from his work and could not get another job anywhere. If this is a crime, only the KGB should be tried for it. (*Report from the Beria Reserve*, p. 49; *Boomerang*, p. 54; *Uncensored Russia*, p. 457: see p. 196 above.)

43. According to the *Chronicle of Current Events*, a Roman Duzhynsky was sentenced in 1965 to four years' imprisonment for involvement in the "national movement" (*Uncensored Russia*, p. 467). Or has Osadchy made a mistake with the first

name and have in mind V. Duzhynsky, a *painter,* who was sentenced to ten years' imprisonment in 1957 for hoisting a Ukrainian Cossack flag over the Lviv Opera Theatre? (*The Chornovil Papers,* pp. 209–210.)

44. Yaroslav Stupak's stunning short story "Pride" (*Vitchyzna,* 1966, no. 12) is written in a thick, rich dialect as the stream of consciousness of Dorko, an old mountaineer. The setting is a snowbound cabin. Unnamed "foreigners" have occupied the villages below and are shooting all the natives on sight. Dorko's son has joined the guerrillas to fight the invaders, and the old man is left with two starving grandchildren and his daughter-in-law, who is dying in childbirth. He steps out of the cabin to go look for his son and is struck down by a bullet. The transparently un-social-realist story seems to have got into print by an oversight, and Stupak has not been heard from since.

45. Mykhaylo Soroka developed a severe myocardium infection on 7 January 1967. A doctor's assistant came to examine him but not until four days later, and Soroka was removed to the medical aid station only three days after that. When Yuliy Daniel complained about this gross neglect, "the medical inspector declared it all irrelevant (the sick man did not die while he was without medical attention) and tried to obtain Daniel's admission that everything in the camp was in order (he needed that for the report). But Daniel refused to make such an admission." (*The Chornovil Papers,* pp. 92 and 96.)

46. Ivan Drach and his colleague Dmytro Pavlychko (b. 1929, a Party member and prominent poet) were members of the Ukrainian SSR delegation to the UN General Assembly in the autumn of 1966. The question of the arrests was not raised at the UN, but the two delegates were asked about them at a literary evening in New York on 11 November 1966. Drach replied in part:

"[A]ccording to all the facts and documents we had before us, which we have seen, have noted—the fact of the matter was that in these people's circles there were individuals who had once been connected with underground nationalist organizations which had existed in Ukraine, even connected with the German Gestapo. And, in fact, they got around many of these people in such a way that there was even a beginning of direct propaganda against our system, our order, so that documents were disseminated—photocopies, retyped, mailed, and handed out throughout the entire Ukraine—in which the nature of our system was described, its hostility to things Ukrainian as such, the red fascism that prevails in our land, and so on. . . . So that, you see, this business has been represented in the press, the Ukrainian nationalist press, not like this, not . . . not in this way. [. . .]

"Actually, I believe that at this time, when we are coming up to the fiftieth anniversary of Soviet rule, we shall do everything so that people who have taken part in these activities to the smallest extent—I think that Bohdan Horyn is among these—well, and Panas Zalyvakha—well, that they will be released in the nearest future. That is what we are actually doing and what we . . . I think that we shall succeed in achieving something towards this." (*Ferment in the Ukraine*, pp. 177–178.)

47. Oleksandr Martynenko (b. 1935): born into a worker's family in the Donetsk Province, Martynenko served in the Red Army and studied at the Faculty of Geology (Department of Geophysics) of the Lviv Polytechnical Institute. In 1962 he was employed as a senior engineer at the Geological Prospecting Institute in Kiev. He was involved in a computer analysis of seismic oscillations and was preparing his candidate's thesis.

Martynenko was arrested on 28 August 1965. On 25 March 1966, at a closed session of the Kiev Provincial Court, he was found guilty of anti-Soviet agitation and propaganda, sentenced to three years of strict-regime camps, and imprisoned at Camp No. 11. For his letters from camp, see *The Chornovil Papers*, pp. 137–138.

48. Leonid Novychenko (b. 1914): leading official Ukrainian critic and literary scholar, author of the standard textbook history of Ukrainian literature, vice-chairman of the Ukrainian Writers' Union since 1969.

At the Fifth Congress of Soviet Ukrainian Writers, held in Kiev in November 1966, Novychenko, who usually follows the Party line, joined many others in sharp criticism of Russification. He rejected the notion, held in some official quarters, that the non-Russian writers in the USSR should switch to writing in Russian. He also raised the question whether the non-Russian cultures were being developed properly. He went on to demand a "profound theoretical comprehension of Lenin's brilliant legacy on the nationalities question" and to attack the prestigious Moscow journal *Voprosy yazykoznaniya* [Problems of Linguistics] for an article which implicitly argued that the Ukrainian and Byelo–Russian languages are doomed to extinction. Finally, Novychenko rebuked the prominent Russian critic Korneliy Zelinsky for arguing from the case of Chingiz Aytmatov, a Kirgiz writer who had changed over to Russian, that other writers should do likewise. *V z'yizd pys'mennykiv Ukrayiny, 16–19 lystopada 1966 roku* [The Fifth Congress of Writers of Soviet Ukraine, 16–19 November 1966] (Kiev: Radyans'ky pys'mennyk, 1967), pp. 222–229. See also John Kolasky's account of the Congress in *Education in Soviet Ukraine* (Toronto: Peter Martin Associates, 1968), pp. 202–203.

Moroz reports the same exchange of comments about Novychenko:

The KGB register of "renegades" is increasing catastrophically. Marusenko (Lviv KGB), in answer to a question from Osadchy: "Why did you not bring Novychenko to Mordovia? He has been saying the same things as we have," replied: "It would not do any harm to bring Honchar [see note 60] also." A valuable admission. This is the type of society served by the KGB. This society is not averse to putting behind bars Honchar and Stelmakh, the chairman of the Soviet of Nationalities, and Malyshko, and many other prominent intellectuals in Ukraine who protested against the arbitrary arrests in 1965. The KGB is an isolated group which strives with all its might to maintain its position on society's neck where it has been sitting since the Stalin era. The ring of isolation around it is irresistibly narrowing in proportion to people's rejection of their shameful, slavish fear. Marusenko admitted this himself. In reply to Osadchy's question: "What is the mood of the Lviv intelligentsia?" he replied: "Some have accepted the line of the Writers' Congress; some vacillate. They do not want to live in the old way, but they do not dare to live in the new way." (*Report from the Beria Reserve*, pp. 41–42; *Boomerang*, p. 47.)

49.   Taras Myhal (b. 1920): writer and pamphleteer, author of numerous calumnies against "bourgeois nationalists."

50.   Captain Harashchenko, the representative of the Ukrainian SSR KGB in Camp No. 11, is also mentioned by Moroz:

Harashchenko . . . when demanding "repentance" from Osadchy threatened to take away his Lviv apartment and "chase him out into the countryside." Harashchenko may be congratulated. Osadchy is the only one among us whom they managed to "re-educate." On the evening of 11 April he wrote a petition for pardon, and expressed the hope that he might benefit the people (?) by working as a lecturer at the university. (Osadchy did not mention whether he counted on any benefit for himself.) A few hours before this, he had written and read to his friends a document in which he denied his guilt, calling the 1965 arrests a blood-letting of the Ukrainian intelligentsia and accusing the investigator, Halski, of rough physical treatment. On the next day, after his comrades had unanimously expressed their contempt for Osadchy, he wrote a new document, *the third in two days,* in which he withdrew his repentance. It is not known how many more repentances and withdrawals Osadchy will write. He can write—after all, he is a journalist. . . . One thing is clear—if Osadchy follows his present course any further, he will not be thrown out of his Lviv flat. And he will be allowed to lecture at the university "for the benefit of the people." Curiously, Halski did not dare to beat anyone other than Osadchy—this is not 1937. But he did beat Osadchy—his ears and neck—as he himself later related. But then Halski is an experienced Chekist; he well knew with whom he was dealing. (*Boomerang*, p. 56; *Ferment in the Ukraine*, p. 150.)

In typing and passing on Moroz's essay, Vyacheslav Chornovil added the following postscript:

The excessively harsh judgment of the fellow prisoner M. Osadchy, obviously due to the recent impression created by his thoughtless act, gives rise to some qualifications. Osadchy's behavior in the camp both before and after 11 April (the statement to the CC CPU "What I was tried for and how" and his literary activity) gives grounds for regarding his "semi-repentance" as a momentary weakness caused by gross blackmail. (*Ferment in the Ukraine,* p. 153.)

51. Anatoliy Shevchuk (b. 1937): a linotypist by trade, he published short stories like his brother Valeriy and was known to have a progressive heart disease and acute rheumatism. He was arrested on 23 May 1966, charged under Article 62 with setting type for illegal literature, and tried at a closed session of the Zhytomyr Provincial Court in September of the same year. He received (along with Zalyvakha) the second highest sentence of those arrested in the 1965–1966 wave: five years of strict-regime camps. For his letters from camp, see *The Chornovil Papers,* pp. 162–166. Three short stories, written in the Zhytomyr KGB Prison, are in *Lykho z rozumu,* pp. 273–286.

52. See note 32 on Ivashchenko, p. 206.

53. The USSR is composed of fifteen Union Republics, and although the Chinese are not a Soviet nationality and the Jews do not have their own Republic, Osadchy is implying ironically that the camp is a microcosm of Soviet society.

54. The Leningrad Union of Communards, led by Valeriy Ronkin and Sergey Khakhayev, was broken up by the KGB in November 1965. Nine people were arrested, brought to trial early in 1966, and sentenced to terms of two to seven years. Their journal carried the epigraph "From the dictatorship of the bureaucracy to the dictatorship of the proletariat." Russian text of two issues published in *Possev* 24 (1967), 4 (1968), pp. 57–58, and 1 (1968), pp. 11–13.

55. A flashback to Mykhaylo Masyutko's trial in Lviv on 21–23 March 1966. Masyutko refuted charges that he was the author of "anti-Soviet" stories and articles which circulated in *samvydav* and turned tables on his accusers by citing numerous violations of the "Leninist nationalities policy" in Ukraine and pointing out that communist political theory

grants all Soviet nations the right of self-determination. For details of Masyutko's trial see *Ferment in the Ukraine*, pp. 9–10, and *Ukrayins'ka inteligentsia pid sudom KGB*, pp. 63–117.

56.   Vasyl Levkovych: arrested in 1946 or 1947 and presumably sentenced to twenty-five years, later amnestied, then rearrested and returned to Dubrovlag. See *The Chornovil Papers*, p. 210.

57.   Osadchy lost the privilege of using, or being addressed by, the term "comrade" when he was arrested.

58.   A prominent landmark in Kiev, on the high west bank of the Dnieper, is the statue of Volodymyr (Vladimir) the Great, Grand Prince of Kiev (c. 978–1015).

59.   This, and the subsequent phrase about a "golden torpor," may be allusions to Pavlo Tychyna's poem "The Golden Echo." Written as a comment on the turbulent times following World War I, the poem uses doves as harbingers of the "Eternal Spirit" that awakens the people to a new life. See C. H. Andrusyshen and Watson Kirkconnell, *The Ukrainian Poets, 1189–1962* (Toronto: University of Toronto Press, 1963), pp. 321–326.

60.   Oles Honchar (b. 1918): prominent Soviet Ukrainian novelist, awarded numerous prizes, Deputy of the Supreme Soviet of the USSR, decorated for war service, member of the Central Committee of the CPU, Chairman of the Writers' Union of Ukraine since 1969.

The publication in 1968 of his novel *Sobor* [The Cathedral], which brought into focus major social problems in Ukraine, set off a storm of controversy. Newspapers were filled with letters expressing indignation at the "distortion of working-class life" in the novel; public burnings of the book occurred, and it was finally withdrawn from circulation. There were also numerous purges (particularly in the Dnipropetrovsk Province, where the novel was set) of those readers who had given *Sobor* a positive evaluation. See *Uncensored Russia*, pp. 291–294. There is no English translation, but see the imaginative German rendering by Elisabeth Kottmeier and Eaghor

G. Kostetzky: Olesj Hontschar, *Der Dom von Satschipljanka* (Hamburg: Hoffmann und Campe Verlag, 1970).

61.   Chornovil delivered a copy of his memorandum on violations of justice in the 1966 trials (*The Chornovil Papers,* pp. 73–75) to Petro Shelest, First Secretary of the Communist Party of Ukraine, on 22 May 1966.

62.   Not translated in *The Chornovil Papers.* See *Lykho z rozumu,* pp. 247–248. In the poem Osadchy writes about a "man in a major's uniform" who amputated his conscience and sold his honor for money. His pockets stuffed with curses and his mouth foaming, he beats up men in dark torture chambers. When he dies, his subordinates will put up an epitaph on his grave: "Here rots the almighty dog who beat up thousands just to become a general."

63.   When the teacher Mykhaylo Ozerny was being tried in Ivano-Frankivsk, one of the factors in the accusation was the word *vatra* [campfire], by which he called the school-childrens' program that is usually referred to by [the Russian derived] *ogonyok.* The prosecutor said that he had not found *vatra* in the twelve-volume Ukrainian dictionary. Ozerny was greatly astounded to learn that a twelve-volume Ukrainian dictionary had been published during the few months of his imprisonment.—*Osadchy's note.*

Mykhaylo Ozerny (b. 1929): a schoolteacher arrested in August 1965 and tried under Article 62 in February 1966 (*The Chornovil Papers,* pp. 152–153). For a transcript of Ozerny's trial, see *Ukrayins'ka inteligentsia pid sudom KGB,* pp. 118–160. The prosecutor objected to *vatra* because it has no cognate in Russian. Ukrainian dictionaries do list the word, but no twelve-volume Ukrainian dictionary has ever been published.

64.   See note 2, pp. 212–213.

65.   Quoting from memory Chornovil's closing statement at his trial on 15 November 1967, to which he had been brought as a witness for the prosecution, Osadchy changes the wording but does not seriously distort the meaning. For the complete text, see *Ferment in the Ukraine,* pp. 159–165.

Notes to the Aftermath

1. *Suchasnist'*, 1969, no. 11, pp. 90–92; *Ukrayins'ka inteligentsia pid sudom KGB*, pp. pp. 15–18.
2. *Ibid.*, pp. 38–39, 47–55.
3. Oleg Penkovsky (b. 1919): a colonel in the military intelligence branch of the Red Army, he was charged with espionage on behalf of the United States and Great Britain and on 11 May 1963 sentenced to be shot for treason. The official record of the trial was published by the Political Literature Publishing House in Moscow in 1963. See Oleg Penkovskiy, *The Penkovskiy Papers*, introduction and commentary by Frank Gibney, foreword by Edward Crankshaw, translated by Peter Deriabin (Garden City, N.Y., Doubleday & Company, 1965).
4. Sergei Kirov (Kostrikov, 1886–1934): a high-ranking Bolshevik whose murder in Leningrad, reputedly inspired by Stalin, precipitated the mass repressions of the 1930's. By verdict of the Ukrainian SSR Supreme Court on 18 December 1934 twenty-eight writers were found guilty of being "White Guard terrorists" and condemned to death by execution.

Vasily Ulrikh (1889–1951): President of the Military Collegium of the USSR Supreme Court, he presided over major trials of the 1920's and 1930's.

Nikolay Yezhov (1895–1939): Secret police official, People's Commissar of Internal Affairs, 1936–1938.

Lavrentiy Beria (1899–1953): Georgian Bolshevik, close associate of Stalin, in charge of secret police and national security. Executed after Stalin's death.

5. Andrey Vyshinsky (1883–1954): lawyer and diplomat. A former Menshevik turned Bolshevik, Vyshinsky was chief prosecutor in the show trials of 1936–1938 where his courtroom

histrionics established the avenger stereotype for later Soviet prosecutors. Vyshinsky was Deputy Foreign Commissar and Minister, 1939–1949 and 1953–1954, and Foreign Minister, 1949–1953.

6. The *troykas* were three-man secret police boards which operated in total secrecy apart from the regular courts and which had the power to deport to a labor colony for five years with the right to add further five-year periods indefinitely when the sentence expired. They were abolished shortly after Stalin's death.

7. Chornovil, *Lykho z rozumu,* pp. 263–268; *The Chornovil Papers,* pp. 155–161. See page 196.

8. Probably the document that Chornovil refers to as "What I Was Tried for and How" (*Lykho z rozumu,* p. 14). It has not reached the West.

9. Dzakho Konstantin Gatuev (1892–1937): Ossetian novelist who wrote in Russian. His novel *Zelimkhan* (1926) depicted the resistance of Chechen-Ingush highlanders to tsarist colonialism.

Ivan Olbracht (pseudonym of Kamil Zeman, 1882–1952): Czech journalist and novelist. *Nikola Šuhaj—Robber* (1933), a prize-winning novel translated into a dozen languages, is the story of a bandit in Transcarpathia who leads a peasant rebellion.

10. Makhtum-Kuli (1733–1785?): Turkmen lyric poet, founder of classical Turkmen literature.

11. Vasyl Mysyk (b. 1907): excellent but little known Ukrainian poet who began his literary career in the 1920's with poems about exotic sea journeys. Severely criticized in the early 1930's for pessimism and romanticism, Mysyk was arrested in December 1934 as a member of the group of twenty-eight writers (see note 4, p. 230), but his case was set aside for further investigation. He resumed his career, largely as a translator, in the 1950's after return from exile and "rehabilitation."

Yevhen Pluzhnyk (1898–1938): Ukrainian writer whose introspective, solipsistic poetry has been compared to Rilke's. Pluzhnyk was arrested and condemned to be executed in 1935, but the sentence was commuted to ten years' hard labor on the Solovetsky Islands, where he died of tuberculosis shortly after his arrival.

12. A *Map of the Ethnic Composition of the Ukrainian SSR*, compiled by V. I. Naulko, was published in 1966 by the Academy of Sciences of the Ukrainian SSR and the Ministry of Geology of the USSR.

13. Roman Andriyashyk (b. 1933): Ukrainian journalist and novelist.

14. Roman Ivanychuk (b. 1929): Ukrainian fiction writer. His book *Mal'vy* [The Hollyhocks] (1968), one of the few competent historical novels to appear in the 1960's, was sharply criticized for failing to apply a class approach and for not presenting images that "express the idea of the fraternal unity of Ukraine and Russia" (*Pravda Ukrainy,* 7 February 1970).

15. Korney Chukovsky (pseudonym of N. I. Korneychuk, 1882–1969): eminent Russian writer who was associated before World War I with *avant-garde* literary circles and collaborated on various papers and journals. Chukovsky is highly regarded for his many portraits of Russian writers, his studies of Nikolay Nekrasov, and his popular books for and about children. He also translated much English literature. His book about Whitman was first published in 1923.

16. Petro Kozlanyuk (1904–1965): prolific Ukrainian pamphleteer and fiction writer. Imprisoned in pre-war Poland for pro-communist activities, he was rewarded after the war with high government positions and numerous literary prizes.

17. Eduardas Mieželaitis (b. 1919): respected Lithuanian poet, Chairman of the Lithuanian Writers' Union, Deputy to the Supreme Soviet of the USSR, awarded the Lenin Prize in 1962 for his book of poetry *Žmogus* [Man]. The line that Osadchy attributes to "Hands" actually occurs in the poem "Minutes":

Invisible fingers snap the thread
of life, tear down all the bridges.
My days are dying like people,
How painful to bear them to the graveyard!

18. From "Les fiançailles" in *Alcools*.

19. *Ukrayins'ke slovo* ("La Parole ukrainienne"), 4 August 1968; *Ferment in the Ukraine*, pp. 189–190.

20. *Ukrayins'ky visnyk, I–II* (Paris: P.I.U.F.; Baltimore: Smoloskyp, 1971), pp. 51–54.

21. In the spring of 1968 leaflets addressed to "all citizens of Kiev" were mailed out. They complained about semi-official restrictions on celebrating 22 May, the anniversary of the return of Shevchenko's remains from St. Petersburg to Ukraine. Late in June, two workers at the Kiev Hydroelectric Station, Oleksandr Nazarenko (b. 1930, a signatory of "The Appeal of the 139") and Valentyn Karpenko (b. 1938), were arrested. Two months later Vasyl Kondryukov (b. 1936) was brought into custody. The three men were tried *in camera* by the Kiev Provincial Court on 26–29 January 1969 on charges of distributing bootleg literature, including "The Trial of Pogruzhalsky," Djilas's *The New Class*, Chornovil's *The Misfortune of Intellect*, Dzyuba's *Internationalism or Russification?*, and several old Ukrainian history textbooks. Nazarenko was sentenced to five years of strict-regime camps, Kondryukov to three, and Karpenko to one and a half. *Ibid.*, pp. 26–29; *Uncensored Russia*, pp. 288–290.

Mykola Beryslavsky (the letter has "Boryslavsky"), a forty-five-year-old teacher and ex-inmate of Stalin's camps, was arrested at Kiev University after he pasted up posters protesting the colonial status of Ukraine, then poured inflammable liquid over himself and tried to set himself on fire. He was sentenced by the Kiev Provincial Court under Article 62 to two and a half years' deprivation of liberty. *Ukrayins'ky visnyk, I–II*, p. 14; *Uncensored Russia*, pp. 295–296.

Vasyl Ryvak (b. 1913?): a leader of the left wing in the Bandera faction of the OUN, imprisoned under the pre-war

Polish regime, emigrated in 1943. Ryvak returned from the United States to Ukraine in 1957 and became a founding member of the officially sponsored Society for Cultural Relations with Ukrainians Abroad. On 4 June 1969 Ryvak was arrested for writing letters to *Pravda* complaining about Russian chauvinism. He was apparently released without trial in January 1970. *Ukrayins'ky visnyk, I–II*, pp. 35–37; *Uncensored Russia*, p. 294.

Stepan Bedrylo (b. 1932): an economist by training, he was employed at the Ukrainian Agricultural Academy in Kiev. Bedrylo was arrested on 20 June 1969 under Article 62 on charges of disseminating Dzyuba's *Internationalism or Russification?* and Moroz's "Report from the Beria Reserve." He was tried *in camera* in Kiev on 5–7 January 1970 and sentenced to four years' strict-regime camps (reduced on appeal to two years). *Uncensored Russia*, p. 296; *Ukrayins'ky visnyk, I–II*, pp. 30–34.

22. *Ibid.*, p. 198.

23. *Ukrayins'ky visnyk, III* (Winnipeg: Novy Shlyakh; Baltimore: Smoloskyp, 1971), pp. 70–71.

24. Hryhoriy Chubay: poet about whom there is no biographical information but whose name frequently appears in the *Ukrainian Herald* in connection with various protests and petitions. For a preliminary rendering of his long poem, "The Search for the Accomplice," see Danylo Struk, "Hryhorii Chubai: Beyond All Expectations." *Canadian Slavonic Papers,* Vol. XIV, No. 2 (Summer 1972), pp. 280–299.

25. *Ukrayins'ky visnyk, III*, pp. 26–28.

26. *Ukrayins'ky visnyk, IV* (Paris: P.I.U.F.; Baltimore: Smoloskyp, 1971), pp. 32–33.

27. *Ibid.*, pp. 166–167.

28. *Ukrayins'ky visnyk, VI* (Paris: P.I.U.F.; Baltimore: Smoloskyp, 1972), p. 10.

It now appears that the 1972 onslaught against Ukrainian intellectuals was on a much larger scale than was known at the time. The latest issue of the *Ukrainian Herald* reports that between January and March 1972 about a thousand searches and arrests were carried out and some three thousand copies of bootleg literature were confiscated in the Lviv Province alone. Arrests were carried out in strict secrecy (under threat of prosecution, relatives of those arrested had to sign a pledge not to divulge the fact), and not even an approximate total of arrests throughout Ukraine could be established. The number of people prosecuted for reading Dzyuba's *Internationalism or Russification?* is believed to run into tens of thousands. Thousands of scholars were sacked from academic posts, and a large number of students were expelled from universities. *Ukrayins'ky visnyk, VII–VIII* (Paris: P.I.U.F.; Baltimore: Smoloskyp, 1975), pp. 125–127.

29. *Suchasnist'*, 1975, no. 4, p. 123.
30. *Ukrayins'ky visnyk, VII–VIII*, p. 123.

Index

Index

Index

Stanislav, Ivan, 103
Stasiv-Kalynets, Iryna, 62, 186, 210
Stetsyuk, Yakiv, 62
Story of My Life, The (Svirsky), 66, 212
Stupak, Yaroslav, 127, 223
Stus, Vasyl, 112, 220
Suknovalenko (zek), 138
Supreme Attestation Commission, xviii
Supreme Court of the Ukrainian SSR, 67, 158, 164, 170, 209, 210, 213
Svirsky, Aleksey, 66, 211–12
Svitlychny, Ivan, 67–74, 199–200
    attacked by Kozachenko, 206
    confrontation of, with Osadchy, 43–47
    Osadchy accused of receiving anti-Soviet literature from, 16, 34–36, 54
    return of, to KGB prison, 191
    visit of, to Camp No. 11, 135–36
Svitlychny, Nadia, 111, 136

Tertz, Abram. *See* Sinyavsky, Andrey
Thirst (Ivanychuk), 174
Tolstoy, Lev, 110
Treaty Between Bohdan Khmelnytsky and Tsar Alexis in 1654, The (Treaty of Pereyaslav), 17, 43, 200
"Trial of Pogruzhalsky, The," xviii–xix, 6, 35, 42, 63, 64, 90, 143, 166–67, 197, 212, 233
troyka, 165, 231

UHVR (Ukrainian Supreme Liberation Council), 26, 201. *See also* UPA
Ukraine, 79–81, 121–23
    historical background on, ix–x
    Osadchy's love for, 19–20
    secession of, from USSR, 199
Ukrainian Herald, 179, 183, 186, 189, 191, 192, 195–96
Ukrainian Rhyming Dictionary (Karavansky), 181, 218
Ulrikh, Vasily, 165, 230
Ulysses (Joyce), 51
United Nations, 82, 84, 171

General Assembly, 223
Human Rights Commission, 207
UNESCO, 113
Universal Declaration of Human Rights, 164, 170–71
    Article 11, 164
    Article 19, 201
UPA (Ukrainian Insurgent Army), 39–40, 98, 101, 201, 204, 213, 217. *See also* Banderites
Upanishads, 116

Valdur (Estonian zek), 113
Vilde, Iryna (pseud. of Polotnyuk, Daryna), 61, 209–10
Vinci, Leonardo da, 14
Vladimir Prison, 83, 110, 179, 180, 181, 207, 211, 213, 214, 216, 218, 222
Volodya (Osadchy's correspondent), 169–70
Volodymyr, Saint (Grand Prince of Kiev), 148, 228
Vynnychenko, Volodymyr, 74, 213
Vyshinsky, Andrey, 165–66, 230–31
Vyshnya, Ostap (pseud. of Hubenko, Pavlo), xvi, xvii, 8, 9, 21, 35, 63, 66, 69, 79, 116, 199, 212

Woe from Wit. See Misfortune of Intellect, The
Writers' Union of Ukraine, xiii, xiv, 50, 206, 220, 224, 228

Yakubyak, Vasyl, 102
Yashchuk, Pavlo, 73, 152, 213
Yevgrafov (zek), 108–09
Yevpatoria, meeting of Ukrainian activists in, 19–20, 200
Yezhov, Nikolay, 165, 230
Yoffe, Captain, 143–44

Zalyvakha, Panas, 111, 113, 140–41, 163, 164, 215, 219, 224
Zarytska, Kateryna, 95, 216
Zbanatsky, Yuriy, 110, 219
Zdoroveha, Borys, 152, 212–13
Zelenchuk, Mykhaylo, 102
Zelimkhan (Gatuev), 172, 231
Zetkin, Clara, 9, 66
Zvarychevska, Myroslava, xix, 59, 62, 157, 158, 182, 207, 209

240